MW00411937

TEXAS PEOPLE'S COURT

THE TEXAS EXPERIENCE

Books made possible by
Sarah '84 and Mark '77 Philpy

TEXAS PEOPLE'S COURT

The Fascinating World of the Texas Justice of the Peace

Mark Dunn

TEXAS A&M UNIVERSITY PRESS
College Station

This paper meets the requirements of ANSI/NISO Z39.48–1992
(Permanence of Paper).
Binding materials have been chosen for durability.

Manufactured in the United States of America

Library of Congress Cataloging-in-Publication Data

Names: Dunn, Mark, 1956– author.
Title: Texas people's court: the fascinating world of the justice of the
    peace / Mark Dunn.
Other titles: Texas experience (Texas A&M University. Press)
Description: First edition. | College Station: Texas A&M University Press,
    [2021] | Series: The Texas experience | Includes index. |
Identifiers: LCCN 2021040591 (print) | LCCN 2021040592 (ebook) | ISBN
    9781623499785 (cloth) | ISBN 9781623499792 (ebook)
Subjects: LCSH: Justices of the peace—Texas. | Small claims courts—Texas.
    | Judicial process—Texas—Cases.
Classification: LCC KFT1720 .D86 2021 (print) | LCC KFT1720 (ebook) | DDC
    347.764/016—dc23
LC record available at https://lccn.loc.gov/2021040591
LC ebook record available at https://lccn.loc.gov/2021040592

To all the justice court clerks.
(Ask the judges they serve; they'll tell you why.)

And to my red-headed angel, Mary,
who was once a JP court clerk herself.

A NOTE TO THE READER

Texas People's Court includes mention by name of over two hundred former and current Texas justices of the peace, along with the name of the county with which they were or are presently connected. For the sake of economy (a precious commodity in a book of this scope), I have often dropped the title "judge" (something easily inferred from a book about judges!).

Contents

Acknowledgments

Wrangling judges ain't easy. In addition to following leads on retired judges who might be willing to contribute thoughts and memories for this book, I reached out to nearly all of Texas's 804 justices of the peace (JPs) during my interview and research phase (in 2019), either by email, telephone, or both. Quite often, I'd call in at the agreed-upon time for our chat and find the judge otherwise indisposed. (Texas JPs are frequently indisposed, given all the unanticipated exigencies of their profession.) In some cases, circumstances required that I reschedule the appointment more than once. And, alas, there were a few judges I really wanted to talk to, and who, I assume, really wanted to talk to me, but we just couldn't work it out.

I am indebted to past president of the Justices of the Peace and Constables Association of Texas, David M. Cobos (Midland County), who helped to get the word out about my book and get the ball rolling with my interviews. Along the way, I learned the importance of this organization and its strong advocacy for Texas JPs and constables. I am also especially grateful for the extra time given to me by those judges who agreed to review the book in its final draft for accuracy, and for the updates I received in 2020 from JPs who were comfortable sharing how they and their staffs were dealing with the challenges of the COVID-19 pandemic.

I should note in the spirit of full disclosure that I made multiple attempts to get in touch with board members of the other group that works on behalf of Texas JPs, the Texas Justice Court Judges Association (TJCJA), but with very little success. Repeated attempts to set up phone conversations with the association's leadership team were, for reasons I could never discern, consistently unavailing.

Unfortunately, the board members of the TJCJA weren't alone in keeping me at a distance. I found myself facing drawbridges raised by other JPs. I encountered judges who said they were simply too busy to speak, or who were disinclined because they didn't think their thoughts or stories would be useful, or who were flat-out-uninterested in having a conversation with me ("Who are you again?" "Who do you work for?"). I have a few theories. First, the unprecedented nature of this fairly intimate look at what it's like to be a Texas JP might have seemed to some of the judges—let's just be honest—plain *weird*. Second, there are some Texas JPs who just aren't the warm and fuzzy types. Finally, there were, no doubt, those current and former JPs who probably thought I was a dirt-digging investigative reporter of some stripe, and that my book would be far from flattering in its portrayal of them.

It was never my purpose to use this project to expose judicial wrong-doing. Though if you're curious about the degree to which some judges *do* feel inclined to color outside the lines, kindly flip to chapter eighteen: "Goin' Rogue."

To my good fortune, two hundred justices of the peace, both currently serving and retired, did speak to me, did open themselves up with warmth and honesty and a good bit of humor—some of it disarmingly self-effacing—and, yes, some of my interviews actually did get pretty warm and fuzzy. To these JPs: Thanks so much for your time, thanks for educating me so thoroughly about your job, and thanks, as well, for making me laugh so hard!

You'll find the names of a few additional JPs in the index. These are judges, both living and dead, some of historic or newsworthy significance, and others whose own impressive careers on the bench helped me to illustrate or expand on the various facets of this profession. Even though they weren't able to speak to me, I went right ahead and put them in the book anyway!

Those who answered the call:

Chris Acord, Grimes County

Henry Alvarado, Sabine County

Margie Anderson, Shelby County

Rodney Baker, Bailey County

Billy S. Ball, Angelina County

Shawnee Bass, Erath County

Matt Beasley, Montgomery County

Debbie Bindseil, Burnet County

Clyde Black, Houston County

William P. Brandt, Tarrant County

Shane Brassell, Hill County

Tim Bryan, Gregg County

Fred Buck, Tom Green County

Sharon M. Burney, Harris County

Tracy Byrd, Randall County

Andrew Cable, Hays County

Sara Canady, Wilson County

Talyna Carlson, Gregg County

Jim Cavanaugh, Brown County

Rodney Cheshire, Angelina County

Nicholas Chu, Travis County

Gina Cleveland, Jasper County

David M. Cobos, Midland County

Cliff Coleman, Bell County

Benjamin Collins Sr., Jefferson County

Sheron Collins, Hale County

Johnny Conine, Comanche County

Kerry Crews, Hunt County

Kelly Crow, Fort Bend County

Larry Cryer, Chambers County

Randy Daniel, Henderson County

Bob Davis, Hansford County

Carl Davis, Anderson County

Ronnie Davis, Liberty County

Sparky Dean, Taylor County

Sergio L. De Leon, Tarrant County

Wayne Denson, Lavaca County

James R. DePiazza, Denton County

Marc DeRouen, Jefferson County

Louie Ditta, Harris County

Brenda Dominy, Cherokee County

Herbert Dunn, Van Zandt County

Irma Dunn, Titus County

Kenny Elliott, Brazos County

Randy Ellisor, San Jacinto County

Theresa Farris, Freestone County

Larry Flores, Frio County

Ed Follis, Lynn County

Leslie Ford, Hutchinson County

Trisher Ford, Tyler County

Sharon Fox, Brazoria County

Stephanie Frietze, El Paso County

Andrew Garcia Jr., Lampasas County

Shanna J. Gates, Frio County

Jon Glenn, Eastland County

Raúl Arturo González, Travis County

Sallie Gonzalez, Cameron County

Rick Grissam, Mitchell County

Sonia Guerrero-Perez, Dimmit County

John Guinn, Coryell County

Mary Hankins, Bowie County
Kyle Hartmann, Fayette County
James Hearne, Crockett County
Jarrell Hedrick, Martin County
Billy Hefner, Colorado County
Jo Rita Henard, Collingsworth
  County
Brad Henley, Hill County
Connie Hickman, Navarro County
Jeff Hightower, Bosque County
Rick Hill, Brazos County
Travis Hill, Lavaca County
Charlie Hodgkins Jr., Palo Pinto
  County
Janae Holland, Wood County
Sylvia Holmes, Travis County
Mark Holt, Walker County
Debbie Horn, Potter County
J. R. Hoyne, Kerr County
J. Treg Hudson, Mason County
Harris Hughey, Denton County
Jon W. Johnson, Smith County
Russell Johnson, Coke County
Jane Jones, Borden County
Keri Jones, Winkler County
Lex Jones, Marion County
Michael Jones Jr., Dallas County
Thomas Jones, Potter County
Justin M. Joyce, Fort Bend County
Jack Keeling, Leon County
Steven T. Kennedy, Uvalde County
Evelyn Kerbow, Crockett County
Matt Kiely, Caldwell County
Glenn E. Klaus, Medina County
Karin Knolle, Jim Wells County

Caroline Korzekwa, Karnes County
Mark Laughlin, Grimes County
Ronald LeBlanc, Matagorda
  County
Sherri LeNoir, Limestone County
Darrell Longino, Polk County
Christopher Lopez, Denton County
Wayne L. Mack, Montgomery
  County
Chris Macon, Ellis County
Stan G. Mahler, Young County
Edward Marks, Floyd County
Katy Marlow, Foard County
Joe Martinez, Gray County
Pam Mason, Donley County
Sharon Maxey, Falls County
Kathleen McCumber, Galveston
  County
John McGuire, Tom Green County
Bobby McIntosh, Uvalde County
Barbara McMillon, Cass County
Don Milburn, Lee County
Kelvin Miles, Parker County
Jackie Miller Jr., Ellis County
Jimmy Miller, Jasper County
Sarah Miller, Erath County
Mike Missildine, Collin County
Wayne Money, Hunt County
Jeff Monk, Johnson County
Susan Moore, Goliad County
Oralia Morales, Brooks County
K. T. Musselman, Williamson
  County
Duncan Neblett Jr., Nueces County
Mike Nelson, Galveston County

Olivia Neu, Cooke County

Teri Nunley, Kendall County

Margaret O'Brien, Dallas County

Stephen Odom, Callahan County

Patricia Ott, Williamson County

David Parker, Kent County

Jerry Parker, Wood County

John Payton, Collin County

Jason Pena, Hidalgo County

Juan Jose Peña Jr., Hidalgo County

Angie Pippin, Fisher County

Nancy J. Pomykal, Calhoun County

Stuart Posey, Victoria County

Cyndi Poulton, Jackson County

Frieda J. Pressler, Kendall County

Bill Price, Coryell County

Rodney Price, Orange County

Tommy Ramirez III, Medina County

Dale Ramsey, Briscoe County

Robin Rape, Brazoria County

Debra Ravel, Travis County

Chuck Ream, Motley County

Kim Redman, Wise County

Jim Riley, Reeves County

Ciro Rodriguez, Bexar County

Yadi Rodriguez, Hutchinson County

Dianne Rogers, Real County

Susan Rowley, Lubbock County

Chuck Ruckel, Collin County

Susan Ruiz-Belding, Frio County

Tom Rumfield, Callahan County

Mark Russo, Rockwall County

Nora Salinas, Brooks County

Julie Sanchez, Hudspeth County

Tisha Sanchez, Palo Pinto County

Donna Schmidt, Cochran County

David Sellers, Runnels County

Jerry Shaffer, Collin County

Mitch Shamburger, Smith County

Bob Shea Jr., Taylor County

Nancy Shepherd, Lipscomb County

Scott Shinn, Van Zandt County

H. B. "Doc" Simpson, Briscoe County

Randall Slagle, Travis County

Beth Smith, Hays County

Brenda Smith, Newton County

Carol Smith, Dallam County

Jack Smith, Falls County

Mike Smith, Harrison County

Jesse Speer, Eastland County

Stacy Spurlock, Jack County

Ralph Swearingin, Tarrant County

John W. Swenson Jr., Clay County

Amy Tapia, Matagorda County

Stephen Y. Taylor Jr., Castro County

Gordon Terry, Garza County

Suzan Thompson, Matagorda County

Mike Towers, Bandera County

Johnny Towslee, Burleson County

Marc Traweek, Yoakum County

George Trigo, La Salle County

Fernando Villarreal, McLennan County

Missi Walden, Ector County

Tim Walker, Lamb County

Rodney Wallace, Cherokee County

Mary S. Ward, Fort Bend County

Stan Warfield, Colorado County
Clarice Watkins, Harrison County
Ronnie Webb, Somervell County
Jeff Wentworth, Bexar County
Donna Wessels, Wharton County
Lisa Whitehead, Burnet County
Jeff Williams, Harris County

Yvonne Michelle Williams, Travis
  County
Donna Wooten, Pecos County
Michael York, Lee County
Douglas Zwiener, Washington
  County

And thank you, Carolyn Duderstadt
(a friend and fellow clerk from days gone by)

Introduction

I was in law enforcement for thirty-nine years. The whole time
I thought I knew everything that a JP did. But I was sadly
mistaken! They do much, much more than I ever dreamed.

—HON. KENNY ELLIOTT, BRAZOS COUNTY

IN THE SPRING OF 2001, my wife, Mary, and I had the pleasure of flying
down from New York to attend the Texas premiere of my Lone Star com-
edy-drama *North Fork*,* staged by the Temple Civic Theatre in Temple,
Texas. To honor my participation in the opening weekend festivities, the
theater presented me with a Texas flag, but not just *any* Texas flag. This
was one of those that get routinely run up the flagpole next to the Texas
State Capitol building for the purpose of special presentation—declaring
the recipient an honorary Texan.

But that wasn't really necessary.

Besides the fact that I had married a Texan (Mary grew up among
the palm trees and orange groves of Hidalgo County) and that my own
family had strong Texas connections,** I held, for four years in the 1980s,
one of the most prototypical of Texas jobs, on par with cattle rancher,
oil rig roughneck, high school football coach, and beauty pageant ad-
judicator.***

I worked in a Texas justice court.

> *Most people think all I do is traffic tickets. Texas JPs wear a
> lot of hats. We do a lot of things.* —Hon. Stacy Spurlock, Jack County

As a JP court clerk, I wore a number of hats; I processed small claims court petitions, scheduled and sent out notices for traffic court, and served as jury room attendant for our occasional six-person jury trials. I helped angry landlords file eviction suits and, conversely, assisted those who found themselves defendants in these lawsuits file their answers. I watched the parents of truants get tongue lashings from my judge for neglecting to send their children to school. I assisted frightened people in filing protective peace bonds. I took payment on uncontested traffic tickets. I don't think we accepted credit card payments in those days— just cash and checks. And you better not write a hot check to the court; we dealt with those, too.

For someone in his twenties who knew that he wanted to spend his life writing plays and novels, the Texas justice court represented a mother lode of opportunities for delving into all the gradations of interpersonal conflict—conflict being the engine of good story-telling. And given the breadth and scope of responsibilities assigned to Texas justices of the peace by state statute, the court became, for me, much more than just a court. It was the perfect vehicle and setting for exploring all the highs and lows, personal triumphs and travails that go along with living as a human on this humanly interactive planet. What's more, I was given the chance to document as a budding writer the kinds of geographically specific transactions that come with those by turns sly, good-ol'-boy winks, two-steppin' swaggers, prim Southern Baptist honey tones, and down-home Texas twangs.

> *I used to pray: Lord, whatever I have to do, make it be exciting.*
> *And He did a good job, didn't He? There was never a dull moment.*
> —Hon. Sara Canady, Wilson County

Texas People's Court: The Fascinating World of the Texas Justice of the Peace takes a sometimes light-hearted, sometimes sobering look at what it's like to be a Texas JP. Even though so much of what a JP does might be regarded as junior varsity on that judicial gridiron, one should never assume, as one judge told me, that stakes won't be high for the parties involved. Here in the Texas justice court, wrongs can be righted and lives changed, for good or bad, in profoundly personal ways. A newly evicted tenant could suddenly find himself homeless. A priceless family necklace might finally be restored to the rightful sibling. The recipient of an occupational driver's license can get to and from work without the fear of being pulled over and taken to jail for driving without a valid license. A death inquest becomes an opportunity for family reflection and valediction, with the attending judge as commiserative witness. (It might even carry significant *national* importance: it was a Dallas County JP, Theran M. Ward, who certified the death of President John F. Kennedy.) Even a joyous wedding has the potential to be either a celebratory life milestone or a burdensome millstone for the spouse who comes to rue this consequential decision!

Stakes are relative. Outcomes can be unpredictable. People can hurt in a myriad of ways and sometimes it falls to a JP to mitigate that pain. On other occasions, it is the justice of the peace's duty to deliver just desserts to those who break the law or insult the concept of human decency.

> *One week I might have multiple dangerous dog case hearings, then the next week, quite a few eviction cases. You never know when the inquests are going to come. And I go to the jail seven days a week.*
> —Hon. Jeff Hightower, Bosque County

Texas People's Court takes up, in each of its twenty chapters, a different aspect, duty, or area of thought related to the profession of Texas justice of the peace. It attempts to put a human face on those responsibilities, attitudes, and perspectives taken from the two hundred conversations I enjoyed with JPs throughout the state—from those who serve in its most populous municipalities to rural county JPs whose jurisdictions include far more dirt roads than paved.

A note about the book's format: I try whenever possible to let the judges speak for themselves. This has required a bit of editing in those instances in which a JP will repeat himself unnecessarily, employ ambiguous pronouns, or bury his punchline in the middle of an anecdote. A lot of Texas justices of the peace talk in what I call "judge lingo," using a vernacular to describe the things they do. It is understood among themselves and their staffs, but might on its face sound imprecise or even erroneous to an outsider. For example, JPs do not "arraign," they "magistrate," though you will find judges in this book who refer to "arraigning someone" as synonymic shorthand for the magistration process (reading rights, setting bond for later appearance, and so forth).

Readers should also be aware that because so much of this book is driven by the conversations I had with JPs in 2019; their thoughts and perspectives reflect the state laws, county ordinances, and justice court policies and protocols that were in place at the time of the interviews. There will be unavoidable instances in which something conveyed to me has changed during the intervening months. Moreover, the COVID-19 pandemic mandated temporary changes to court operations and services beginning in the spring of 2020. Some of those changes, especially those related to technological applications, have proven so helpful to some justice courts that they have been made permanent.

I was inspired by a particular judge with whom I spoke, a "robed wrangler" who seemed to embody the spirit and mettle of the Texas JP. Judge Steven T. Kennedy (Uvalde County) reminded me in the following personal anecdote why I wanted to write this book.

There was an inmate that eluded custody in the district courtroom and he took off. He ran down the stairs and out the door. There was a deputy right behind him—a big ol' chubby guy. I knew the deputy wasn't going to catch him and I was physically fit for an old man. I ran the inmate down, and I'd like to tell you that I tackled him and did something real special, but he flat played out and fell down, then I ran up behind him and put my hand on him and said, "Don't you go anywhere!" because I was out of breath too!

I'm ruling that a true judicial wrangling, even though I didn't happen to ask Judge Kennedy if he'd been wearing his robe at the time.

NOTES

North Fork was later published with the title *Cabin Fever: A Texas Tragicomedy.*

**My mother, a student at what was then called Texas Woman's College, broke off her engagement to a Texas Aggie. Had they married, my roots may have gone even deeper into that good Texas soil. On the other hand, I wouldn't have been me.

***I had the chance to speak to a gentleman in Callahan County named Stephen Odom, who had worked in the oil industry, had been a cattle rancher, was a coach, and was employed in a justice court . . . as justice of the peace. I don't believe there's a beauty pageant judgeship in his future, but you never know.

TEXAS PEOPLE'S COURT

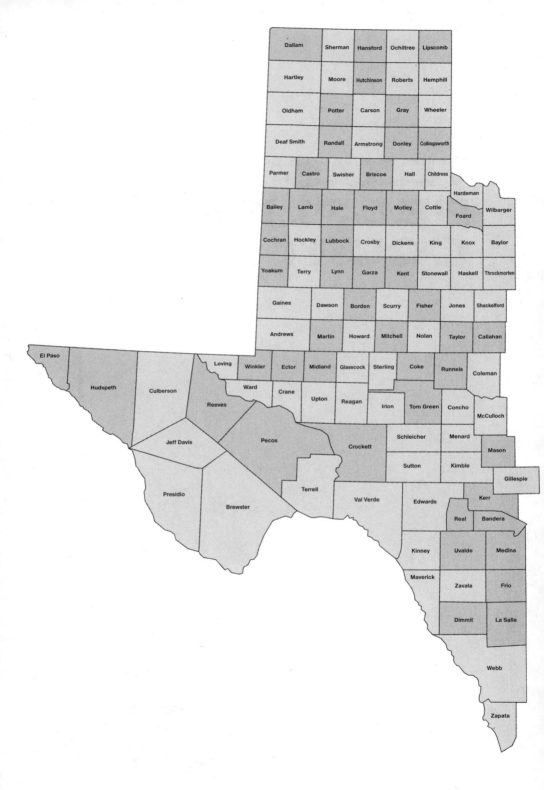

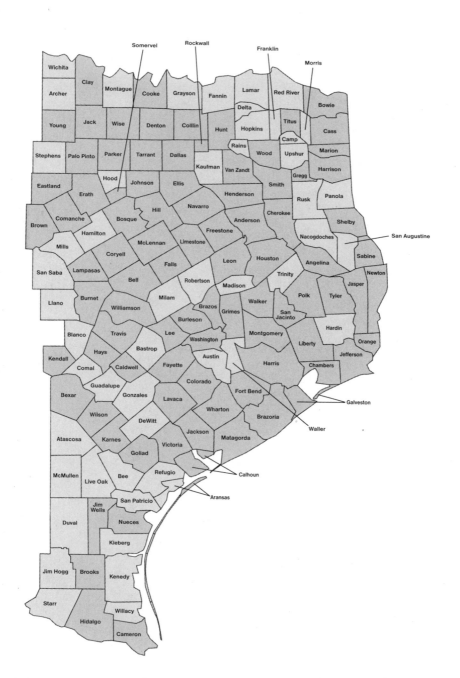

1

Human Drama, Texas-Style

I love cases where it looks like there's gonna be tons of wild stuff.

—HON. CHRISTOPHER LOPEZ, DENTON COUNTY

ON AUGUST 23, 2019, Orange County justice of the peace Joy Dubose-Simonton was required to perform one of a JP's most painful duties: certify the demise of someone she knew—in this case *two* people she knew. In fact, the judge had just visited with the couple less than an hour before their sudden, violent deaths. Nineteen-year-old Harley Morgan and twenty-year-old Rhiannon Boudreaux were killed when their car was struck by a pickup truck. Harley had just pulled out onto Texas 87 following a visit by the couple to the judge's office. They'd been attending a wedding ceremony.

Their own.

And it was Dubose-Simonton who had married them.

The judge had signed the marriage license for the two high school sweethearts (actually, they were middle school sweethearts who had fallen in love in the eighth grade). He was a night baker at Dunkin' Donuts. She worked at Walmart. They had big plans for all the years of married life that lay ahead, their "happily ever after." Now they were gone, and it would eventually fall to Dubose-Simonton, one of Orange County's four justices of the peace, to sign her name again—this time to Harley and Rhiannon's death certificates. In this county—like 240 others in the state of Texas—the JP doesn't just marry people, she also serves as a county coroner.

The summer before, three hundred miles to the west in Wilson County, Judge Sara Canady was required to conduct inquests involving a double homicide that occurred only a block from her court in Floresville. Canady knew the young woman who'd been killed; she had worked as a clerk in the judge's office through a work-study program for which Canady served as mentor. The young man who had also been killed was a classmate of her son. There was one thing more: because it was Canady's week to be on call, she ended up having to set bond for the murderer—the woman's husband.

Over in Montgomery County, only five weeks before the death of the newly married Morgans, Judge Wayne L. Mack married a couple for whom death was a different form of intruder. Dean and Monica Berckenhoff's young son Colton had died in a freak accident seven years before, though the manner of his death allowed for the harvesting of several of his organs. Colton's heart went to a twenty-year-old youth minister living in Fayetteville, Arkansas, Travis Stufflebean. Travis's heart had been dying—literally—and after five unsuccessful open-heart surgeries, his only chance for survival had been the transplant. His body accepted Colton's heart without complications.

Monica's sister, Amanda McDonald, and their parents, the Guys, flew Travis over to Montgomery County from Arkansas to surprise Dean and Monica as they took their vows.

Judge Mack was in on the plan. At the end of the wedding ceremony, Mack asked if anyone had anything to say before he pronounced the couple husband and wife. That was the cue for Travis's appearance. He carried a stethoscope. The Berckenhoffs' other two children were there, standing with their parents before Judge Mack. Travis's appearance brought their late son back into the family circle. Both the bride and the groom listened to Colton's heart beating vigorously inside Travis's chest.

Because the wedding was covered by several local media outlets, Mack was able to convey to a wide audience the desperate need that patients on donor waiting lists have for organ donors. (As of September 2020, there were almost 110,000 individuals waiting for transplants; each day an average of seventeen people die before they can be helped.*)

"One of the things I really love about my job," said Mack, "is being able to celebrate new beginnings. In my duties as a coroner I see a lot of death. This was an opportunity to celebrate in tragedy that their son was able to give life."

> *What I enjoy most about being JP is being able to help people in a time of crisis. It's not a glorified job. We do a lot of dirty work: getting down, getting dirty. But the gratifying part is being in a position to help, and when I can't, directing them toward those who can.*
> —Hon. Thomas Jones, Potter County

Every day hundreds of Texas justices of the peace will interact with members of their communities (in addition to those just "passing through"—or, rather, trying to *speed* through their counties!). A visit with a JP might have nothing to do with marriage or death (or even eviction, traffic tickets, or a neighbor's wake-the-dead broken muffler). Rodney Baker (Bailey County) told me that sometimes people just come in to talk. It may be a friendly visit—a number of small county judges have open-door policies—or the visitor may be in need of help or guidance on some specific matter that will never wind up in court. Not every Texas JP serves as his precinct's local wise man; nonetheless, the unique role of justice of the peace gives these men and women special tools and perspectives useful in trouble-shooting, problem-solving, and anxiety mitigation.

> *Some people just need someone to listen to them.*—Hon. Mary Hankins, Bowie County

Residents in hundreds of JP jurisdictions throughout Texas are grateful to have someone who is willing to listen, and sometimes even to understand all the particulars of what they're going through. I like the way that Mike Smith (of Harrison County) puts it:

Some JPs live in large areas where they are so busy they can't take time out of their day to talk to their constituents. People like myself that live in smaller areas, if somebody has a question they want to ask, my door is always open and they know they can come in. A lot of older people will bring in their mail and ask: Is this is a scam or is this the truth? It's great to sit down and talk to people and know that you play a part in trying to help with what some consider menial problems, but to them they aren't.

Larry Flores (Frio County) has the same relationship with his constituents.

You never know what you're gonna do as a judge in a small town. Sometimes you're helping them fill out applications for food stamps or you're looking over something else that doesn't have anything to do with your field. It's just an honor when they come to you for whatever reason. They think that in a small town you're the only one that can help them. Which I'm really not, but just the fact that they come to you—that's pretty awesome.

JPs have seen it all. Or at least quite a bit of it. Jon W. Johnson (Smith County) put it this way:

People don't realize that technically there are hundreds of duties that go along with being a JP, from deciding to put down dogs when they bite people to taking care of malnourished horses when people are cited for starving their livestock. You've got to decide where those horses are going to go and who's going to take care of them. This job has more variety than any job I've ever done.

The example offered by Connie Hickman (Navarro County) addresses the many chilling ways that a JP might be involved with a local tragedy. She speaks at national forums in support of the work done by Texas justices of the peace.

I have lots of conversations with people. Texas's courts are so different from other states.' People are appalled that Texas JPs can go out and pronounce. For example, I had the Cameron Willingham case, where he killed his three children. I pronounce them dead, issue a warrant for the person who did it, set his bail, and put him in jail. Other judges in other states just don't do that large array of things.

Tim Walker (Lamb County) is even more succinct:

I had a pretty good idea of the width and boundaries of the job of justice of the peace. I just didn't know how deep the water was!

One of the judges with whom I spoke put his role in ministerial terms: a justice of the peace is a civic pastor, someone who listens, who tries to help (almost all JPs keep lists of community resources available for those in need), who is required not only to dispense justice but also to impart understanding, and, when possible, to navigate with delicacy, humor, and evenhandedness all the drama and emotion playing out before them.

> *Some cases come through that are so hilarious you just have to try to make it through. And bad things that occur that are ingrained in your mind and your soul that you'll never forget.*
> —Hon. Connie Hickman, Navarro County

In some cases, the drama and emotion simply involve letting off steam. The justice of the peace controls the valve. Carl Davis (Anderson County) told me:

A lot of times when a person comes in, they have a ticket. They're upset because they got stopped. They're upset because they got issued the citation. They're upset because they have to pay it. A lot of times just listening to them . . . I'm not giving a lot of feedback—I can't discuss the case with them, and the way I don't discuss it with them is that I listen to them. I say, "Is that right?" Once they vent and tell their side of their story, they feel a lot better.

And then they pay and go home.

On other occasions, that penchant for altruism and community service, which seems to be chromosomal in a majority of JPs, places them right inside their local school; Talyna Carlson (Gregg County) mentors and tutors at-risk kids. Caroline Korzekwa plays a larger role in Karnes County beyond serving as one of its four justices of the peace:

I'm very community oriented. I drive the school bus. I've been part of the band boosters. I've been on the church committee for the picnic. I'm just a very involved person. With the JP job, all those things work hand in hand. When kids wind up in my court, I supervise them on the community service.

Korzekwa said that years later, some of those kids will come back to visit . . . and to thank her. "I never wanted to get in trouble again, Judge, because I don't *ever* want to work that hard again!" She added that this is true: she didn't have a lot of repeat offenders.

Making that extra effort can pay off in spades, as lives are changed for the better and problems find resolution in both judicial and extra-judicial ways. (More than one JP has played the role of mediator in an effort to avert formal litigation between neighbors, friends, and family members).

There are judges who are hand-holders. Others exercise tough love. Brad Henley (Hill County) likes to remind people that they aren't alone. Everybody makes mistakes. Even JPs.

I make mistakes, but so far, I've gotten them all corrected without anybody being the worse for wear. I just want people to know that we're all in the same boat here. We're all human. I do all my credit card cases on the same day and I tell everybody just to relax. We'll get it all worked out. Nobody's going to jail and nobody's going to get killed over credit cards.

In S. R. Binder's 1997 Texas documentary *Hands on a Hardbody*, which tells the simple yet powerful story of a group of Longview, Texas, residents vying to win a Nissan hardbody truck in an endurance contest reminiscent of Depression-era dance marathons, competitor Benny Perkins becomes the philosophizing conscience of the competition. With down-home breviloquence, he explains how such contests maintain their special appeal. Benny suggests that "it's a human drama thang."

Sleep-deprived contestants trying to keep their hand fixed to a truck in a literal last-man-standing competition—which several years later claimed the life of a young man at that same Longview Nissan dealership, when he committed suicide in the midst of the contest—display emotions that are raw, that are primal, that are fraught with the very kind of drama to which Benny refers. Likewise, justices of the peace, including the one who, no doubt, presided over that suicidal competitor's inquest, face a jumble of emotions from their constituents that are equally as raw and equally as dramatic.

Human drama finds its way into JP courts in ways that might have Benny nodding . . . or smiling . . . or wincing empathetically. And the contest aspect of justice court dealings is undeniable, for a good deal of what winds up before a Texas JP or in front of a panel of jurors unfolds in the form of contest, contention, and conflict in need of either bench-trial adjudication, jury verdict, or some form of cool-headed, compromise-infused settlement.

That drama can be, paradoxically, both frightening and immensely satisfying for the judge who knows how, with a nod to Mr. Dickens, to revel in the seasons of Light and weather the seasons of Darkness. Judge Canady has seen both the best of times and the worst of times in her county. She worships at the First Baptist Church in Sutherland Springs, where, on November 5, 2017, twenty-six congregants lost their lives in the deadliest mass shooting in the state. She has also seen her community come together in an amazing and inspiring way. "We're so inextricably linked," she says. "You cannot tease that apart."

We have learned that the human spirit will always outshine anything we are put through.—Hon. Leslie Ford, Hutchinson County

In his job as JP for the West Texas county of Reeves, Jim Riley and his three fellow justices of the peace have had to contend with the day-to-day turbulence associated with a modern-day boomtown (or, rather, boom county). The fracking frenzy—which, like the country's historic gold rushes, fomented a twenty-first-century form of entrepreneurialism on steroids—tripled Riley's eviction docket. Longtime tenants who had been paying two and three hundred dollars a month in rent were subsequently forced to shell out as much as $1,500 for the same lodgings. Everyone in Reeves County, apparently, turned into a landlord, asking for and receiving top-dollar rents. Ad hoc RV parks and fleets of trailers known as "man camps" sprouted up like mushrooms. Those who couldn't pay the county's increasingly inflated market-rate rents had to vacate, and all too often it was the judge's job to hear whether or not the law was being followed.

I spoke with Judge Riley at the height of the boom.** He told me he was performing three times more death inquests than he used to. US Route 285 had a nickname: "the Death Highway." Vehicle crashes in the county rose 300 percent in a decade.[1] Suicides among the army of oilfield workers, untethered from family and anything resembling a normal life, shot up. Riley magistrated a large increase in drunk driving cases, and cases involving the possession of crack, meth, and whatever else would get a roughneck through the well-paying but soul-draining job of drawing oil from the battered ground beneath Reeves County.

Riley said he took all the human drama in stride. Reeves County is his home. He was born in the very county building where he was serving as JP. It used to be a hospital. (Judge Riley noted that his clerk's office was once the X-ray room, and he expected some day to see her glowing!)

Booming oil counties, big-sky ranching counties, cotton counties, wheat counties, rice counties, citrus counties, suburban commuter counties, bustling skyscraping urban counties—each of the 254 counties of Texas possesses a distinct personality and profile. But they also have something very much in common: they are the collective home of nearly thirty million Americans,*** many of whom will find the comedy and tragedy of their lives played out before over eight hundred justices of the peace.

Signatures on pieces of paper that blissfully cement lives or that acknowledge the expiration of a life.

Matters of the heart, both figurative and literal.

Hard-bodied Texans (not infrequently suing for ownership of hard-body trucks).

Human drama, Texas-style.

(We'll talk about the cows later.)

NOTES

*According to the US Department of Health and Human Services.

**As I was finishing this book, the COVID-19 pandemic was delivering a gut punch to the West Texas fossil fuel industry. What is unclear is whether the Wild West fracking boom market that Judge Riley and I discussed in October 2019 will have cycled into bust territory for the long term by the time this book is published, though Riley's observations remain retrospectively valid, and could very well become valid again in the future. Thus is the nature of the boom-and-bust Texas oil business.

***According to the 2020 census, the population of Texas is now 29,183,290.

get ladled onto the plate of a Texas JP, she has an added advantage: she knows the public. She's assisted them at the counter and taken their calls.

And she knows which clerk's desk drawer has all the paperclips.

Debbie Bindseil (Burnet County) has clerked in several different courts and admits that being clerk in JP court is the hardest. While busy, urban justice courts move more toward clerical specialization (criminal supervisor, chief clerk for civil matters . . .), small-county clerks "have to do it all." In Bindseil's court, that's one full-time and one part-time clerk.

I have one clerk. She tells people that she works for Judge Henley. I tell her, no I work for her, because she's the only one around here who knows what's going on! I'm real proud of her. I've known her all her life.—Hon. Brad Henley, Hill County

The most consistently positive thing said to me by the judges I interviewed was praise for their clerical staff. "They protect the judge," Bindseil told me. "A good clerk is going to keep you out of trouble both civilly and criminally. They try to keep the judges from hearing things they shouldn't hear." This last bit is important; a litigant who speaks ex parte willy-nilly before a judge will force that JP to go through the hassle of recusing herself in the interest of showing fairness to the opposing side.

Clerks also help the judge remember deadlines and timelines as directed by the Texas Rules of Civil Procedure. Not keeping on top of those pesky rules can get a judge into trouble, which can result in embarrassing grounds for appeal.

There are judges who joke that all they do is come to the court and sign their name. This comical exaggeration does have a whiff of veracity; in some JP courts, the clerks do a good deal of the heavy lifting. (In one county in West Texas, an arrangement has been made with the county judge to have her clerk appointed as a fully invested interim judge for those times when the JP has to leave the county.) It's best, though, when judge and clerk are lifting together. That can be easier than it sounds when, because of the small size of the county, the judge must serve as both JP *and* as her own clerical staff.

Clarice Watkins (Harrison County) was a DJ before she became a JP. During her quarter-century in radio, she had a Sunday morning gospel program and spun a lot of contemporary music platters. Later, Watkins worked as clerk for a justice of the peace. When that judge left and a new judge came in, she lost her job because "he wanted his own people." But Watkins kept close. Circumstances eventually required the new judge to resign, and she was the logical person to replace him.

At the risk of spoiling this rosy outlook when it comes to the importance of JP court clerks, there was at least one JP I interviewed—Ed Follis (Lynn County)—who said he was completely comfortable doing his own paperwork and didn't cotton to the idea of having a clerk. I asked him if his commissioners couldn't give him somebody to help out just a little. "Don't need them," he replied. "Don't want them in my way. I don't want to train them and the county doesn't need to be out the extra expense. I'm doing all right."

I do believe he was.

Incidentally, Judge Follis probably wouldn't have a problem with my using the verb "cotton." He's a former cotton gin manager. He isn't the only one I interviewed. Marc Traweek (Yoakum County) told me that dealing with the problems that go along with that profession teaches you how to deal with people. "Being the manager of a cotton gin," he said, "was like boot camp for being a JP."

FARMERS, RANCHERS, COWBOYS, COWGIRLS

The late Jimmy Miller (Jasper County) couldn't believe he ended up as a judge.*

There are a lot of people who wouldn't have predicted this either. If they'd had social media back when I was a boy, I probably wouldn't get to be a judge now. I rodeoed and I rode those old bulls, and I hunted and I lived in rural Texas. The old men taught me a long time ago that there were two seasons for deer: salt and pepper.

I spoke with quite a few ranchers and farmers—those who used to run cows and till the soil and those who still do, even while serving in their local justice court. Johnny Conine was a rancher. "I worked for a stocker-feeder operation here in Comanche, a pretty big one," he told me. "I run my own cows. I'd calved about eight hundred heifers that year the JP position came open, and I thought, I'll give it a try and see what happens." ("Giving it a try" involved defeating several opponents in the GOP primary.) One of the hardest parts of the job of justice of the peace, Conine added, was having to be indoors so much.

Over in Donley County, not only did Pam Mason and her husband raise cattle and quarter horses, she helped to form a landowners' association devoted to wind turbine placement in her part of Texas. She also sold insurance and worked with her brother in the development of a method to remove poisonous hydrogen sulfide from gas wells.

Mary Ann Luedecke (Jeff Davis County) is also a cowgirl judge. In 2011, before becoming JP, she fought alongside hundreds of firefighters to contain the Rockhouse fire, which ultimately consumed almost 315,000 acres of land near Fort Davis, including her own spread.

J. Treg Hudson (Mason County) wasn't just a rancher and construction worker before he became JP; he also shod horses for about ten years. He's worn a lot of different hats and strongly believes that a varied professional background is a helpful thing for a JP to have. (By the way, Judge Hudson is the only JP I interviewed whose dad played on a winning Super Bowl team, the New York Jets, with the win in '69. Jim Hudson had also played for the Longhorns and was on the team that won the 1963 national championship.)

Bob Davis (Hansford County) quit being a cowboy in 2001, but there was a time in his life when that was all he wanted to do.

I ended up doing several things related to the cattle world, roped forever—spent twenty years or so going to three or four team ropings a week, if not more. But I was never good enough to make a living at it. I grew up taking care of cattle. I grew up on horseback. I was selling feed for a feed company when I decided to run for JP. Somebody asked me, "What the hell qualifies you to be a judge?"

I said, "I never read much law growing up, but I had a lot of law read to me!" That was my campaign slogan from then on.

In his first race for JP, Davis lost the Republican primary, which, without a competitive general election, is usually determinative in his county. But that didn't stop him from running a write-in campaign in the fall.

And he won.

Some JPs are married to ranchers, like Jo Rita Henard (Collingsworth County). Henard likes the free time she says being a small-county JP gives her. She spends that time painting horses.

I spoke with a lot of JPs who either used to be farmers or still are. Rodney Baker (Bailey County) has both farmed and sold crop insurance; he still keeps his hand in the insurance business because it gives him a chance to talk to the farmers in his area. Billy Hefner (Colorado County) is still a rice farmer; his father was a rice farmer and his son is also keeping it in the family. Ronnie Davis (Liberty County) was also a rice farmer before he became JP. Karin Knolle (Jim Wells County) grew up in a dairy farming family, going back several generations. She was also a substance abuse counselor and worked with students at high risk for drug and alcohol abuse.

The late Joe B. Evins (Hidalgo County) started out as a migrant farm worker in Texas's Rio Grande Valley. He later moved up to the job of fruit and vegetable grader and packer. After serving as the head of a tank crew in Gen. George S. Patton's US Third Army during World War II (Evins participated in both the Battle of the Bulge and the liberation of France), he went on to hold several political and judicial offices, including being a JP. He served for twenty-five years as district judge.[1]

During Judge Quail Dobbs' fifteen years on the bench in Howard County, if you just happened to slip up and call him a bozo or a clown, he more than likely wouldn't have taken offense. He'd probably just correct you with a smile: "I used to be a clown . . . for thirty-five years, a *rodeo* clown!" And Dobbs was *good*. He ended his career in grease paint by fulfilling his dream: going to the National Finals Rodeo as barrel man. One presumes there were plenty of smiles in his courtroom from 1999 to 2013.[2]

Paul Desmuke was another JP who loved to perform. He joined the Miller Brothers' 101 Ranch Wild West Show after serving as Atascosa County's justice of the peace, and when the traveling show went bankrupt during the Great Depression, he performed at the 1933–34 Chicago World's Fair. Former JP Desmuke threw butcher knifes at his wife, Mae.

With his feet.

He couldn't throw them with his arms. He didn't have any.[3]

Chris Acord (Grimes County) grew up on a dairy farm and has no problem with being on call twenty-four hours a day, seven days a week. In the dairy business, those sorts of hours are a given. Acord still raises cattle and does custom hay baling. He also used to be an ag teacher, which brings us to . . .

TEACHERS AND SCHOOL ADMINISTRATORS

Before he became a justice of the peace, Jerry Shaffer (Collin County) was a college professor. He's also been a high school football coach with two state championships to his credit. Shaffer doesn't find the transition from educator to JP all that unusual. When it comes to "dealing with human beings," he said his teaching and coaching experience has been good preparation. He's on personal terms with all kinds of "personalities, interests, and foibles."

Still, learning to be a judge isn't easy. Shaffer noted that one of the biggest challenges when he became a JP was learning the law and having to figure out how to apply it. He was no longer the teacher; he was the student.

I had to learn things like when can we issue a capias pro *fine or an* alias capias, *when do we issue a bench warrant, when can we have a failure-to-appear—all these little details, how they all work out. The mechanics of it all—here's the form we use and here's how we fill it out. The clerks look at it from a pragmatic point of view; I look at it from a theoretical point of view.*

This makes perfect sense; Judge Shaffer used to teach mathematics and physics.

> ***Once a teacher, always a teacher.****—Hon. Sharon M. Burney, Harris County*

I talked to quite a few former teachers, most of whom couldn't help bringing some of their educator instincts and tactics into the courtroom. Sara Canady (Wilson County) told me she's "taught everywhere from pre-school to prison," including a stint as an English instructor in Chiayi, Taiwan, so she's always looking for ways to improve the minds of those who appear before her, even if her schemes may be considered a little unorthodox. Take those situations in which defendants want to get a traffic citation dismissed.

If you look in the code of criminal procedures, there are several conditions: (a) You pay a special deferral fee. (b) You must go X amount of days (30–60–90) with no other traffic citations; you have to have a clean record for X amount of days. And then the code says: "And any other reasonable conditions imposed by the judge." *So here's my reasonable condition: You write me a three-page essay on the importance of driving safely. If you really wow me, I can reduce the days on deferral.*

I joked that as a writer, I'd have an unfair advantage in her court. She responded that she'd then feel obligated to ask five pages from *me*.

I asked her about the kinds of essays she gets.

Most of them start out like this: "I have to write this essay because I want deferral, even though I think it's unfair that I have to do this, but I'm doing this because I have to. I have done some research. Here is the research. Here is a personal story. When I was a new driver . . . it was important for me to drive safely. The end."

Her "reasonable condition" receives a full range of responses from traffic defendants. One young man was particularly livid over the inconvenience. She explained to him that what he heard from her clerk was correct:

"If you've already had a driver's safety course in the last twelve months, sir, you don't qualify to take the class."

"Well, I just don't understand! Why would you make me do this? I work full time and this is my weekend with my seven-year-old son and I don't want to spend all this time writing this stupid essay!"

"Then I'll make this concession for you. If you will just write me a one-page essay and have your son draw me a picture and fax that in by Monday, I'll give you a 30-day deferral."

I could see the smoke coming through the phone.

"You mean you're gonna give my son work too? *All right then!" And he slams the phone down.*

On Monday Judge Canady's court got a fax. The clerk took it to the judge. "Look at this! Oh, this is so cute! A picture of his dad in his truck!"

Mike Smith (Harrison County) coached high school football for thirty-seven years and taught government and economics. Tim Walker (Lamb County) was also a coach—football and baseball. He taught drafting and woodshop.

Rick Hill (Brazos County) spent six years in the air force before starting a career in teaching and education administration. He found that he couldn't "knock on a door or make a phone call without someone saying,

of duty in Vietnam, served as constable, and then got his law degree and has practiced as both district attorney and defense attorney.

Judge Jeff Monk of Johnson County boasts a more colorful professional background than most of the erstwhile lawmen and lawwomen with whom I spoke. He was a police officer, but also a marine, a member of the state narcotics task force, railroad conductor, and a film and television actor (appearing in the miniseries *War and Remembrance*). He wanted my readers to know that he is nothing like the comically compulsive TV detective Adrian Monk.

Jim Cavanaugh (Brown County) was also a police officer, but that constitutes only a small corner of his extensive resume. He served the FBI both in high profile cases and as an undercover agent from 1971 through 1996. He worked in hostage negotiation, and was very busy in the 1970s given the rash of airline hijackings in that decade. Cavanaugh also taught abnormal psychology as it relates to criminality. Nowadays, he isn't just a JP; he and his wife raise and sell miniature donkeys.

After a career in law enforcement, Michael York (Lee County) was ready to segue into the next chapter of his life. It was the romanticism of Texas JPs and the Wild West, he admitted, that attracted him to the profession. That and the fact that he was "getting old." "Criminals don't grow up," he said. "The people who chase and arrest them do." Like a lot of the JPs I talked to, York didn't much care for the part about having to campaign for the job. In his case, his first campaign for JP lasted a year. He told me there are two ways to run a political race: scared or unopposed.

Johnny Towslee (Burleson County) knows the criminal side of the court from all angles. Not only was he once a police officer, he comes from a family of judges. His father is a retired district court judge and his sister is a currently serving judge in district court. Towslee also owned his own bail bond company for a while. He said that as a JP who is also a magistrate, he looks at eligibility considerations when he sets bond in the same way he considered those very risk factors when he was the one putting up the bonds.

Benjamin Collins Sr. (Jefferson County) spent a lot of years as a deputy constable serving eviction and small claims citations, and was forever wondering about the people the law required him to interact with for only a few moments. As a judge, he now has the chance to hear their stories, to dig into the reasons folks find themselves in bad straits. It humanizes them, he said, in a way that simply handing them a citation or subpoena doesn't.

Judge George Trigo has found that his experience as a peace officer and the education he's acquired as a criminal investigator have given him a decided advantage when it comes to performing his inquest duties, especially when a homicide might be involved.

Smaller counties—I don't mean to demean anybody—but they don't have the best trained officers. So when I get called to a death scene, I try to look for everything. I was called to a death scene early in the morning—the victim of a train accident. It's usually rare when we go to a train accident to find the body intact, but when I went to turn this young man over, the only thing I could see was an injury to the left side of his head. I sent the body in for an autopsy.

The young man *had* been hit by a train, but he had also been hit by something else—*someone* else.

About two or three years later they arrested two brothers who had beat the man up and then put him on the tracks. I did suspect, first thing, that he might have been killed someplace else and then put on the tracks. I'm always suspicious. I tell people that I've only trusted one person in my life and I wasn't even sure about my mother sometimes. When I went to DPS school, the first thing they told us was if you want to be a good police officer, be a nosy SOB.

And nosy officers can, as Judge Trigo demonstrates, go on to make good justices of the peace.

Mike Missildine (Collin County) used to be the constable in his precinct. He finds that his previous job has been invaluable, especially when it comes to signing emergency detention orders.

I've been out there and I've executed those warrants. I know the questions to ask, I know what the officers are going to be looking for. Also, it's about getting down and seeing what kind of problems this person has. Is he violent? Is this a substance abuse problem, and not really a mental health problem, though substance abuse can be considered a mental health problem. There are deep questions that a lot of judges don't know to ask because they haven't gone out and executed these warrants.

Before becoming a justice of the peace in Burnet County, Lisa Whitehead served as an assistant to the county attorney. Assisting in the preparation of cases that would be prosecuted by her office in justice court gave her a familiarity with how the court operated, which in turn helped her when she became a JP herself. But there was also an advantage to *leaving* that job. As a JP, she no longer had to go in and out of an office whose glass door bore an inconvenient abbreviation of her job title, which was assisting with criminal cases: "Lisa Whitehead, Criminal."

> *I prefer being a JP to being a deputy sheriff. The hours are better, and now I don't have to fight with drunks in the middle of the parking lot.*—Hon. Trisher Ford, Tyler County

Judge Ralph Swearingin did a bunch of things that prepared him for being a JP, including serving on the Supreme Court committee that wrote the Texas Rules of Civil Procedure (helpful, especially if you're a Tarrant County JP spending 90 percent of your time with civil litigants). Swearingin shared with me a prescient moment spent with his grandfather as a kid. They were sitting on the porch and the old man predicted that Ralph was going to be three things when he grew up: first a lawyer, then an FBI agent, then a judge. Ralph's grandfather had a gift for prescience; not only did Swearingin go on to be a lawyer and judge, he's also a graduate of the FBI National Academy.

Not all ex-law enforcement Texas JPs come from Texas. J. R. Hoyne (Kerr County) started out on the Chicago police force. (He's also got a brother who's a cop in Chicago and one who is a police chief in California). There aren't too many Chicago families who get to brag about having a Lone Star judge in the family.

EVERY OTHER GIG AND PROFESSION UNDER GOD'S WARM SUN

Those JPs who weren't lawmen, lawyers, farmers, ranchers, teachers, or former JP court clerks have held so many different jobs over the years that it's a wonder the TV quiz show *What's My Line?* ever had to go off the air.**

In my training session when I became JP, there was an insurance agent, someone who had formerly been in law enforcement, and a retired school superintendent. I was one of two or three lawyers. It's nice to have that diversity of experiences!—Hon. Nicholas Chu, Travis County

Here's a sampling of the many and varied previous occupations:
—K. T. Musselman (Williamson County): Uber and Lyft driver while he was campaigning for JP; political reporter and blogger; and Democratic party campaign consultant, organizer, and activist.
—Stephen Y. Taylor Jr. (Castro County): truck driver.
—Steven T. Kennedy (Uvalde County): gas measurement technician for Enron (he left before the collapse).
—Mark Laughlin (Grimes County): John Deere tractor product salesman.
—Dianne Rogers (Real County): EMS administrator, store clerk, T-shirt maker.
—Bobby McIntosh (Uvalde County): technician for Southwestern Bell Telephone.
—Ronnie Webb (Somervell County): mechanical maintenance supervisor at the Comanche Peak Nuclear Power Plant.
—Sheron Collins (Hale County): worked at Walmart, first as cashier, then in the accounting office.
—Harris Hughey (Denton County): regional sales manager for a national wholesale apparel company.
—Teri Nunley (Kendall County): freelance court reporter.
—Don Milburn (Lee County): glazier.
—H. B. "Doc" Simpson (Briscoe County): worked in a service station, for a local undertaker, was executive vice president for a bank, and owned his own Chevrolet dealership.
—Jon Glenn (Eastland County): crane mechanic.
—Chris Macon (Ellis County): firefighter and paramedic. (When he became JP, he replaced another firefighter JP!)
—Clyde Black (Houston County): regional security director for Domino's Pizza.

—Gordon Terry (Garza County): tire salesman.
—Wayne Money (Hunt County): car salesman and life insurance
    agent.
—Larry Cryer (Chambers County): owner of a concrete contracting
    company, pool company, and pest control company.
—Charlie Hodgkins Jr. (Palo Pinto County): manager of explosives
    for one of the largest drilling and blasting companies in the
    Southwest.
—Fred Buck (Tom Green County): owner of a local moving company,
    constable.
—Jack Smith (Falls County): owned an advertising agency and wrote a
    humor column for *Wacoan* magazine.
—Randy Daniel (Henderson County): member services manager for a
    rural electrical co-op and mayor of the city of Athens, Texas.
—Brad Henley (Hill County): auctioneer.
—Christopher Lopez (Denton County): hotel manager, personal
    trainer, yoga instructor, yoga studio manager.
—Margaret O'Brien (Dallas County): industrial hygienist, who
    implemented Occupational Safety and Health Administration
    (OSHA) regulations and conducted incident investigations. She
    also worked in semiconductors, first for Motorola and then for
    Texas Instruments, and was also a part-time realtor.
—Sara Canady (Wilson County): babysitter for the children of the
    JP who preceded her.

Jerry Parker (Wood County) joked that before being a justice of the
peace, he'd done everything but star in silent movies. Back in his native Louisiana, he owned a service station, ice business, and washateria,
hauled shrimp from Louisiana to Texas, and worked in the state penitentiary. In Texas, he served as a field officer for the Parole Division of
the Texas Department of Criminal Justice. After retiring, and "sitting
around watching too many re-runs of *Martha Stewart*," he took a job as
marshal at a local golf course. One of the golf course regulars turned him
on to the possibility that this jack-of-all-trades might make a good JP.
    Mark Russo (Rockwall County) and I both agreed that at least one
of the special skills he acquired in professions not typically viewed as
pathways to the job of justice of the peace, was, surprisingly, just what

he needed. Not only was Russo a chef and worked quite a bit in TV and radio, he also spent twenty years in the ring as a professional wrestler.

Wrestling was very translatable to the courtroom. It helped me to get a good read on people, to get a feel for who I could trust. You don't get into the ring with someone you don't trust. You learn how to exercise good judgment. If you don't use good judgment in the ring, you can hurt someone. The same applies in the courtroom. I want to create a safe environment in my courtroom.

Sharon Maxey (Falls County) worked as secretary and bookkeeper for her husband's grain elevator business. He later became a constable and she later became JP in the same precinct. Since having a JP and constable who were married to each other and serving in the same precinct had never happened before (as far as anyone knew), the commissioner's court sought an opinion from the Texas attorney general, and were told that it was perfectly legal just so long as the couple avoided problematic interactions, such as the signing of warrants, that presented a perceived potential for bias. Because I didn't wish to sound disrespectful, I refrained from sharing with her the picture in my head of the judge handing her constable-husband—in the midst of their nightly pillow talk—papers she wished him to serve the next morning.

I was pleased to have the chance to talk with Ciro Rodriguez (Bexar County), who became a JP after a dozen years as US congressman. He had previously been a community mental health worker in the field of substance abuse. Judge Rodriguez said that going from being someone who makes the laws to someone who makes sure that those laws are followed wasn't easy. He's always been committed to helping kids get the most from their educational opportunities; the chance to address truancy as a JP really appealed to him.

Carl Davis (Anderson County) also worked in the mental health field before becoming JP. He was a counselor, housing coordinator, and case manager, and has a degree in psychology. We spoke about one of the duties of the JP for which Davis's background was invaluable: emergency detention orders. These are the warrants that allow people to be picked up who are posing a threat to themselves or to others; they authorize an evaluation pursuant to a possible formal mental health commitment.

Garza County JP Gordon Terry worked in his county's new prison. This led to time spent as a private contractor in Abu Ghraib prison in

NOTES

*When I was checking in with some of the JPs I'd interviewed in 2019 to find out how they and their staffs were weathering the COVID-19 storm, I learned from Judge Miller's wife, Drue, that her husband had succumbed to the virus in August 2020, and that she had temporarily stepped in to fill out the months remaining in his term until the next election. I was reminded how much I'd enjoyed talking with her late husband; his warmth and humor made him one of my favorite interviewees.

**Shameless plug for my previous book: In *Quizzing America* I do a deep dive into the world of 1950s quiz shows and how they reflected life in that decade.

*** Judge Payton was once the undisputed *Guinness World Records* holder for youngest judge. His claim narrowed to "youngest *elected* judge" when an Indiana justice of the peace named Marc L. Griffin came forward thirty-seven years after having been *appointed* to his judicial office in 1974 at a younger age than Payton.

3

Sue Me, Sue Me, What Can You Do Me?

Some of these small claims issues need to be left between the participants and God.

—HON. FRED BUCK, TOM GREEN COUNTY

THE "PEOPLE'S COURT."

Kyle Hartmann (Fayette County) sums it up this way:

Part of what makes justice court great is being able to have litigants represent themselves. It's not up to the citizens who come in to know how to make a formal motion. In the higher courts they have to communicate everything through their attorney. In our court, it's up to us to find out in plain English what they're asking for. If you bog justice court down with too many rules it would completely defeat the purpose.

Back in the old days, things were even more relaxed when it came to lawsuits at the justice court level. This is what former Erath County JP Sarah Miller told me. She served from 1975 to 1999 ("I came in with the dinosaurs," she quipped).

There weren't the things they have to do now. I had a lot of people come in and say, "I'm gonna file on so and so. His animals are eating all my hay."

I'd say, "Do you mind if I call that person and tell him you're up here and fixing to file on him, and see if you two can't get together at the local café and work this out?" I had very few cases that ever went to trial because I got them together in a neutral place and they sat down and worked out their problems.

Court 101:

The plaintiff has to give all the evidence. The defendant doesn't have to provide any evidence. Sometimes the plaintiff just tells you a story. It's not about who is telling me a story. What proof did I get? If the plaintiff doesn't prove their case, the defendant doesn't have to say a word. They can ask for a direct verdict and it's over. But your average person doesn't know that. I've had people with a big case who didn't bring me a single piece of paper, not one piece of evidence—just a story.

Next up are cases involving businesses and their customers.

Businesses sue their patrons for not paying (or not paying in full) for products and services rendered. But those who patronize businesses can also file suit for not receiving what was promised. And things can get messy. Sometimes, literally messy. Mark DeRouen (Jefferson County) found this out when he was hearing a small claims case in his court.

The plaintiff was suing his dentist for his false teeth not fitting him properly. During the trial he walks up and literally pulls them out and puts them on the bench. "I'm setting these up here for you to give back to the defendant. I no longer have use for them." I respectfully requested that the bailiff get some towels and I made the gentleman clean the bench and take the teeth back. I wanted to maintain my cool, but I was definitely stunned and disgusted. There was spit and everything on my bench.

Newton County JP Brenda Smith can count herself lucky not to have had a similar encounter with evidence in her very first small claims case: a loaned potty chair that was never returned!

Margaret O'Brien likes the civil cases that get filed in her court in Dallas County—even the ones that make mountains out of molehills. She said that she once had to hear a small claims case over a $34.99 hubcap.

Justin M. Joyce (Fort Bend County) and I discussed how his court is impacted by an increase in religious, cultural, and ethnic diversity in his community. This often manifests itself in the small claims court suits that get filed in his precinct. Judge Joyce believes that these cases are inevitably shaped by attitudes that came over from the "old country": landlords who don't want to return security deposits to vacating tenants, people who don't adhere to the terms of their contracts, a pervasive mindset that everything is negotiable. Joyce likened it to haggling over the price of goods in an old-world marketplace.

And speaking of old-world approaches to transacting business, there are times when the arrangements don't involve an exchange of money. Andrew Garcia Jr. (Lampasas County) advises people not to barter. If someone is going to fix your truck, he says, then pay them to fix the truck. Civil trials go much easier for a justice of the peace who doesn't have to deal with an "if you do this, I'll do that" situation, which can easily end up with the "this" not getting done right or the "that" not getting finished to the liking of the other party.

The third category is family member vs. family member.

When I was speaking to Gordon Terry (Garza County), I asked him about his *Judge Judy* cases—the shorthand I sometimes used for neighbor vs. neighbor small claims cases. He responded, "What about family vs. family—your *Jerry Springer* cases?"

Michael Jones Jr. (Dallas County) hears a lot of small claims cases of this kind—one family member suing another. He said that you work through these just like you do with other civil cases; you still base your decision on the evidence. This isn't always easy, though, because emotions are apt to get in the way.

Small county JPs like Jarrell Hedrick (Martin County) see their share of these suits.

When you're in a small county where everybody knows everybody else, sometimes that's good because you know where they're coming from and how to help them—if you can help them—but sometimes it's bad because, dang it, I like this kid. I wish he hadn't done this. I had a case the other day where I had two brothers fighting over a house. I've known them for years. They regretted that I was the one to have to hear the case. We got it settled, but it wasn't fun.

Last, but definitely not least, is "the man" vs. "the little guy" (or vice versa, otherwise known as David vs. Goliath).

When I was working as a JP court clerk in the mid-1980s, my wife, Mary, and I didn't have a single credit card between us. Now credit cards are an omnipresent part of American society and a real bugbear for every one of Texas's 804 JPs. Debt-holding parties wishing to avail themselves of the courts to recover what they believe they're owed may file in the justice court precinct where the debt was accrued. And because of the recent increase in the court's monetary jurisdiction from $10,000 to $20,000, they are doing this in even greater numbers than before. Credit card cases can sometimes be the only civil cases that many rural JPs hear.

Douglas Zwiener (Washington County) rules on lots of them.

It's my prerogative to set a hearing on credit card cases and here is why I do that. Sitting in my lobby one day was an elderly lady and she had a tissue in her hand, crying. I said, "Ma'am, what's the matter?"

She said, "I don't know why I'm here."

"Well, did you get a letter from the court?" She handed me the summons for civil court. I said, "Ma'am, this is nothing but a debt claim. Somebody says you owe them money."

She said, "I've never had a credit card in my life."

"Well, did you maybe co-sign for your son or daughter or another family member?"

"No."

The trial got underway. The woman reiterated that she'd never ever had a credit card. The representative for the plaintiff said otherwise: not only did she have a credit card, but she'd abused her privilege.

It turned out to be a case of mistaken identity. Zwiener discovered that the social security number was off by one digit. He dismissed the case.

That's my hallmark case for making them all come to a hearing and prove up. These guys are professionals and they're really good at what they do, but they do make mistakes and that's why we're here: to make sure that justice is served.

He is joined by many judges who make sure that the mistakes credit card companies make (and those law offices that buy up credit card debt for the collection potential) don't hurt his constituents. Having to devote so much time to credit card cases raises the hackles of a lot of judges with whom I spoke. Jo Rita Henard (Collingsworth County) says these cases are "overpowering her." The fact that there are only around three thousand people in her county tells you everything you need to know about the impact that unpaid debt is having not only in Texas, but throughout the country.

At the same time, it reminds us of an important point about life in twenty-first-century America: we have become a J. Wellington Wimpy society.* Far too many people adhere to his motto, "I'll gladly pay you Tuesday for a hamburger today." There are JPs who understand all too well that a lot of those who find themselves dragged into justice court on cases involving outstanding credit card debt aren't total innocents. Donna Wessels (Wharton County) has seen quite a few repeat offenders—folks, she says, "who just run up each card to the max and can't pay for it."

> *I had somebody sue Borden's milk for $10,000 because they said they drank a glass of milk and it made their stomach hurt.*
> —Hon. Matt Beasley, Montgomery County

In general, civil trials require the use of a different part of a JP's brain than, say, criminal cases, administrative hearings, and inquests. Judges in higher courts may have a hard time understanding the important role that intuition and common sense play in justice court. Here is Chris Macon's take on it. He's one of Ellis County's four JPs—a colleague of Jackie Miller Jr.

In justice court, the rules of evidence are out the window. Justice court is the people's court—the lowest court in the tier. The justice court, the Appeals Court, and the Supreme Court in Texas have the greatest latitude. We've got a lot of leeway, a lot of gray, a lot of play room. The courts in between—the county, district, and federal courts—are well-defined procedurally. In justice court, as in the Supreme Court, you can be all over the place.

I get cases all the time where an attorney will "move to exclude," or they'll want to keep out evidence or whatever, and I'm like, "No. We'd like to see this." I'll get two attorneys or maybe get a defendant with an attorney and the plaintiff is pro se, and the plaintiff will start rattling off stuff—they may have pictures and they may have a contract, and I'll say, "Bring it up here and let me look at it." I'll look at it and say to the attorney, "Here. You want to look at this? Because I want us all on the same page, I'm going to allow it."

Sergio L. De Leon (Tarrant County) agrees that "most cases in JP court are common sense kinds of cases."

You don't need a legal background to decide them. What's right is right, what's wrong is wrong. If a judge is savvy enough to ask the appropriate questions and knows how to ask those questions of the litigants, then he or she can get to the truth and can make their ruling accordingly. The tricky part is when a rule does apply, and you have to watch out for these because there are so many. For example, the clock starts to tick whenever a discovery order has been granted. Judges do have to watch the clock.

Mike Smith (Harrison County) cited a good example of how common sense and an intuitive sense of fairness play a crucial role in a JP's decision-making process when it comes to small claims cases:

Let me tell you about a case: There was this small town and they had this golf course. Two eighty-two, eighty-three-year-old men who played golf with each other every day kept a running score card. They played a dime a hole. Well, one of the gentlemen got to the point where he couldn't play anymore, and he found that the other man owed him $456, so he sues the man for the $456. What is the judge going to do? Where is the law for that? What statute do you go to on that?

But that's how this court originated. It is for situations just like that. Somebody came in one day saying, "I loaned my son $650."

I say, "Do you have a piece of paper?"

"No, he's my son. Why would I draw up a piece of paper with my son?"

They expect you to make a decision when they come to you, because that's the kind of court it is.

As ridiculous and seemingly trivial as some small claims suits are, Theresa Farris (Freestone County) reminds us that JPs are still dealing with people's lives. "It's high stakes stuff if it's happening to *you*. A JP shouldn't just treat it as if it's nothing. I like to treat people just like I'd like to be treated."

Trisher Ford (Tyler County) looks at her job in the very same way.

This is the people's court. We've seen it all, from, "You've chopped down my bush," to "You have my photo frames." At first, you're thinking, photo frames? Then you listen to their story and you think, oh, I have a photo frame from my grandmother, and I wouldn't want anybody taking it. Regardless of whether they win or lose, they're gonna be heard. And they don't have to hire an attorney to do it. They feel comfortable walking in here; it doesn't matter if they make a dollar a day or a thousand dollars a day. They can pretty much have their voice heard.

How *do* you decide? Judge Glenn E. Klaus (Medina County) shared a little of his process with me.

I usually find something in a case that I'm going to hang my hat on. At some point, something is brought up from either side which I'll note down, and then I'll go back to it later. Sometimes you just split it down the middle. They're both right, they're both wrong. It can make everybody mad, or it makes everybody happy, because they just want their day in court.

One of the things that John McGuire (Tom Green County) likes about his job is getting quickly to the bottom of frivolous lawsuits and "making the right judgment." Some of the people that McGuire sees "know dang good and well they don't have a case," but they'll file anyway.

There are other ways that the JP court can be manipulated when it comes to small claims suits. Michael Jones Jr., who sees a lot of small claims cases filed in his precinct in Dallas County, cites as a definite red flag a plaintiff suing for the maximum damages allowed by the court. This can indicate that his justice court is being exploited for a purpose that might be better served in some other manner (either through filing in a higher court or by means of some other remedy).

Jeff Wentworth (Bexar County) is quite familiar with these suspicious filings. At the time we spoke, the monetary jurisdiction in justice court was still $10,000 and below. "Whenever someone sues for exactly $10,000," he said, "you know it's worth more than that, but they know they can't sue for more than that." Still, Judge Wentworth feels obligated to ask how they came up with that amount.

Some of the plaintiffs will tell him flat out: "Well, Your Honor, that's the maximum you can sue for in this court."

In county court, you have to have a lawyer.

And you have to pay for parking.

The rules now allow a justice of the peace in civil trials to ask questions that level the informational and evidentiary playing field when litigants come in who are not smartly prepared and who sometimes even proceed quite bunglingly in presenting their side in the people's court. It's no easy task for a JP to make sure that a plaintiff or defendant doesn't lose just because of a clumsy or incomplete presentation. A justice of the peace, especially in the presence of a well-prepared attorney representing the opposing party, must—in addition to making sure that all the facts get out—refrain from giving the impression of showing favoritism toward the babe-in-the-woods pro se litigant. John W. Swenson Jr. (Clay County) agrees that it can be a "touchy situation" making sure that a case or defense is helpfully developed without putting the other party to disadvantage.

There are times when there is a paucity of dispositive evidence, and a judge will have to make a ruling based on which party has offered the most credible testimony. Judge Terry calls it "going with a gut feeling as to who is telling the truth and who isn't."

A good number of cases arise from written promises made and not kept, and signed contracts that are breached. But Judge Macon reminded me that handshake deals are still a part of doing business in the state of Texas.

We actually see quite a bit of it. It basically comes down to how prepared you are and what you do in fact have in hand to back up your testimony. I have to weigh into account the credibility of what you present to me and that's what I go with. It's quite shocking to me with the landlord/tenant cases I see, though, how many people have verbal agreements on renting residences these days.

Judges who come out of law enforcement can be intimidated by civil cases because of their lack of experience in this area. Not Mike Missildine in Collin County. He says it's the investigator in him; he takes advantage of the opportunity that Texas law gives him in the people's court to develop a case, "to see where the bread crumbs lead." He enjoys working toward what he calls that "aha! moment," in which he's able to bring both parties to a logical conclusion.

Teri Nunley (Kendall County) first worked as a court reporter in district court. Her former job gave her a familiarity with the civil side of the Texas judiciary, although she is struck by one of the differences between the two courts.

The courtroom is where I've spent all my days. Civil cases seem really easy to me here at the justice court, because I've seen major district court civil cases. All my small claims cases seem like nothing to me compared with people suing the Goodyear Tire Company over a bad accident where deaths were involved, or suing doctors and hospitals for malpractice. All the civil cases in JP court are important to the people involved, but it's easy for me to listen to the facts and try to put away the emotions.

Though she does wonder, on occasion, why she's having to hear a particular case.

I had one a week or two ago for $100. I thought, Y'all couldn't handle this over a phone call? To file suit and have it served is $131!

Jeff Monk's court in Johnson County is one of those around the country that have been trolled by *Judge Judy* field researchers on the hunt for juicy, poachable cases with high entertainment potential. Monk said if the researchers found something they liked and it met certain criteria with the producers, the show would send out letters to both parties to see if they'd like Judge Judy to take over. If the plaintiff and defendant agreed to appear on the show, a letter of dismissal went to Monk's court, and the lawsuit was magically transformed into a form of televised mediation, as Judge Judy Sheindlin was no longer an acting judge, but only playing one on TV. Monk told me that some people turned down the offer because "the fifteen minutes of fame just wasn't worth it."**

There are judges who can dispense with a contested small claims case in less than five minutes, especially if one side doesn't have a leg to stand on. But some cases aren't cut and dried at all. They're *uncut* and quite squishy. They require multiple witnesses, or there's a long history there that factors into present-day circumstances. Suzan Thompson, who used to be a JP in Matagorda County, shared her most memorable civil bench trial with me. It was also her longest.

The landlord was suing the tenant, who had actually vacated the property, but he was still suing for damage to the property. Normally these cases go an hour, two hours, but both parties—both the plaintiff and the defendant—had attorneys. I thought maybe another thirty, forty-five minutes and we'll be done, and I remember this specifically because it was during the closing of the O. J. Simpson trial. That's significant because my trial went on for over five days! Oh my goodness, it was insane. They had so many witnesses brought in. I had pages and pages of notes from the testimony. After they'd finally closed, I was like, "Thank you!" I remember having previously asked one of the attorneys, "Are we gonna do the O. J. thing this week, or can we just get on with this?" I rendered my decision on the same day they acquitted O. J.

Apparently, they ended up doing the O. J. thing.

NOTES

*Did you know that Popeye's friend Wimpy actually had a first and second name?

**I recall that when I got hired to be a clerk in Judge Debra Ravel's office in the fall of 1983, the first thing I said to Mary when I got the news was, "I'm going to work for a female Judge Wapner." Judge Joseph Wapner's *The People's Court* was the first big arbitration-based reality TV court show, and I was a big fan.

4

Bag and Baggage

A lot of times people just have a verbal agreement with no written lease. You do have to wade through what the truth is, and usually there's two sides and the real truth is in the middle.

—HON. TIM BRYAN, GREGG COUNTY

JUSTICE COURTS HAVE ALWAYS had original jurisdiction in eviction cases, no matter how much the rent is. Because of this, eviction laws have been written to try to keep things simple. Who has the legal right to occupy a particular piece of property? That's the principal issue. Because evictions are supposed to be filed in the justice court precinct in which the property is located, the number of cases a JP will hear is dependent on how many apartment complexes, public housing units, nursing homes, rental houses, and grown sons living in the family basement one finds in a particular precinct. For example, in Grimes County, most of the county's apartment complexes have been built in Precinct 3—which makes Mark Laughlin the "eviction judge."

From my many conversations with Texas justices of the peace, I've come to realize that there are a few JPs who seem hardwired to lean in favor of an eviction suit plaintiff and a few others who like to tip the scales in favor of the eviction suit defendant. One hears in some counties, "Oh, he's a landlord's judge," or "She's much more of a tenant's judge." But the general feeling is that most JPs will try hard not to exercise bias in favor of either side. Like Judge Tim Bryan (Gregg County), they endeavor to take every case on its own merits, an approach that puts them face-to-face with both abusive landlords and problem renters.

I was naïve. When I got into law enforcement, I thought everybody did the right thing. I quickly realized that's not the case. What I found with evictions is that not only do I feel it's my responsibility to apply the law, but it's also my responsibility to make sure that we don't have predatory landlords out there cutting off the power and removing the doors because the tenant isn't paying the rent. That's specifically prohibited by law. We have to step in sometimes to fight for the rights of the tenant or to guide the tenant in how they can file a case to get their door back on its hinges, because the landlord has to follow the rules just like the tenant does.

There have been extraordinary cases where the forty-year-old son is evicted because he won't get a job, or the boyfriend and girlfriend are together and he doesn't want her there anymore. But it's mostly pretty cut and dried. The landlord does have the right to the property if someone isn't paying their rent, but I do think it's important, rather than just running them in and out like cattle, to be compassionate to people, because being evicted can be the worst thing in their life. We had a lot of people losing their houses because they were losing their jobs in the oil industry, so I do think that instead of just saying, "If you can't pay, you can't stay. Get out!" it's important to say to them, "The law is clear. I'm here to apply the law. But you can make it through this."

Then there are the landlords who bend over backward for their tenants. Sheron Collins (Hale County) had a gentleman who fit this description in her courtroom.

Here in Hale County we have good landlords who try to work with folks, and the back rent ends up being ridiculous. But when you're behind two or three thousand dollars in back rent, it's time to go. I will tell you that on one of our evictions, I had the tenant come in and say, "Well, I took his $100, and then I just decided I wasn't gonna move."

I couldn't understand what she was talking about. I said, "You took his $100?" The plaintiff was just sitting there with this look on his face like, oh my goodness, she actually said that out loud. I asked the tenant, "Why would your landlord give you $100?"

"Well, he told me that he was gonna have to pay $100 to come to court, so he just gave me the $100 to move out."

I looked at the plaintiff and I said, "I've heard of a move-in allowance, but I've never heard of a move-out allowance."

Well, it didn't work. The landlord had been doing this and it had been working until he hit the one who took his money and wouldn't move. I've known this landlord ever since I've been in this courthouse. I said, "Sir, I think you have more money than sense."

Eviction cases are sad cases, where people fall on hard times and they can't pay their rent. But the landlords fall on hard times if they can't collect the rent. —Hon. *Bill Price, Coryell County*

Donna Wooten (Pecos County) was one of two judges who told me that she'd had to sign a death certificate on someone she'd just evicted. In Judge Wooten's case, not only had circumstances required her to rule for the landlord, she then had to issue a writ of possession (which authorizes the constable to remove the individual from the premises) when the tenant refused to abide by the court's decision.

The landlord had given him a year of free rent for his trailer because she didn't have the heart to kick him out. He was a disabled vet, a horrible alcoholic, and a known drug abuser. She finally got to the point where she was selling the trailer park and the buyers needed all the tenants out. He was promptly evicted. It was pretty black and white. The landlord came back for a writ of possession. Our constable didn't want to move his things to the curb. The man said he'd be gone by noon. I got a phone call right as I was getting ready to leave for lunch. The man shot himself.

I did an eviction, writ of possession, and then a death certificate.

The other judge was Lisa Whitehead (Burnet County).

We had an eviction in the summer, somewhere around August. This was a fairly nice guy, but he'd do drugs and what-not, and the law was being called on the people who would come there, so it was a lease violation as opposed to a rent violation.

And then toward the end of August, I was called to do an inquest for a gentleman who was found in his car. It was him. He died in his car from—I guess he had it running with the air conditioner on and he must have fallen asleep. He'd done some drugs, he fell asleep, the battery died, the windows were rolled up, and he just basically cooked in his car.

So even a simple eviction can turn into something awful.

Gina Cleveland (Jasper County) sees a lot of family evictions. She told me that most people don't understand that if you want a relative out of your house, you still have to go through the legal eviction process. There are times when a JP has to move quickly because abuse is involved.

Michael Jones Jr. (Dallas County) deals with situations in which a parent has to use the justice court to remove a son or daughter who won't leave otherwise.

They don't want to own up, they don't want to leave. They run the parents' bills all the way up and don't want to pay for them. Some of the situations become disrespectful, some even become violent.

One day I said to Charlie, my clerk, "Look at this. I was quick today. It's almost eleven o'clock and I finished my eviction docket and nobody cussed me out today!"—Hon. Sharon M. Burney, Harris County

Ciro Rodriguez (Bexar County) has seen more than one instance in which a grown child takes over the house and the mom ends up being shuttled vagabond-like among the other family members.

One of the ones that irritate the hell out of me is the guy who comes in here dressed in a suit, all cleaned up, who's been living in his mama's home for fifteen years. He's never given her a nickel and she's having to go from sister to brother to daughter, not able to live in her own home. And the guy feels he's entitled to it.

Judge Rodriguez recalled another eviction defendant who said he had every right to stay in his grandmother's house after her passing because she'd always told him, *"Mi casa es su casa."*

Wayne Money (Hunt County) is also a tough-love kind of judge when it comes to family evictions.

When Mom and Dad have to kick the kid out of the house, it's not just tough, it's sad. That kind of eviction also makes you mad because of how kids take Mom and Dad for granted. The real dose of life is this: get out on the street and make your own living, whether it's shining shoes on the corner or working the back of a trash truck or waiting tables. Before you make your fortune, you've got to work for a living.

In case you're curious, Jerry Parker (Wood County) set me straight on how you serve legal notice-to-vacate on someone in your family. I wondered if you had to put the notice on your front door for all the kravitzing neighbors to see; the law actually allows a family member to serve written notice to vacate to another family member by simply handing the person the piece of paper or tacking it to their bedroom door.

A lot of factors figure into the eviction suits JPs must hear—some of them meteorological acts of God. Three weeks after Hurricane Harvey struck the Texas Gulf Coast, Justin M. Joyce noticed a big increase in eviction cases filed in his precinct in Fort Bend County due to people being thrown out of work because of the storm and therefore not being able to make their next rent payment.

Circumstances were different during the COVID-19 pandemic: a statewide moratorium on evictions was declared. Then on September 1, 2020, the Centers for Disease Control released an order creating a federal moratorium on residential evictions for nonpayment of rent for "covered persons," effective through the end of the year. The CDC moratorium was extended through January 31, 2021, by the federal stimulus bill signed December 27, 2020. Emergency orders issued by the Supreme Court of Texas allowed for a temporary halt to residential evictions in rental situations in which tenants were able to sign declarations of their inability to pay their rent due to financial hardship related to the pandemic.

The declaration also included the statement, "If evicted I would likely become homeless, need to move into a homeless shelter, or need to move into a new residence shared by other people who live in close quarters because I have no other available housing options." This language was important and clearly related to the primary purpose for the federal-mandated moratorium, with that purpose stated unambiguously in the declaration's extended title: "Declaration Under Penalty of Perjury for the Centers for Disease Control and Prevention's Temporary Halt in Evictions to Prevent Further Spread of COVID-19." The upside for tenants was that a lot of Texas renters wouldn't be thrown out on the streets at the height of the pandemic for failure to pay their rent; the potential upside for all of Texas was that a roving population of homeless Texans wouldn't, ostensibly, be spreading the virus hither and yon.

But the order, in effect, offered only stopgap relief. Tenants were still liable for all the back rent and related fees they were accruing. And property owners—especially small mom-and-pop landlords—couldn't evict tenants who, for a good many months, were paying only part, or, in many cases, *none* of the rent they owed. Nor did thousands of these landlords, many struggling economically themselves, hope to ever receive all the back rent owed to them. Making matters worse were those who never let a national crisis go by without a bit of creatively applied opportunism. As Jim Cavanaugh (Brown County) told me in the midst of the pandemic, "It hasn't taken long for the 'frequent flyers' to realize that if they can get into any rental property, they cannot be evicted for non-payment. They have had a free ride since April or May and cannot be touched until January 2021."

When I spoke to Judge Whitehead in the fall of 2020, she described one particularly nervy eviction defendant who apparently decided that he'd see if he could make the CDC moratorium on evictions work to his benefit.

I'm hearing a case next week. A woman asked a friend of hers she'd known for twenty years to house-sit for her over a weekend. When she came back, he'd moved all his trucks, his boats, his trailers, and his cats onto the property. He just moved in. She had to move to a hotel for a few days because she was afraid of him.

All in all, Texas JPs were forced to tread unprecedented waters and navigate through often untenable situations representative of some of the worst fallout from the pandemic in their beleaguered communities.

Ironically, it isn't always a struggling economy that places renters into the kind of dire financial straits that threaten their ability to stay in their homes. When it comes to putting people out, bag and baggage, the culprit might just be the opposite. In vibrant growth counties like Travis, market forces driven by a land-office real estate boom have caused property values to escalate, and those who occupied these properties—especially low-income Austinites—have found themselves squeezed by rent increases and buffeted by frequent and confusing changes in ownership and management. When they are hot commodities, apartment complexes frequently change ownership (which means they also change management) and the tenants, some of them long-term, are left reeling.

Back in 2019, Travis County JP Yvonne Michelle Williams explained to me how this worked in her precinct, whose low-income residents had been experiencing both gentrification pressures and simple profit-motivated greed.

The average property that I see now—I've been seeing the same properties for eight years—they've been bought two times over in the past three years. When the boom happened, tenants would come in and say, "I don't even know who to talk to because they've changed managers five times just since I've been here."

The new owners come in and they say, "We can get more for these properties if we raise the rent. And all the people who have been owing rent for the last month and half, get rid of them!"

I know when this happens because my docket will be mostly one apartment complex, because the new management came in and said get them out.

Before the pandemic, Judge Williams's court scheduled two eviction dockets a week, which meant that she spent a nice chunk of her county's taxpayer dollars hearing eviction suits. A big pet peeve of hers is managers who use her court as a vehicle to help them collect their rent. They file an eviction suit to light a fire under the tenant, but then end up dismissing the suit once they've gotten the next month's rent and the late fee plus the court costs from the tenant.

Judge Rodriguez shares that concern in Austin's sister city San Antonio. As home prices have gone up, large parts of the city that were formerly havens of affordability for low income folk have been bought out. Rents have risen, people have been evicted, and there has been no place for them to go.

> *Let me tell you when I feel bad. For the first six months of my job, I couldn't eat lunch on eviction day because I had to put people out.*
> —Hon. Yvonne Michelle Williams, Travis County

I haven't spoken with a single Texas JP who said they enjoy evictions. It's one of the toughest parts of the job. "They can really be a challenge, and touching," says Irma Dunn (Titus County).

You don't want to kick people out of their houses. But you have to understand the other side: the owner needs to make a mortgage payment on the house and you can't be living there for free. Sometimes the people are like, "You're only doing this because I'm black or because I'm Mexican."

I say, "Uh-uh. That's not gonna work in this courtroom. One of my clerks is white and one is black and I'm Hispanic. You got a lot of love in this office!"

A JP is torn between compassion for the renter being put out on the street and empathy for mom-and-pop property owners who can't pay their mortgages and their property taxes if they aren't getting rent money from the people who live there. They aren't excited about filing eviction suits on their tenants, but circumstances give them no choice. Dianne Rogers (Real County) has landlords in her court who want to give their tenants a break, but can't do so without placing themselves in financial jeopardy.

Still, it can be especially difficult for a Texas JP to evict people from their homes when, as Ronald LeBlanc (Matagorda County) reminded me, there are small children involved. Judge Jones has a list of community groups and churches that assist evicted families. Other JPs also provide lists of resources to help the families get through this transitional period.

> *The good thing about an eviction is that it's black and white. You either paid your rent or you didn't. It's not one of those things you really have to think about. The bad part is that it's usually not one person you're kicking out of the home—it's a family.*
> —Hon. Kim Redman, Wise County

Setting aside the emotional component, evictions, except for those few prickly exceptions having to do with he-said/she-said oral agreements or fuzzy lease terms, are fairly straightforward, not to mention grounded in solid logic. Joe Martinez (Gray County) does a fine job of laying out that logic.

Society has to have an orderly way of dealing with problems so that the parties don't go into an anarchy situation. The law is not there to persecute you. The law is there to create an orderly transition in a difficult situation that you cannot continue in. You can't stay in someone's house and not pay the rent. The law is there to assist the person in this dilemma.

Nancy Shepherd works in the Lipscomb County courthouse. The town of Lipscomb is one of the tiniest county seats in the state, with fewer than fifty people living there. On the other end of the population spectrum sits Nicholas Chu, who serves as one of five JPs in Travis County, with its estimated current population of over 1.2 million. Prior to the pandemic, Judge Chu was hearing thousands of eviction suits a year; Judge Shepherd in her busiest year: maybe five.

Since an overwhelming majority of eviction cases are won by plaintiffs, who can usually prove, without doubt, that their tenants aren't paying the rent and need to go, I asked a few of the JPs who handle a considerable number of eviction cases to give me examples of suits in which the law would require a judge to rule for the defendant, or tenant. Duncan Neblett Jr. (Nueces County) offered a couple:

One is where there isn't a written lease. The other is that, "I know the rent is $500, but he said I could work half of it off by painting the walls and keeping the grass cut," and then you get into a swearing match where, "Yeah, I said that, but he used the wrong color of paint on the wall," or "He didn't mow the yard right." If they don't have it in writing, it's just a he-said/she-said. There are definitely situations where the tenant has a legitimate reason to resist an eviction.

Sergio L. De Leon (Tarrant County) cited an instance in which intuition told him the defendant was telling the truth. But how to prove it?

I had an eviction case right before the Thanksgiving holiday. The landlord was seeking to evict an exchange student from Africa. The student was pleading with me that he had paid the rent and had put it into the overnight box before the holiday. The plaintiff said no, it didn't happen. I put myself in the young man's shoes and called for a brief recess. I asked the plaintiff to call her office and have people look all over and see if they could find the young man's rent check. She did this and came back in and asked for a dismissal. It was behind one of the plants by the window. You have that kind of latitude as a justice of the peace in terms of getting to the truth of things. Had it been someone else, maybe they would have been stern and not listened.

For this man, he had justice. He walked away with a good feeling about the American judicial system.

Jeff Wentworth (Bexar County) told me that one of the hardest parts of his job is dealing with intransigent landlords (or managers for large corporation-owned apartment complexes) who refuse to work with tenants in getting the back rent paid so they won't have to move out. He related the story of a woman in San Antonio who was both blind and deaf who still got herself to work every day at the Lighthouse for the Blind—a three-year tenant who fell one month behind in her rent only to have to face an eviction suit filed by the Florida-based real estate company that owned the apartment complex and had a very rigid policy when it came to renters in arrears. Such a policy baffled him.

The most surprising thing for me since I became JP has been this attitude that some of these landlords have toward tenants. I don't believe they appreciate what a genuine hassle it is to have to move and then have a blight on their record that's not going to help their credit or their employment or anything else. Moving is just a major problem for a lot of people. It really bothers me when you have a landlord and tenant before the bench who haven't talked about the case at all and the landlord gets up there, and let's say the tenant owes $1,500 in back rent, the landlord wants it all, and the tenant says, "Well, I have $1,000." Let's say we're trying this case on a Tuesday and the renter says, "I get paid on Friday and I can pay it all off then."

I'll say, "Well, good." And then I'll turn to the landlord and say, "So you'll have your $1,500. That's what you sued for."

The landlord will very often reply, "No. We just want possession."

It's "company policy."

Sylvia Holmes (Travis County) has observed evictions and landlord/tenant disputes from all angles. In her private practice, she represented landlords. But when she was associate director of Legal Services for Students at the University of Texas (UT), she represented UT students in a variety of legal matters, including disagreements over the withholding of security deposits when tenant-students moved out. I mentioned to Judge Holmes that when my wife, Mary, was a student at UT, she and her roommate used the services of a university attorney to win treble damages when their own security deposit was unfairly withheld. Judge Holmes replied that from her own observation of such cases, they're pretty evenly divided between landlords trying to take advantage of students who have no desire to fight them in court, and those shifty Joe College-types who actually had done something that forfeited their deposit under the terms of the lease ("That cartoon Bevo spray-painted on the living room wall was there when we moved in, Your Honor, I swear it!").

For Judge Holmes, one of the hardest parts of being a JP is hearing nursing home evictions. Holmes argues that society needs to be better prepared for all the legal issues that will accrete alongside a rapidly aging population, including the financial impact of long-term rehabilitative care, or, to put things more bluntly, the fact that because of advancements in modern medicine, older Texans are living much longer than they used to (and longer than their children expected them to!).

The smaller the county, the more familiar become the faces of those filing and contesting eviction suits in a JP's court. Ronnie Davis (Liberty County) told me that there are some people who get filed on for eviction every two months.

I had one a while back; the man owed $1,700, I evicted him, they rented to him again, and then turned around and evicted him again. A lot of it is comical.

One house renter had two-hundred-and-some-odd bags of trash in the yard. The property owner had pictures of it. I told the tenant when I evicted him, "I don't want one bit of trash in that yard when y'all move out of there."

Later, Judge Davis saw the "after" pictures. "You could eat in that yard," he said. "It was just as clean as it could it be."

The landlord told me, "They'd done just like you told them. Didn't leave any trash in the yard. They put it all in the attic."

In the final analysis, evictions require a JP to make a consequential decision about the fate of someone in a bad situation that may or may not be of their own making who is occupying a physical space they may no longer have the right to occupy. For a Texas justice of the peace, one eviction can ruin your whole day . . . or night, as Stan Warfield (Colorado County) explains:

I don't like to do evictions, particularly when it's an eighty-three-year-old woman who is blind, has been living in the house for eighteen years, has turned her business over to her kids, the kids stopped making the mortgage payments, and she gets foreclosed on and evicted. There is nothing the judge can do. I don't usually lose sleep over my decisions. I lost sleep over that one.

But if you're the right judge in the right county at the right time, there just might be something you *can* do. Ralph Swearingin (Tarrant) is a problem-solver. (His most recent project involves improving the system that relies on JPs to make decisions regarding emergency mental health detentions.) When it comes to evictions, Judge Swearingin has figured out a way to lend a hand to suddenly homeless Fort Worth evictees.

I'm in here within the first four to six weeks of my first term and I have an eviction case. A lady is standing there. She's holding the hand of a child probably five or six years old. I say, "Ma'am is there anything you'd like to tell me?"

She says, "Yes, judge there is. I had one child who died, I have one in the hospital not expected to live, and you're telling me and my small child that we're out on the street."

There was dead silence in a very full courtroom. It caught me off guard. I took a gigantic swallow, and I said, "Yes, ma'am. I'm sorry, but I am."

I went home that night and I told my wife, "I believe that God did not intend for me to be in this place and to do nothing." So I started making phone calls, and one thing led to another. I got with some people—the main focus was Tarrant County Human Services—who had a bundle of money and they weren't really sure how they were going to spend it, so I proposed to them an eviction assistance program. It's now been in place here since I've been a judge. With anybody who, through no fault of their own—maybe they're ill, maybe they're taking care of somebody who's ill, maybe they're facing family violence or loss of a child or family member, whatever it may be—I can nod my head and my bailiff knows. He follows them outside the courtroom and he tells them that there is a program and we can't tell you if you qualify, but here's the phone number. Through that program, the other JPs in Tarrant County and I have helped a lot of people over the last thirteen years. It's not just temporary assistance; it involves trying to find an avenue to meet their needs.

I believe that maybe that was part of my purpose for being here. I sleep at night knowing there is a program to help people.

5

A Jury of Their Peers

ALTHOUGH BENCH TRIALS—THAT IS, trials in which the judge herself decides the outcome—are far more common in justice court, some litigants choose to consign their fate to a jury of their peers. It's a very American tradition. Though trial by jury can be traced back to ancient Greece and was one of the explicit rights demanded by the Magna Carta, the United States stands alone among the nations of the world today in routinely using juries for both criminal cases and a wide array of *non*-criminal lawsuits.

Jury trials in Texas justice court can be dry as dust or one of the most enjoyable forms of entertainment around, offering up different variations on the theme of human conflict: lawyer vs. lawyer; lawyer vs. pro se (self-representing) litigant; and pro se vs. pro se. Sparky Dean (Taylor County) is amused by how some of those who choose to represent themselves in front of a jury will prepare for their day in court: they watch television. (Specifically, their favorite legal dramas!)

We had a jury trial several years ago. One of the witnesses comes up and I say, "If you'll state your name before giving your testimony."

The guy goes, "My name is so-and-so," and the defendant jumps up and objects.

I'm not paying a lot of attention because I'm sitting there writing, and you do that rewind in your mind—wait a minute. He's just giving me his name. I said to the young man, "What are you objecting to?"

All of a sudden, there's that deer-in-the-headlights look. He says, "Judge, I object to what he's saying."

"But he's just telling me his name. How can you object to his name?"
He says, "That's what they do on TV."
He had studied for court all night long by watching Perry Mason, *right? I'm like, "Oh, God bless you."*

Darrell Longino (Polk County) pointed up the pitfalls of putting a pro se defendant before a jury. The case involved alleged health and safety code violations.

It ended in a mistrial because the defendant was so vocal and ani-mated, he was throwing his arms around and spitting on the jurors and scared them to death. I warned him three times, and ended up holding him in contempt. It was the first time in twenty-three years I'd ever held anybody in contempt. But he wouldn't stop.

I had the jury removed and took care of the contempt. I knew they were tainted and there was no way they could come out with a just verdict after he'd scared them like he did, so I had to declare the mistrial. The case was refiled. Before we went to the next trial, we had a pre-trial hearing and we set rules that allowed him to enter things into evidence, but he couldn't go down any rabbit trails.

Longino reported that this next trial went smoother. Once he knew what he was and wasn't allowed to do in mounting his defense, the defendant kept the flutter and sputter to a minimum.

> *I like the courtroom, more so when there's lawyers around. Things move faster. Pro se defendants don't know what they're doing. A lawyer will eat a pro se's lunch.*—Hon. Jack Keeling, Leon County

I spoke with quite a few judges about what happens when a self-repre-senting litigant finds himself going toe to toe with a lawyer. The law al-lows JPs in such cases to make sure that a pro se plaintiff in the throes of panic doesn't forget to tell the jury what it is he wants. After all, pleading your own case before a jury of your peers isn't something us non-lawyers do every day. Glenn E. Klaus (Medina County) enjoys studying the interplay between lawyer and layperson in his courtroom (almost as much as he likes watching "rock 'em, sock 'em" bouts between attorneys).

When you have a pro se plaintiff or defendant opposed by a party with an attorney, a lot of times the attorney will cut the other party a little slack, but I can always tell when they've had enough and they're going to drop the hammer. Even the county attorney prosecutors in criminal cases will cut the defendant a little slack. But you get one of these attorneys overdosed on Matlock, *they don't do that.*

Scott Shinn (Van Zandt County) thinks the rule change that now permits a JP to help develop a case does tend to propel pro se jury trials forward at a much faster, smoother clip.

For example, I had a jury trial before the rule change where a plaintiff presented a beautiful case and should have won, but he never told the jury what he was asking for, and I had to do a directed verdict. Now I can say, "Okay plaintiff, are you through with your case? Be sure to tell the jury what you're asking for before the defendant presents his case." I think it makes a huge difference and gives us the freedom to move these cases along. People don't lose now just because they forgot to tell the amount of money they wanted.

Every JP has a different opinion when it comes to the juries that serve in their court. Sometimes the opinion amounts to, "It's anybody's guess just *what* a jury is liable to do." Even the jurors themselves don't always know what they're going to do, or at least aren't able to come to the required consensus: a 6–0 verdict in criminal trials, a 5–1 verdict in civil trials.

In the case of the former, hung juries can get hung up by that one hold-out juror, who can both gum up the works and leave his fellow jury members seeing red. Billy S. Ball (Angelina County) recalled a particular traffic case in which he could hear "five angry jurors" in his jury room, ready to let the defendant loose, but the sixth juror—a former cop—wasn't having it. (The antithesis of Henry Fonda's reasonably doubting Juror #8 in *Twelve Angry Men*.) Who would Ball have sided with, had this been a bench trial? He didn't even have to think about it: the five angry jurors.

Jurors in justice court can be counted on to do one or both of the following: put themselves in the shoes of the defendant, or put the defendant in *their* shoes. With regard to the latter, this can involve exercising just a little animosity toward the party or parties responsible for sticking them in a jury box and jury room when they'd rather be doing something else. Jackie Miller Jr. (Ellis County) put it this way:

If you make your juries stay in here a long time—you've got two attorneys battling it out on a civil suit, and it's been four or five or six hours—I tell these guys they'll convict Jesus Christ, because they want to go home; they've got kids, families. And I don't break for lunch. But I do find that most jurors do take their civic duty very seriously.

Stan G. Mahler (Young County) has noticed that in certain traffic cases in which it's up to the jury to set the fine on a guilty verdict, the jurors will "really hammer a defendant." But Mahler also sees jury trials in which a defendant's fate is determined by good, old-fashioned fellow-feeling. Judge Miller has noticed more jury acquittals for professional truck drivers than drivers of cars because of concerns about the truck driver being able to make his living.

There are those who decide to let the judge be the one to decide their fate, and there are those who prefer to roll the dice with a jury. It can be a good move if your case requires some degree of kindness and understanding, but juries don't always see things this way. Joe Martinez (Gray County) doesn't get a lot of jury trials in his court, maybe one a year. He thinks his litigants don't want to inconvenience their neighbors by forcing this particular civic responsibility on them. (Besides that, he doesn't think his is all that exonerating of a county.)

It's like their own peers are going to be skeptical of them because they're called up for an offense. They're probably thinking: if you got cited for it, there must have been something you did wrong. They don't really put up with a lot of stuff here.

> *You know, juries are actually harder on defendants. They'll hit them harder on the fines.*—Hon. Ciro Rodriguez, Bexar County

Yvonne Michelle Williams saw this happen in her courtroom in Travis County:

A lady asked for a jury trial because she got a handicapped parking ticket. Seriously? Do you know why she asked for a jury trial? Because she

was on one of the Dell campuses on a Sunday morning around nine a.m.
while it was raining. There wasn't a soul in the parking lot. There were
about five hundred empty spaces with about twenty handicapped parking
places up front. She was parked in one of them because she was moving
her office. I don't know what the deputy was thinking. He pulled up and
gave her a ticket. I would have just fined her a dollar. The jury found her
guilty and fined her $600!

Judge Williams also had an eviction case in her court in which the
defendant asked for a jury trial, and things didn't go as predicted then
either.

The defendant was a young white woman going to UT and guess who
the foreman of the jury ended up being? A white female of her age who
wore the same kind of clothes and who could identify with this woman.
The landlord was a foreigner with a strong accent. When the jury came
back in, it was a shock to everybody, including the woman, because they
delivered a verdict in her favor! Shocking because she had just been buying
time. Had the plaintiff said to me, "I want a judgment notwithstanding
the jury's verdict, because they aren't following the law," I would have said
yes, but I can't tell him this. He has to make that decision.

Having worked in district court as an assistant DA, Travis County
JP Raúl Arturo González talked to me about the difference between
juries in the higher courts and those that get picked for justice court
trials. The jury pool is smaller in JP court, with only six seats to be filled
(and no alternates), and you're much more likely to find jurors willing
to serve since their civic duty might last only a few hours as opposed to
several days. As a result, there are fewer folks balking and trying to beg
out of serving. "The matters at hand aren't going to be as complicated,"
he added. "You don't have as many witnesses. There aren't as many
questions to answer."

If there are attorneys involved, they're not going to have as many
juror challenges for cause. Things do tend to clip along; JPs like to keep
their trials lean, knowing that court time is too valuable to allow for a
parade of witnesses who will basically be testifying to identical facts.
Judge González says that self-represented litigants in jury trials can be
quite long-winded, though, and sometimes a judge will have to do a bit
of gentle prodding to get them to present evidence and testimony that
bolsters their side.

I may prompt them a bit: "Tell the jury why you're asking for this. Tell them at the end what it is you want them to do. Don't just assume that they've read your petition." I get very few deer-in-the-headlights litigants, though. They've lived through this disagreement. They want to get some closure and I don't even think they mind losing, just so long as they get their chance to have their say and they have six people tell them either, "Hey, you're wrong. We just don't see it your way," or, "We agree with you."

I asked González if he ever had pro se plaintiffs and defendants who liked to go all "Matlock and Mason." He said sometimes he'd watch them get up from the counsel table and invade the personal space of the witness on the stand (such as when sharing a piece of evidence) even when they didn't have a reason. The protocol, González says, is to ask questions from the table and not get in people's faces.

Juries are always surprising JPs, not infrequently ruling differently from how the judge would have ruled in a simple bench trial.

Sharon M. Burney (Harris County) remembered a particular day when she'd scheduled back-to-back jury trials. One was an eviction case in which the defendant had asked for a jury trial because he felt a jury wouldn't have to guess at what it felt like to be in the middle of a hot and humid Houston summer without air conditioning. His landlord hadn't seen fit to get his to work, so the defendant sure as hell wasn't going to pay the man rent.

Of course, Texas law is fairly clear on this. You can't refuse to pay the rent if there are things your landlord is or isn't doing that make you miserable; there are other civil remedies for such derelictions. The tenant saw things differently and he hoped the jury would agree. It did.

Had this been a bench trial, Judge Burney admitted that the law would have required her to rule for the landlord, so the defendant was smart to take his chance with a jury. He also sounded pretty lucky. Burney made no mention to me of whether she was asked by the plaintiff to overturn the verdict because of the possibility that it contravened the law.

The second jury trial was one of the wildest Burney had ever had in her courtroom, and definitely the day's main event. A man was suing a female coworker for $10,000. His reason? She sliced him with a box cutter. The woman countersued, also for the court's maximum. *Her* reason? All the verbal abuse that had allegedly precipitated the assault. The testimony included an unexpurgated string of vulgarities to which the defendant said she'd been subjected. There was testimony from the plaintiff's other girlfriends. There were graphic references to things that go on in bedrooms that don't involve sleeping. There was a history here: calls to the police, even restraining orders . . . The proceeding would not have been mistaken for a Southern Baptist potluck.

In the end, the jury ruled against *both* of the disenchanted lovers. Judge Burney went to the jurors, and, in releasing them, told them that in terms of pure entertainment value, they'd really lucked out; after all, they could have gotten the broken air conditioner case.

Edward Marks (Floyd County) has overseen very few jury trials in his small county, yet he, too, can point to that *one*. It was a doozy—a civil trial. The plaintiff and defendant were feuding brothers.

Another judge asked me if I'd sit in on this one because she had to recuse herself. I said sure; I'd never done that. When I got down there, she said, "Judge, this thing is gonna get a little 'western' before it's over with." These brothers were constantly at it.

We had to stop the proceedings at one point and sequester the jury because one of the brothers thought he was having a heart attack. EMS was called in. I said, "Do you want to keep going?"

They did.

The sheriff was standing in the courtroom and I had to say to the brothers, "If you don't start acting like human beings, I'll have the sheriff take you to visit one of our county's fine accommodations."

They said, "You can't do that!"

I said, "You'd be surprised what I can do."

The plaintiff brother was asking for $10,000, but the jury awarded him $5,000. This made him so mad he took his walking stick and started beating the hell out of his brother. He wins the civil trial but he goes to jail for assault!

> *Some of the defendants in criminal cases who demand jury trials—the more they talk, the worse it gets, but it's their deal.*
> —Hon. Fred Buck, Tom Green County

In some Texas justice courts, a jury trial is the infrequent exception. For this reason, judges might be intimidated by the process of summoning potential jurors and overseeing the juror selection. Jury trials represent one of those rare times a JP is asking something of his constituents rather than the other way around. It's a different dynamic. The judge becomes observer, game referee, train conductor. It's the jurors who take the train to its destination.

JPs wish there were some way to thank juries for their service besides a simple vocalized expression of gratitude. Former Travis County JP Debra Ravel had the chance to do just that for her jurors.

The jury finished up and I told them they'd really worked hard and I wanted them to know that it was my birthday and that I'd been given an awfully large birthday cake that couldn't possibly be eaten by all of us—would they consider staying and joining us for my birthday party? All but one or two did stay, and they all sang "Happy Birthday" to me.

Months later, it was getting close to the filing deadline for the 1986 election. The state rep from our part of town came in to see me and he said, "You won't believe this, Debra, but if you're running again, the Republican party has decided not to run anyone against you. It turns out that a woman who is extremely powerful in the Republican party was on one of your juries, and after the jury reached a verdict, she attended your birthday party. She thought you were one of the most gracious and pleasant people she ever met. She stood up and made a speech and was resolute about not running anyone against you."

And they kept their word.

Judges who preside over more than just the occasional jury trial can really grow to like them, like Tim Bryan (Gregg County).

I feel jury trials are the best because I don't have to make a decision at all. I have to make sure the rules are followed. Sometimes I think it's funny that people think they have the best case in the world, then you put it before six reasonable men and women in Gregg County, or any county, and they see through all the lies. They make a determination as to who is credible and what evidence is important. To me those are the easiest cases. All I've got to do is sit up there and make sure everybody gets along.

This is why Judge Dean also likes jury trials:

With a bench trial, you're really having to pay attention to what people are saying, since we don't have a court reporter and we're not a court of record. In JP court, a change made a couple of years ago now allows a judge to ask questions in a case. You're fixing to have to determine somebody's innocence or guilt, or this person versus that person, who's telling the truth, who's not telling the truth, who's got the best case, how the evidence is presented. In a jury trial you just sit there. You're an umpire watching the game from the best seat in the house.

Those umpires got to watch very few jury trials in 2020, because in-person trials-by-jury were suspended once the COVID-19 pandemic took hold of the state. And while so many of Texas justice courts' operations were forced to go virtual during the many months of the pandemic, holding a jury trial through video conference was something that all but one Texas JP decided not to tackle, so the constitutional right to a trial by a jury of one's peers was suspended for the duration. Some of the judges I checked back with in 2020 were happy about not having to deal with jury trials during that anomalous year; others really missed them.

During this period, enterprising defendants and their creative lawyers, aware that requesting a jury trial on a criminal charge would lead to an automatic continuance, used a defendant's constitutional right to trial by jury as a means to postpone the disposal of their cases. Many of these were weak cases that would more than likely result in fines and other inconvenient consequences for defendant misbehavior.

> *The Texas Supreme Court and the Office of Court Administration have put a hold on all justice court jury trials until sometime after January 1, 2021. Traffic court defense attorneys have caught on to this, and our jury trial list is growing!*—Hon. Darrell Longino, Polk County

The one virtual jury trial that did take place in a Texas justice court during this period was sufficiently groundbreaking to make the national news. Nicholas Chu in Travis County had the honor of conducting it. Judge Chu had expressed his desire to the Texas Office of Court Administration to hold a criminal jury trial remotely. The district clerk liked the idea, since a judicial experiment like this was best attempted first in a state justice court with its much smaller jury pool and its cases offering fewer complications. The trial took place on August 11, 2020.

What we decided to try was a class C misdemeanor speeding ticket: "speeding in a construction zone with workers present." It can't be addressed by taking a defensive driving class; you have to either go to trial or plead. The defendant wouldn't lose anything by going to trial. I had an attorney who was willing to represent her pro bono because he'd wanted to be involved in a virtual jury trial. The county attorney's office agreed to do it. We thought if worse came to worst, the defendant would have the right to a de novo appeal up to county court.

The jury split the baby. They found the defendant not guilty of speeding in a construction zone with workers present. They did find her guilty of speeding. I assessed her a dollar fine; she was a good sport about being a guinea pig. We've all agreed that I'm the first judge to preside over a criminal jury trial virtually, probably the first in the world.

Judge Chu told me that the trial was streamed live on YouTube, where it garnered 15,000 views at one point. We both marveled over the fact that 15,000 people from around the world tuned in to watch a Texas woman contesting her speeding ticket! Chu made the point that such an opportunity is a result of the unique nature of the Texas justice court system: the courts are small enough to be used as laboratories for innovation within the American judicial system.

What Chu didn't tell me is that the trial conceivably earns the distinction of another judicial first: it was apparently the first jury trial in American history in which a cat was seen "frolicking" behind one of the jurors.*

It can get interesting when it's a justice of the peace herself who is called for jury duty. When I spoke with Trisher Ford (Tyler County) she had just received a jury summons, but she didn't think she'd get picked from the pool because she was the very judge who'd issued the arrest warrant on the defendant.

Tim Walker (Lamb County) made the astute observation that perhaps the reason there aren't more jury trials in JP courts is because people who don't want to hire a lawyer to pinch-hit for them before a jury of their peers are fearful that they themselves won't be able to effectively sway those peers. Of course, there are those pro se plaintiffs and defendants who are confident they can deliver a performance worthy of a TV lawyer, law degree or no law degree. One of the sadder displays of such moxie involved a woman who had been filed on for eviction in Theresa Farris's court in Freestone County. The defendant asked for a jury, so Judge Farris really had to hustle since the trial had to be heard within six days.

The woman knew the law and was smart enough to do what needed to get done, but she was crazy. They found her naked in the bushes next to the retirement apartments where she lived. She would do strange things, like take people's animals, and she came to the trial with her dress on backwards. This one was hard. The jury decided to go ahead and evict her. She didn't appeal it.

When a civil case is heard by a jury, who usually has the edge—the plaintiff or the defendant? According to Judge Fred Buck (Tom Green County), it's more often the plaintiff. He's found that plaintiffs are usually much better prepared to go to trial than the party they're suing.

Not that there aren't plaintiffs who don't fumble this rule of thumb in comic fashion. Randy Daniel (Henderson County) oversaw a jury trial in which his six jurors returned to the courtroom after an interminable three-minute deliberation. The case involved two feuding female neighbors, one of whom accused the other of damaging her car by throwing a rock at it. The accused denied the accusation. Judge Daniel, learning that the plaintiff didn't actually see the defendant lob the destructive rock, asked for evidence. The plaintiff produced the evidence: A plastic bag containing a rock.

Yes, *that* rock.

NOTE

* This wasn't the last cat to earn celebrity in a virtual Texas court proceeding during the pandemic. Several months later, on February 9, 2021, District Court Judge Roy B. Ferguson (394th Judicial District), found himself and other virtual-court participants facing a very cute—but hilariously shifty-eyed—computer-generated feline that was inconveniently blocking lawyer Rod Ponton's visage in a particular hearing. The lawyer was having difficulty turning off this chat filter, the problem made worse by the fact that the kitten seemed to be speaking for him. Circumstances at one point led attorney Ponton to plead before Judge Ferguson, "I'm here live; I'm not a cat."

Dead Reckoning

ER doctors won't certify a death? So who do they call?
The retired school principal!

—HON. RICK HILL, BRAZOS COUNTY

WHEN IT CAME TO inquests, Judge Debbie Horn (Potter County) thought she knew the job.

I was kind of arrogant. I thought, I'm just going to step right in and it's going to be an easy ride. I wasn't prepared for the smells. I wasn't prepared for the grief and emotion, the families grabbing you and hugging you. You are part of a life-altering moment for them. The emotion is overwhelming. Or they start screaming at you to get out of their house. I've had husbands refuse to let me come in. Law enforcement will step in and say, "If she doesn't come in, we can't proceed. If we have to make you leave, we will do that." I've only had that twice. It breaks your heart.

One of the most important duties of a Texas justice of the peace is performing death investigations. Only fourteen counties have—because of their large populations—handed the job over to a designated county medical examiner (ME).* Because of this, Texas JPs who work in a county that boasts an ME actually get to do something that most JPs do not: sleep.

Those justices of the peace in the 240 counties without their own MEs are always on-call whenever the grim and importunate need arises to investigate the cause and circumstances of any death that occurs within their jurisdiction. Article 49.01 (2) of the Code of Criminal Procedure requires them, first and foremost, to ascertain if the death "was caused by an unlawful act or omission."

The job is not an easy one. In larger counties that still require its JPs to perform inquests, this aspect of a JP's responsibilities can, some weeks, swamp everything else. In counties with smaller populations, the calls are less frequent but no less sobering.

Sometimes the emotional response isn't sadness, it's outright fear. Andrew Cable (Hays County) was on the scene for one of those.

I was in this one house that stunk really bad, and I told the deputies and the family, "Hey, open up those windows!" So they opened the windows and I reached over the body to turn the ceiling fan on. As I turned that fan on, I looked down at the deceased person and the body had goosebumps all over it. I looked at the detective and he looked at me and we both went running out of the house screaming. There were deputies—full-grown men—running out of that house. I called the medical examiner and I asked, "Is this normal?"

He goes, "Oh, yeah. Skin is a texture. It's going to react to cold and hot like anything else."

By the time Jon W. Johnson had completed his first six months in office, he'd already handled over seventy inquests. Johnson serves in Smith County, which has the third highest annual number of deaths among Texas counties without MEs. Signing death certificates is a big part of his job. Because a death call can take precedence over everything else he does, there have been times when Judge Johnson has had to excuse himself from the courtroom, sometimes right in the middle of a trial.

I'll tell the people in the courtroom, "I'll be back in an hour." Inquests are my top priority.

We have three major hospitals and they're all Level III Trauma Centers. A lot of times I'll get called at night from the emergency room and they'll say, "We have a victim of either a car accident or a heart attack. They found him lying on a street corner."

I'll say, "Where's he from?"

"Well, he came in on the helicopter."

The person might be from two counties over where they don't have a major hospital. They airlift him to Tyler, where he passes away.

And it becomes Judge Johnson's job to sign off on how he died.

Sometimes with an inquest, it's a puzzle. It can get really interesting,
trying to put the pieces together, if you have the pieces. Sometimes
you don't have any.—Hon. *Tracy Byrd, Randall County*

Johnson's Smith County colleague Mitch Shamburger has performed
so many inquests over the course of his nearly thirty years on the bench
that he decided to write a book about them. In his autobiographical
volume *Inquests: Living with the Dead,*[1] Judge Shamburger chronicles
his years as a county coroner. His catalog of the numerous ways he has
seen people in his county give up the ghost gets chillingly specific at
times. For example, he recounts the bewildering array of materials he
has seen employed as suicide nooses, from nylon rope to clothesline to
the tie of a terry cloth robe.

Kerry Crews (Hunt County) has found that his long career in law enforcement, which included serving as a criminal investigator and police
chief, plus his work as a volunteer fire fighter prepared him for doing
inquests. Unlike most JPs who send bodies away for autopsy and then
await the results, Crews has actually observed several of these forensic
procedures firsthand, and, as a result, has a better understanding of how
medical examiners arrive at their determinations.

To autopsy or not to autopsy? That's the ticklish question faced by
many Texas justices of the peace. The procedure is expensive and it's the
taxpayers who foot the bill. There are JPs who lean more toward fiscal
responsibility and won't authorize one unless they deem it absolutely
necessary (or unless the law requires them to, such as in the death of a
child under the age of six). There are others who find autopsies invaluable in trying to answer troubling questions. Donna Schmidt (Cochran
County) told me of a death inquest she performed in which the wife of
the deceased was fearful that her husband had choked to death on pills
she'd given him. An autopsy ordered by Schmidt proved that it wasn't
the pills at all, but an underlying health issue that had caused his sudden
demise. Judge Schmidt was able to give the widow peace of mind that
she wasn't to blame.

During the 2020 COVID-19 epidemic, I asked David Cobos (Midland County) how autopsies were being performed with the looming possibility that an unattended death was caused by complications from the virus. He said it was paramount that the coronavirus first be ruled out before proceeding. If a test showed that it was present, the autopsy wouldn't move forward. The epidemic also made JPs a lot more reluctant to attend death scenes in person if the cause of death could be ascertained remotely.

Before 2020, when it came to whether or not to send a body off for autopsy, Nancy J. Pomykal (Calhoun County) walked that fine line right down the middle.

Nowadays, autopsies cost almost $3,000 and then there's another $850 for transportation to and from the ME's office.** Of course, the commissioners and some of the judges will say, "Well, he just died of a heart attack." If it's expected, if it's been diagnosed, if they're older, they're taking medications, and more than likely that was *the reason they passed, then, yes, I will forego an autopsy.*

But we had a man in his early sixties who passed away about three years ago. They had taken him to the hospital because he couldn't breathe, and he died. They didn't even call the JP out. They just said, "Well, the doctor's gonna put this down as a heart attack."

The girl who operates the funeral home called me. She said, "Judge, I just don't feel right about this. Would you take a look at it?"

I opened an inquest on this particular individual. They got him up to Austin and it ended up being a pulmonary embolism that actually killed him, so it was definitely not *a heart attack, and there were several contributing factors to his death that he hadn't even known about. The doctor had been ready just to sign off on it. Even though it wasn't my case, I called the hospital and said I was going to conduct a death inquest because I have jurisdiction throughout my county.*

Judge Pomykal also told me that a Texas justice of the peace has the legal right to set aside a death certificate signed by a doctor if she suspects foul play.

The main role of a justice of the peace is to rule out foul play and make sure there are no suspicious circumstances. We do have the authority to issue a warrant right there if we have enough probable cause and a suspect.

From my conversation with Rodney Price (Orange County), I got
the sense that one of the skills of a justice of the peace is the ability
to know when to an order an autopsy. He has seen relatives of elderly
family members who were under a doctor or nurse's care demand that
the county pay for the procedure because of suspicions that there was
something seriously amiss with that care.

*A lot of times the family will request an autopsy. And when you talk to
them, well, the family member just got released from the hospital. They
say, "We think there was malpractice there," and they're talking to a lawyer and they want to build their case. I had one last week where a lady
died in hospice care and, as you're probably aware, a hospice death has
an attending physician, and an autopsy was not called for. The family
wanted to spend the county's money based on a suspicion or charge that
care wasn't taken with this person.*

A family can order their own autopsy, but they will have to bear the
cost. "They can spend the $7,000," Price told me. "The county can't afford
to donate that money to help them bolster their case," especially a case
that may be completely unfounded.

Darrell Longino (Polk County) has found that in many situations
in which it's the family pushing for the autopsy, once they learn that
they—and not the county taxpayer—will have to foot the bill for this
investigative procedure, they'll change their minds. But there have been
times, Longino told me, in which the family does go ahead and order the
autopsy for themselves and they end up learning that the cause of death
was a hereditary illness no one was previously aware of and that might
conceivably show up in other family members.

Homicide? Natural death? Accident? Or suicide? Judge Herbert Dunn
(Van Zandt County) has tracked a disturbing trend in the suicides for
which he conducts inquests: the deceased are getting younger. When
I spoke with him, he remarked that the last one he had done was an
adolescent who had just turned fifteen.

Rick Hill (Brazos County) pointed out that authorizing an autopsy on
a suicide victim can get snagged up on other considerations.

*Early on in my career, there was an A&M college student who got high
on mushrooms, freaked out, and shot himself in the head. He's on life
support in the hospital. He's an organ donor, but the police say, "We can't*

*let him donate organs because that might mess up the autopsy. We might
not be able to figure out what happened."*

*So I'm sitting there thinking, I know why this guy died. I had some
conversations with the hospital staff and with the family and law enforcement. I said, "We already have the blood draw, we can already analyze his
blood and see what he had in his system, so I'm going to authorize organ
donation."*

*They recover his organs and I don't think much about it until about
a month later I got a card. It said, "Judge Hill, I want to thank you on
behalf of our family and the many recipients who received transplants. A
fifty-year-old man received the heart. A male in his twenties received his
lungs. We gave the left kidney and pancreas to a male in his thirties and
the right kidney to a ten-year-old male. Also, corneas and bone marrow
were recovered. Your support made it possible for several others to live
with a better quality of life. Thank you."*

*And guess what? When I got the autopsy report back from Travis
County, it said he died from a gunshot wound to the head.*

Rick Grissam (Mitchell County) said that when it comes to unattended deaths, it's always best to first rule out homicide. Once this is
eliminated from the list of possibilities, it clears the way to discovering the actual cause of death. Grissam has seen presumed suicides that
ended up being homicides. It's a murder mystery mainstay: the murder
that was set up to look like death by one's own hand.

It actually happened on April 7, 2006, in McLennan County, and the
murderer almost got away with it. The body of his victim, a thirty-one-
year-old schoolteacher named Kari Baker from Hewitt, Texas, didn't
undergo an autopsy for four months. JP Billy Martin hadn't believed it
was needed. The judge testified that he got a call from a Hewitt police
officer the night of Ms. Baker's death who reported that police investigators had determined the cause of death to be suicide. After all, there
weren't any bullet holes or stab wounds and there—*right there*—was an
open bottle of sleeping pills and a typed suicide note. In other words,
"We got this one, Judge." Judge Martin further testified that he decided
not to even go to the scene. He said that what the officer had reported
was "good enough" for him, and then went back to sleep.

Four years later, Kari Baker's Baptist minister husband, Matt, was
handed down a sixty-five-year sentence for killing his wife and covering
up her murder.[2]

Controversy whorled all around the demise of a famous non-Texan who died in his sleep on February 13, 2016, when, in the absence of the two Presidio County JPs, County Judge Cinderela Guevara was called upon to handle the inquest for the late Supreme Court justice Antonin Scalia. As had Judge Martin, Judge Guevara conducted her inquest over the phone and did not authorize an autopsy. Nor did Scalia's family wish one, since the judge had been "having health issues pertaining to his heart" and "there were no signs of foul play." Still, there were internet conspiracists and radio hosts of a certain political bent who sniffed a treacherous plot—perhaps emanating from the White House itself—to remove Justice Scalia by murder most foul. The theory went viral when the host for Scalia's West Texas quail hunting holiday, rancher John B. Poindexter, in an unfortunate choice of words, told the *San Antonio Express-News*, "We discovered the judge in bed, a pillow over his head." The word "over," Poindexter subsequently corrected himself, meant, in effect, "above," as in, "positioned between Scalia's head and the bed's headboard."[3]

Whether an autopsy is called for or not, it's important to get the death certificate right. Tim Bryan (Gregg County) exercises great care when it comes to filling out death certificates since they can be important to the payout of insurance benefits and to any post-mortem litigation. He told me about a truck-driving student who died in the sleeper compartment of the truck's cab when an accident befell the truck while in the hands of the vehicle's other driver.

Knowing that there would be some kind of litigation, it's important to know exactly what caused the man's death. At some point his family might have to petition the company to give them some money to satisfy what that young man might have made in his career as a truck driver. And I knew that death certificate would be part of the case.

Judge Bryan gave me another example: a marine corps veteran who committed suicide. The Veterans Affairs (VA) doctor who had been seeing the man believed that the death was related to post-traumatic stress disorder; Bryan wanted to make sure that this fact was noted on the certificate since it affected the kind of benefit the VA would give.

What if the death isn't a recent one? Sometimes bodies aren't found for days, even weeks. Joe Martinez (Gray County) remembered one of his JP colleagues telling him about a recluse whose corpse wasn't discovered until "all the tissue had emaciated away and all that was left was bone with a thin veneer of some kind of skin tissue on top. He was practically skeletonized—about as decomposed as you can get without falling apart."

When Judge Longino was sheriff, he led the search for a woman who, in the throes of some form of dementia, had wandered away from her house. It wasn't until after he'd become justice of the peace that her body was found. Now it was his job—with the assistance of an anthropologist—to confirm that this was indeed the same woman who'd gone missing.

Discovering the remains of someone long-deceased isn't the only time a Texas JP might require the assistance of anthropologists and other forensic specialists in determining the cause and manner of a death. In 1993, all four of McLennan County's JPs were required to perform inquests related to the law enforcement siege on the Branch Davidian cult compound outside Waco. Four ATF (Bureau of Alcohol, Tobacco and Firearms) agents and six cult members died in the initial raid attempt; seventy-six Branch Davidians perished when a fire engulfed the buildings during a second assault. The JPs found themselves partnering with a large battery of pathologists and forensic experts: noted Smithsonian Institution forensic anthropologist Douglas Ubelaker, three anthropologists from the Tarrant County ME office, five pathologists, thirty-five forensic dentists, three toxicologists, ten criminologists, seven fingerprint technicians, in addition to support staff and lab technicians.[4]

Incidentally, David Pareya, one of those four JPs, was thrust back into the national spotlight twenty years later when disaster struck his hometown of West on April 17, 2013. An ammonium nitrate explosion at the West Fertilizer Company's storage and distribution facility not far from Pareya's house killed fifteen, and the judge was called upon to perform the related inquests. Pareya told local reporters even before the dead had been identified that he was "probably going to know every one of them." He was right. Twelve of those who died were first responders.

And the explosion didn't just hit close to home for the judge—it actually hit his home, significantly damaging it in the blast. Judge Pareya himself narrowly escaped personal injury when the windows of the Chevy pickup he was in shattered. "All I've got is the clothes I have on and what's in my pockets," Pareya told the press on the day of the explosion.[5]

About two years later tragedy struck yet again in McLennan County. Pete Peterson, one of Pareya's fellow JPs, was required to perform inquests on biker gang members killed in a Waco shootout. Then, in his role as magistrate, Judge Peterson had to set bond on the 177 surviving "members and associates of the Cossacks Motorcycle Club and the Bandidos Motorcycle Club," who were charged with engaging in organized criminal activity. The amount? A cool million dollars each.[6]

Suzan Thompson (Matagorda County), who retired at the end of 2018 after thirty-six years on the bench, said that inquests were handled differently when she came into office in 1983. A JP who was called to the scene of an accident or potential murder was required to spend the whole day there. Nowadays, she said, a JP's time is better managed. Judges have learned to put more faith in their investigators to gather the needed information in less complicated cases.

As a former justice court clerk in Wise County, Stacy Spurlock processed the paperwork on inquests. Spurlock, now serving as Jack County's at-large JP, remarked that "it's definitely different being 'on the scene.'" She sees the inquest calls as team-building opportunities for each of her county's different first responders. She also said she hadn't been aware of the struggles that the funeral homes go through when they have to come and pick up the body.

The sheriff had a missing person. She'd disappeared from her home. They'd been looking for her for three or four days. They found her in her car in a ravine. They had to get a wrecker service to pull the car out and then set it down on the ground so they could get inside. There were two men from the funeral home, a couple of sheriff's deputies, and a couple of first responders there, all trying to get her body out of that car. When they'd pull on her, something would come off. There is no way to describe that smell. All those poor men were up there gagging and tossing their cookies. It was really, really bad. I was looking at them. "People don't even realize you do this stuff. That is hard stuff."

Evelyn Kerbow (Crockett County) knows firsthand what funeral homes have to deal with. Her husband, Bruce, owns the funeral home in their town. He accompanies his wife on late night death calls.

> *Law enforcement isn't supposed to move anything or let anyone out or in until the JP gets there. Everything is supposed to be left in the same condition when law enforcement went in.—Hon. Nancy J. Pomykal, Calhoun County*

JPs and members of their local law enforcement agencies work hand in hand at death scenes, but there are parameters that have to be respected. As Mark Holt (Walker County) explained, those parameters become even more important when deadly force is involved.

When we have an officer-involved shooting and I show up, being from law enforcement myself, I know how important it is to not mess with the crime scene. You don't touch stuff until it's done. On one occasion, the sheriff walks up to me and goes, "Well, if you'll just go pronounce him dead and back away, then we can do our deal and you can do your deal."

I said, "Well, if he's not dead yet, you need to do CPR on him."

Otherwise, Judge Holt told me, it's the JP who has sole custody of the body and who basically decides when anyone can "do their deal."

A lot of people in law enforcement and in the media, and quite a few JPs themselves, use the verb *pronounce*—as in pronouncing someone dead—as a kind of shorthand for the inquest process. The judges know what the word actually refers to and are likely to use it informally in conversation, as some did when they spoke with me. Others, however, might be inclined to take its meaning literally. Local news reporters, for example, will often revert to the phrase, "pronounced dead by Justice of the Peace such-and-such" in their stories; apparently, they haven't gotten the memo yet. Judge Holt went on:

A lot of people have that misconception that we pronounce them dead. We do the inquest. We don't "pronounce" them. In the state of Texas, the statute reads that any credible person can pronounce someone dead. If you come on a tragic traffic wreck and you see a guy almost decapitated, you yourself can go, "That guy's dead." Certifying the death is what we do.

Holt has three units of Huntsville Prison in his precinct, including the high security unit.

I get the calls for those. I also have the infirmary. All the inmates in the state of Texas are brought to my precinct to die if they're in prison. That's where they take them.

Any time an inmate dies, there has to be an inquest and they have to be sent for an autopsy. They just changed it so that if they know that there was nothing suspicious about the death, the family can say, "Please don't do an autopsy. We just want him back." Because autopsies are very invasive.

Holt remembered a time when the JP in his precinct had to come in and certify death by execution, but he hasn't had to do this.

Mike Towers (Bandera County) told me that deaths that occur in law enforcement custody can be a pretty serious business, and have to be handled carefully.

We had a death in the jail about a year ago and there were a lot of questions. What happened to him? Did one of the other inmates kill him? Did the jailers kill him? You don't want a guy with a badge investigating it. You need someone there who is an independent person like a judge, so we investigate the case. We do the manner of death. The forensic pathologist does the cause of death. A gunshot wound: Is that a suicide? Is it an accident? What happened? That's up to our interpretation. When you have something like an in-custody death, it's very important to not only maintain propriety, but also the appearance of propriety, by having an independent arbiter examine the facts to make a ruling and not just do whatever the sheriff says.

There are occasions when a JP can't make a proper determination without formalizing her investigation. Judge Pomykal said she has had a couple of such inquest hearings and there have been times she's had to threaten to hold a formal hearing because "I wasn't getting out of law enforcement what I needed."

Formal inquest hearings represent one of the few times a justice court becomes a court of record. A court reporter is engaged and witnesses can be "placed under the rule."***

Mike Smith (Harrison County) cited an instance in which a formal inquest hearing seemed all but mandated by the circumstances.

Here's something that people don't understand: On most insurance policies, if you commit suicide you only get what the policy says if you take your own life. But with a double indemnity policy, which I seldom see anymore, on an accidental death they pay double. I had a guy standing on the side of the road at 2:30 in the morning and telling his girlfriend to come pick him up because his car had broken down. They got into a big argument and he said, "Well, I'm just gonna kill myself. I'm just gonna step out in front of a car."

This poor man—just driving his car, no way did he do anything wrong—and this other guy steps out in front of it and gets killed. Well, this was one where I had to hold a hearing. I had the attorneys present if they wanted to come and all that stuff, and what we had to decide is how do we know this was suicide. Well, we knew it was suicide because the girl was talking to him on the phone when it happened and the phone was still on when we found him. So we have this hearing, and after going over the autopsy and the blood report on the driver, well, I ruled it a suicide. It cost the family about $150,000 because they had double indemnity insurance.

And couldn't collect it. According to Judge Smith, the guy meant what he said.

> *I did ninety-one inquests in 2018. Mine is the largest precinct in the county and has the new Trauma II hospital. You take the phone in the shower with you. You don't have a choice.*—Hon. Beth Smith, *Hays County*

Death usually comes unannounced. When it does, Texas JPs have to be ready to jump. Judge Jon W. Johnson (Smith County), like Judge Beth Smith, jumps a lot.

I may work forty hours a week in the courtroom, but I never know whether I'm going to spend the night sleeping or working all night long at a homicide. You stay with the body until the funeral home comes and gets it. Law enforcement is responsible for the crime scene. I'm responsible for the body.

> *My truck is like a driving file cabinet. I have forms to every funeral home, to every forensic center. I have all the information on death inside my truck. I have a whole kit I've developed with police officers and crime scene investigators. My wife calls the truck "Dr. Death."*
>
> *When I interact with families, I feel like I'm doing good in a really bad situation. Even though I don't know them, I want to show them that I do care. I'm there for them if they need anything.*
> —Hon. Matt Beasley, *Montgomery County*

One of the biggest challenges for an inquest JP is dealing with the family. Sometimes when a judge arrives at a death scene, the family is there. It might be only one person—perhaps the grieving spouse—or it could be everyone related to the deceased within the tri-county area. "Does this complicate things?" I asked Judge Pomykal. Most definitely.

It happened to me just the end of June. A young man unfortunately passed away suddenly from what we suspect was a drug toxicity or over-dose. I knew the family. I thought, well, I'll call them when we know what's going on. Well, they were there when I got there! That quickly. You have to be real careful. You have to secure the scene.

Judge Donna Schmidt (Cochran County) told me about one inquest call she made in which there were at least fifty family members gathered on the lawn when she arrived and even more there when she left. The whole thing had a sideshow or spectacle aspect to it, she said. Even worse, the family had decided to take matters into their own hands prior to her arrival and cut down the body of the deceased, who had hanged himself, thus compromising the investigation.

> *I often tell families that the reason I am here is because I am writing the last chapter of your loved one's life.*—Hon. Bill Gravell, Williamson County[7]

The smaller the county, the stronger the likelihood that a JP will have known the individual who died, or at least be somehow connected to the person. When Judge Tim Bryan was called out to the home of a woman who had passed away, he found about forty people gathered on the back porch. To Bryan, this was a huge indication that the woman had left behind a great number of people who loved her. "I can't tell you how many times," said Bryan, "and this is the saddest part of my job—when I'd go somewhere and find that someone had died alone." In this particular case, the woman's last name was the same as one of the surnames in Bryan's own family.

So, I see that name and discover that these people are my relatives. I was at the house pronouncing a relative of mine. One of the cousins I was close to was one of the cousins this family was close to. We had such a good connection that day—they didn't have a church home and they weren't real sure about the funeral—that they asked me to officiate the funeral of their grandmother. My father was a Baptist preacher, but I'd never done that before. It was a great honor for me to serve in that way.

It's a unique fact of life that we're all gonna die, and I think it takes special people like JPs all over the state of Texas who really strive to try to make this part easier on our constituents. At the same time, we have a responsibility to make sure that the loved one, the deceased, wasn't murdered or there is nothing suspicious about their death. We have to speak for them. They can't speak for themselves.

Judge Bryan has witnessed both the best and the worst kind of behavior from grieving families.

I heard it explained that grief is love with no place to go. So we do really stupid things when we're grieving. Some families fight over money. I've had them fight over salt and pepper shakers while I'm standing in the room with their loved one and the body's not even cold. I don't think they mean to be foolish. People are overwhelmed with grief and don't know what to do. I do think it's important that we as public servants channel that and try to get them to something more positive.

> **With a lot of these people, they die without a will. I'm trying to conduct an inquest and furniture's going out the back door.**
> —Hon. Clyde Black, Houston County

Marc DeRouen (Jefferson County) has seen his share of unexpected behavior from mourners.

The family members were going so crazy. The officers couldn't keep control, and they were actually asking for backup. I got hit in the head with a water bottle after one of the sisters threw it—top off—across the room at her sister. When it came across, it clipped the top of my head and got water all over my face. The officers got pretty serious with the folks then. It was about to be taser time. I didn't feel threatened. It wasn't like they were attacking me. It was family member against family member, and I was in the middle of it.

Benjamin Collins Sr. (Jefferson County) could write his own chapter in that book.

At times, with all the family showing up, they get in the way. We have the police there and they're trying to secure the scene, but the family wants to come in and see. Well, not right now! When they bring out the person in the body bag, we've had to call the ambulance because the family members start passing out. They even bring their children. That's what really bothers me: bringing the grandkids to the house, knowing that Grandma has just died and we've got to bring out that bag.

You never know what to expect when you get a death call. Theresa Farris (Freestone County) would be among the first to tell you.

I had a call out at Richland-Chambers Reservoir. A lot of nice, big weekend homes there. When I got there they said, "It's just a head."

I didn't know what to expect. When I was walking up, it smelled horrible, and I was thinking, "That one head smells this bad? What is that? It smelled like rotting fish. I walked up to this new home on the lake. This head had washed up out of the water onto the sidewalk. The body had been chopped up. You could tell it was perfectly cut. They had a leg that showed up in Lake Bardwell around Ennis.

I had to send that head in for an autopsy. Then the leg. We connected the two. They held the head for quite a while to figure out who he was.

The stink came from one of the game wardens who'd thrown the guts of some fish into the back of the truck and forgotten about it. The head didn't smell like anything.

Former Erath County JP Sarah Miller has also performed some unusual inquests. She once had to deal with a body that had been run through a tree chipper. Well, not the whole body. She told me that the hands and hair and skin wouldn't go through the chipper, so the murderer put them in plastic bags and buried them. I was curious to know what a body looks like when it comes out of a wood chipper. Her unflappable response: "A jumbled *mess*!"

During the catastrophic 2015 Blanco River flood in Hays County, Judge Andrew Cable found himself stuck with a dead body in the back of his pickup truck and an extra-ornery Mother Nature preventing him from performing his inquest duty as JP.

The night of the storm we didn't know what was taking place. It had just been raining for days. I get called out to this ranch where this guy had killed himself. I get there about 11:30, 11:45. The officers are there and they say they can't get their vehicles down there or they'll get stuck. I've got four-wheel drive, so I take my truck and the funeral home guy is there, so—and this isn't normal—we put the body in the back of my truck. But I can't get my truck into four-wheel drive, so the deputies are hopping up and down back there, trying to get traction, then the funeral director says, "Hey, you've got to stop. This body's going to get to the morgue with post-mortem bruising." We strap the body down and I finally get the truck into drive and I get it back to the highway.

The deputy behind me asks, "Where are you going?"

"To get this body out of the back of my truck."

He said, "Well, you can't use the Blanco bridge." I pull up to the bridge. Water is literally ten to fifteen feet over that bridge. There are cars and structures floating over it.

Then our county commissioner pulls up behind me—because nobody can get across—and he walks up and goes, "Mr. Cable?"

"Yes?"

"Is that a body in the back of your truck?"

"Yes, sir, it is."

"Are you going to be removing it soon?"

"Yes, I am."

"Okay. Carry on."

In my conversation with Justin M. Joyce, I learned that his precinct in Fort Bend County is perhaps the most religiously diverse of any besides Harris County. We discussed the impact this has on his inquest responsibilities, especially given the large population of Muslims and Hindus. He told me that sometimes religious requirements related to the disposition of a dead body can get in the way of governmental requirements. A family will ask that an autopsy not be performed for religious reasons, or there is a request to be able to bury the body in the ground no longer than forty-eight hours after demise.

Jerry Parker (Wood County) recounted a special case that presented its own challenges related to the practicalities of laying a member of a particular religion to rest.

One Saturday evening, I was on call, and my wife had fixed a nice beef stew and I got a bowl of it when the phone rang. It was a lady calling: "Judge, I need you to come and pronounce my father's death."

I said, "It doesn't work like that. You need to call dispatch, and then they call me." I went and sat down. I knew I had time to finish my stew before dispatch called and told me where the body was.

I get out there and the fire department is there and the ambulance, and the odor was bad! I could smell it before I went in the house. I go in and he's been dead for three days. His wife and daughter were in there. I went in and looked at the dead person. These black trash bags were tied around both legs up to his knees. I interviewed the family and I said, "Why are these black trash bags on his legs?" They said that the bugs were getting to him. "Why didn't y'all call when he died?" They said they belonged to a religion where they believe that you don't do anything to the body for three days in case the person rises like Jesus did.

Not too long ago, the commissioners in Fort Bend County gave a big assist to its JPs. As this large county of over eight hundred thousand moved toward the eventual establishment of a medical examiner's office, it hired death investigators to take some of the burden off Justin Joyce and his fellow judges. Joyce recalled that when he was an inquest judge, he had to deal with an estimated four hundred deaths a year in his precinct alone. He spoke to me about the difficulty of getting up and leaving a courtroom full of people midway through a jury trial to go off on a death call. Still, the deceased's family shouldn't be kept waiting either: The body can't be picked up by the funeral home without the JP's authorization.

I asked justices of the peace whose counties are close to or share a border with Mexico if their courts have experienced any repercussions from the current immigration crisis. Several told me that the number of inquests they'd been called on to perform on newly arrived undocumented immigrants has been on the rise. Most perish in the intense South Texas heat. Judge Sonia Guerrero-Perez, whose county, Dimmit, meets the border in one corner, said that she was summoned to just that kind of death call only a couple of weeks prior to our conversation.

It was about 106 degrees outside, about 2:00 in the afternoon. I was called out to the ranches, which is the area that the individuals cross

through. The border patrol was chasing a group, and this particular in-
dividual was in distress. He started taking his clothes off because he was
so hot, and he ended up passing away. When they were working on his
body, I do remember that either the EMT or the paramedic told me that
his body temperature was 108 or 109. It was sad to see. We were out there
for two-and-a-half hours, but I was able to go in and out of a police unit
to cool down and drink my water and go back out when needed. Because
the individual died so far into the brush, we were not able to walk in,
and border patrol had to carry him about a mile and a half so I could
pronounce him dead. The border patrol agents had to be seen by EMS as
well because it was so hot.

Nora Salinas (Brooks County) is often called on to sign death certificates on the remains of unidentified undocumented immigrants found
in her South Texas county; sometimes all that is left is a long-decom-
posed skeleton. When the investigation can determine the identity of
the deceased and the remains can be sent back to the family for proper
burial, Judge Salinas takes special satisfaction in the closure that this
represents both for the family and for herself.

The usual protocol is for a local law enforcement agency to bring a
death to the attention of the justice of the peace to conduct an inquest.
Barbara McMillon (Cass County) related to me an unusual situation in
which she got the jump on law enforcement. A woman she knew brought
a second woman whom the judge didn't know to speak to her about the
possibility that her boyfriend had killed his mother. The elderly woman
had lived for a while with the couple after the boyfriend removed her
from her nursing home. When the concerned woman returned from a
two-week trip out of state, she discovered that her boyfriend's mother
was no longer there. The boyfriend said she'd "gone to visit relatives in
Dallas."

She hadn't. It turns out that while the girlfriend was away, her boyfriend's mother had passed away and he'd buried her in the backyard
and kept quiet so he could keep receiving her Social Security checks. It
was determined that he hadn't killed her, but the situation had confirmed
the girlfriend's concerns, her friend's concerns, and, ultimately, Judge
McMillon's concerns, which she said investigators in both the sheriff's
office and the district attorney's office hadn't shared. Judge McMillon
was proven right, but having her suspicions validated carried no joy.

I have worked numerous inquest scenes over the years but none as sad as this one. The son had buried his mother in a small two-foot-by-three-foot grave, and laid her in a fetal position, wearing her nightgown. As I looked into the small, dark, damp, and cold grave, I have never felt so helpless and sad during my career.

Judge Gordon Terry (Garza County) described his inquest duties as an assault on multiple senses:

I just went to do an inquest on a friend of mine, six months younger than me, and I was thinking, the things that bother you on an inquest are the sights, the sounds, the smells. Those three things: seeing the bodies— victims of gunshots, car wrecks, or whatever. The sounds: you're with the grieving families. It's always my hope that I don't come across as callous or cold when I have to ask my questions, when I have to get the information I need to do my job. And the smells. *We get deaths where people have been in the home for a week. In the summertime. With no air conditioning.*

Handling an inquest involves more than just showing up at the death scene, trying to determine "cause and manner," and then helping to arrange for the removal of the body. Two months after a terrible traffic accident in his county that took the lives of three children, Michael York (Lee County) was still dealing with the bureaucratic aftermath.

Not only are you out there doing a job, you're doing the inquest, but then it's not done. You've got to go back to the office and categorize and label those pictures, you've got to deal with the funeral homes and the death certificates and the hospitals and the family members. I'm still not through with that particular case.

Even though Galveston County has its own medical examiner, Mike Nelson did inquests for fifteen years because he wanted to learn all the facets to death investigation. As a result, he became a helpful member of the medical examiner's team.

At the other end of the spectrum, Scott Shinn (Van Zandt County) sometimes finds himself doing the work of his county's local lawmen.

Inquests are an adrenaline rush like playing a sport. I hate to say that, but it's true. You're there trying to investigate the cause of death. I'm sure we miss it sometimes, but ultimately you are there figuring things out. Our county is pretty rural and our law enforcement doesn't have all the means that other agencies have, and sometimes our guys get it wrong, so sometimes I find something they don't find. I actually had an instance where I found the bullet casing they didn't find.

I asked Chris Macon (Ellis County) if having been a firefighter and paramedic ever comes in handy when determining the cause of death. "All the time," he said. He also told me that other judges pick his brain when it comes to questions about their own inquests.

Before taking office, Judge Marc DeRouen had the chance to go out on a few inquest calls with his predecessor, Judge Bob Morgan. Jefferson County is a large county, which makes it a high-volume inquest county.

One of the first I did was for a guy who'd jumped off the Rainbow Bridge between Port Arthur and Bridge City. It gets a lot of jumpers. As we were coming back to the office, we got a call on a guy who was murdered in an apartment complex. I was freaking out. I said, "You've got to be kidding. Is this what you do all day long?" You go to the bridge, a guy had jumped. You're sweating out there with the mosquitoes and everything. We get in the truck and we haven't gone two miles when PD calls and says we've got a homicide at such-and-such apartment complex. It's my first time to see a guy shot, with blood all over the mattress. And I'm thinking, I don't know if I'm cut out for this. The judge assured me that this was not the norm.

Well, yes and no. DeRouen told me that the last week he was on call, he had to deal with seventeen deaths. And when it comes to how an inquest will play itself out, all bets are off.

There was an inquest I had about four years ago. I go in. Nice family. One family member is sitting at the table in a little breakfast nook area, one's sitting in a chair. So I sit down on the couch and I'm gathering the information. It's their mother that's passed away. I'm asking about her health and what all she's been through. Both the sons are there with their wives. The home belongs to one of the sons. "I moved Mom in because she was starting to get feeble and not eating properly."

So we're sitting there talking, and I said, "If you don't mind, if the officer can take me, I need to go and see where your mother is."

They said, "You're sitting right next to her."

She was a very frail, thin lady. She had died on the couch and they just threw an afghan over her. I had no idea I'd been about six inches away from her. It just looked like a pile of blankets. The family probably thought, This judge must be really *comfortable doing inquests!*

Some inquests are easy; others you wouldn't wish on your worst enemy. Judge Matt Kiely was the justice of the peace on scene for the worst hot air balloon accident in US history. The crash, which killed sixteen people, happened on July 30, 2016, and occurred just fifty yards inside Kiely's precinct in Caldwell County. The balloon struck power lines and then crashed into a field near Lockhart.

Once I got on scene, instinct and training kicked in. I've got to make sure the funeral home transport I use is going to be able to handle this. Are we going to have enough refrigeration? Is the medical examiner we use going to be able to handle all sixteen bodies at her location? What we did was we sent eight bodies to her, my funeral guy took the other eight bodies and held them in refrigeration, and once she was finished with the first eight autopsies, they kind of flip-flopped where he brought the other eight bodies over. We had to do dental records on all of them.

For Kiely, this is the starkest possible example of what a Texas justice of the peace might be called to do.

People that don't know what we really do—and that's what really cracks me up during the election season—all these people who don't have a clue, but they say they can do the job better than we can, and it's like, can you handle sixteen dead people who've fallen out of the sky and burned to death?

In spite of his inquest responsibility, Kiely's job was made more difficult by a fellow JP who decided to intrude upon the investigation. (According to past complaints filed with the State Commission on Judicial Conduct against this judge, he had a history of overstepping his authority in the county.) Nor was the FAA (Federal Aviation Administration) all that helpful. "They came in thinking they could do whatever they wanted to."

And then there was the FBI.

The guy who was second in command and I got into it. He tried to tell me that I needed to step away, and I said, "You may be a federal employee, but there ain't nothing against you going to a county jail. If you try to remove me from this scene one more time, that's where you're gonna go, because you can't hinder my investigation. I'm allowing you onto our scene to help the NTSB (National Transportation Safety Board) do their investigation."

Later, Judge Kiely sat down with his emergency management coordinator, Martin Ritchey, Congressman Lloyd Doggett, and a representative from Senator Ted Cruz's office to share the details of the inquest investigation.

Once I told the congressman the cocktail of medications that was inside the pilot, he said, "How does this happen?" If this had been a commercial airplane, the county would have been reimbursed all kinds of money. The property owner would have been reimbursed money. But because it was a hot air balloon and it was considered recreational, the county ended up having to pay for all of this: $75,000.

The legislation that resulted from all of this didn't come quickly or easily. Following the accident, Congressman Doggett doggedly urged the FAA to adopt a safety measure, which the NTSB had long recommended, requiring balloon operators to obtain a medical certificate. He was not alone in pushing the FAA to do the right thing. Ultimately, the amendment he authored, as part of the Federal Aviation Administration Reauthorization Act, did pass and was signed into law by President Donald Trump on October 10, 2018.

Nowadays, Judge Kiely conducts classes for the Texas Justice Court Training Center (TJCTC) related to the kinds of aviation fatalities that JPs have to deal with. He says that whether he likes it or not, having handled all sixteen of the inquests in the Lockhart hot air balloon crash, he's become the expert.

Unfortunately, Kiely does have company when it comes to having to deal with problematic bureaucrats and agencies in the course of doing his job as inquest JP. Judge David Pareya told the *Waco Tribune-Herald* that after he and his fellow JPs showed up at the Branch Davidian compound in the wake of the first deaths, it was, of all people, a Texas Ranger captain who gave them the most trouble—a man who was clearly unaware of a JP's statutory authority over death inquests and the removal of bodies. Pareya recalled the captain telling them that he "didn't want us 'coon-pawing out there at my scene.'" Fellow JP John Cabaniss educated the ranger, who registered surprise: "So you mean to tell me that there is a law that requires me to use *y'all* to remove those bodies?" Judge Cabaniss reiterated their authority, then paused and looked up, as Judge Pareya remembered it, and said, "Just one more thing. For the benefit of us novices in the back, please define what coon-pawing is."[8]

Believe it or not, I heard one inquest story that actually had a happy ending. It came from John Guinn (Coryell County).

One morning I walked out of my house and saw the pickup truck driven by the elderly gentleman who delivers my Austin American-Statesman, *just sitting in my driveway. I peered in the window. "Oh crap," I went. "He's dead." I didn't take his pulse or anything; I called the sheriff's office and I said, "I think my deliveryman just died in my driveway out here." I no sooner got off the phone, though, when there he was—standing next to the truck.*

It turned out that he had hit a deer and fractured his radiator. He couldn't go anywhere, "So," he said, "I just decided to take a nap in your driveway."

I had already pronounced him dead. I had to call the sheriff's department and say, "Please disregard that last call."

(I didn't ask the judge if he got his newspaper.)

Because of accommodations that had to be made starting in 2020 due to the COVID-19 pandemic, inquest JPs found themselves conducting fewer in-person death investigations. They ended up during this period signing off on an unusually large number of death certifications over the phone. The possibility of viral exposure was simply too high for some judges to risk infection except in cases in which an on-site investigation was strongly indicated. Some JPs did continue to make in-person death calls, like Shawnee Bass (Erath County). She told me, "I've done some of my inquests over the phone with the agency sending me pictures, but for the most part I usually go to the scene."

> *At the end of the day, I was elected to serve. So serve I will continue to do, rain or shine, COVID or no COVID.*—Hon. Cliff Coleman, Bell County

The last word in this chapter goes to Sharon Fox (Brazoria County), who draws the perfect distinction between person and job. Making that distinction is something that she and her fellow JPs strive to do on a daily basis.

There was a couple at our church that we took on like a second set of parents. He was in hospice and died from cancer; we went running over to the house when this happened. I went in just as friend and family. Back then, we still went to hospice inquests in this county. I sat there and cried just like I would over any dear friend who'd died. And then I said, "Well, time to go to work." I went outside. I got my clipboard and my pen, and the tears were gone. I had my paper in my hand and I did my job. That's one of the first times I realized that God had given me a file cabinet in my brain for this and I open it when I need to and then I shut it.

Reader, kindly turn the page. Sometimes the drawer to that file cabinet sticks.

NOTES

*Bexar, Collin, Dallas, Denton, Ector, Fort Bend, Galveston, Harris, Johnson, Lubbock, Nueces, Tarrant, Travis, and Webb Counties.

**Inquest JPs send their bodies to medical examiners in other counties to undergo autopsies.

***"The rule" refers to removing a witness from the courtroom so that she can't hear the testimony delivered by other witnesses.

I'm Blessed That I Don't
Dream about Them

Most of the time I can make it back to the car before I start crying.
Some are harder than others.

—HON. SHERON COLLINS, HALE COUNTY

FOR THE ENTIRE FOUR years I worked as a clerk for a justice of the peace in Travis County, I wasn't aware that most JPs in Texas also served as county coroners. This was because Travis was one of the few counties in the state that had its own medical examiner, so its justices of the peace weren't required to go out on inquest calls at all hours.

My judge didn't talk about this thing that she didn't have to do, and so I was spared from hearing at the time about the most unsettling part of a Texas JP's job. There are large-county JPs who told me in our conversations that if they had to conduct inquests, they'd probably seek some other line of work. "Thank God Denton isn't an inquest county," said Judge Harris Hughey.

My stomach couldn't take it. I don't know how those guys do it. If we didn't have a medical examiner from Tarrant County who did our inquests, I probably wouldn't have run for JP, just because I know my limitations and this would be difficult for me to do. I admire the JPs who do it.

In fact, Jackie Miller Jr. was appointed to the job of JP in Ellis County because his predecessor "couldn't handle the deaths."

He just couldn't deal with the whole idea of going out and not knowing if you were going to see somebody that's passed away from a heart attack or natural causes or a car wreck or a hanging. He just wasn't one who could turn it on and off. You never know what you're going into. I'm very blessed that I don't dream about them, I don't think about them. I say a prayer when I leave the house. By the grace of God, no matter how hard they've been, I haven't moped over them. And that's a blessing.

I asked Judge Miller if he'd ever performed an inquest on someone he knew well.

One of the hardest ones was my high school football coach. Riding up on a traffic fatality and seeing his brain in his lap. I can't see his face anymore. But I knew it was him when I saw the car—he'd been broadsided by a dump truck. For me, I still see him the way he was then, on the day he died, not shouting at me on the football field.

Carol Smith (Dallam County) is thankful she doesn't have to do a lot of inquests.

That's probably the toughest thing for me. They're still hard. I had a kid early one morning who flipped his car in the median. He was just tired. He had been driving all night. When I get out there, he's lying in the bar ditch. I could just see my son. He had the same build, same dark hair. You just can't get those images out of your mind.

I had a mental health meeting at the hospital with some other judges, and they were talking about the need to get someone in here for the officers and for the jailers, like if they have to cut someone down who committed suicide—the traumatic stuff. I said, "You know, I go home and cry. You deal with each one that comes and you do the best you can." I knew this was part of the job when I took it. I know about a judge who won in the Panhandle who, when she realized she'd have to go out on death inquests, just quit. She walked out the door and they had to appoint a replacement.

> *I've done 260 inquests since taking office six months ago. You witness over and over again the most traumatic thing in a family's life. Yeah, it changes you, I think.—Hon. Matt Beasley, Montgomery County*

Death doesn't respect the calendar or the clock. It is messy, it is inconvenient, and it is cruel, especially to those left behind. To the Texas justice of the peace who must effect a careful and thoughtful governmental response, it is also about answering the "why," and dealing with all the nuts and bolts of the "what next?" The job of determining cause and manner of death for those who pass away in their precinct or county demonstrates the mettle, the grit, the tough leather hide that goes along with being a Texas JP. The job is especially tough in Texas counties with only a single JP, and there are quite a few; judges in counties with more than one JP often take turns being on call for the whole county. It's a duty that is tempered by a genuine, very human reaction to encountering death, sometimes at nearly unimaginable points of extremis.

Deaths that occur in the very early part of a judge's first term are the hardest. Brenda Smith (Newton County) took office on April 17, 1996. Within hours of her swearing in she was called out to the local sawmill, where one of the workers had been electrocuted—a man she knew. Fortunately, one of the other JPs in the county was there to help out.

One of the first inquests that Jasper County JP Jimmy Miller investigated involved a ten-day old baby.

I went home and I thought, Lord, what did I get into? I'm fixing to go back and run that road maintainer!

(Before he become JP, Miller had been a heavy equipment operator on Jasper County's road and bridge crew. Together, his crew took care of 180 miles of roads.)

Yet Judge Miller learned to take things in stride.

I drew from an old, old judge who told me when you go to a death scene, whether it's natural or suicide or whatever, that body is no longer a person. It's a piece of evidence. I know that sounds cold, very cold, but it has served me well.

Several judges I spoke to validated the theory that deaths often come in threes. Lisa Whitehead (Burnet County) said there would be some days she'd have three inquests in one day. For Gordon Terry (Garza County), the old adage has painful personal resonance.

We had a trooper that died in a car crash maybe ten years ago. We'd just had two deaths in our county—a helicopter crash and a car crash fatality, I think. The trooper had come in that morning and we'd been talking, and as he was leaving, I just said, "Have a safe day and be careful out there."

And he said, "Well, you know, bad things come in threes."

Well, we got a call that night that he was out making an emergency call and he crashed his car into a concrete culvert on Highway 84.

Sometimes the number is higher. K. T. Musselman (Williamson County) told me that the first weekend he was on call after taking office, he had twelve inquests.

> *My first few months in office, almost every death I went to ended up being a suicide with a shotgun. One was a twelve-year-old boy. I'll never forget that.*—Hon. Sharon Fox, Brazoria County

The most difficult deaths to certify? Babies and young children, and those who take their own lives, especially teenagers. Michael York (Lee County) told me about one especially disturbing inquest.

About ten years ago when I was a deputy I went to a call where a two-year-old girl had drowned in a stock tank. The mom and dad were doing CPR on this child, who I knew was dead when I took over the CPR. I went to the autopsy. I was in the same room with the doctor, taking notes and taking pictures during the investigation. I'll never forget how mad this little old medical examiner lady got because of what she was finding had been done to this little two-year-old girl. She'd suffered severe child abuse over a prolonged period of time. She documented the bruises and the abrasions, and I was horrified. I had never seen this in my life. Two years later, I was sitting at the coast with some friends of mine when their little two-year-old girl came out of my blind spot and jumped up on my lap and wanted me to hug her, and all I saw was that other little girl. I couldn't do anything.

Unless you find a place to put it, you're never through with it.

Judge York told me that both parents ended up in prison. He also said that his area's local mental health authority had started a new program directed toward first responders. He was involved in bringing it to his county. "When I started law enforcement, you didn't talk about this. You toughed it out. We don't do that anymore."

Shawnee Bass (Erath County) finds that inquests are getting harder for her. The community of first responders she belongs to plays a vital role in helping her get through the difficult call-outs.

It seems like the longer I'm in, the harder the inquests are and the more they get to me, I guess. It wasn't that way to begin with. I think when it really started to be more difficult was last December when I had two little girls killed in a car wreck. The first responders and the officers—having them is the only way I can deal with it.

After the 2017 Sutherland Springs church shooting in Wilson County, Governor Greg Abbott facilitated grant funding for special counseling for the community. Judge Sara Canady found a counselor with whom she connected.

I see her once a month. It does pile up. The counseling is tremendously helpful. I think it's healthy to get counseling. I think it's good for me as a community leader to be able to say, "I get counseling, too." It's not shameful at all and I'd rather say I'm not flipping out. I'm not going off the deep end. Because I've seen judges go off the deep end. I've seen judges who wouldn't admit that this was too heavy for them and when they tried to carry the load, they just explode.

JPs who do inquests see people at their most vulnerable, and the job taps into that vulnerable part of themselves. Cliff Coleman (Bell County) was called to McLane Children's Medical Center in Temple. A baby had died of SIDS (sudden infant death syndrome).

She's there—a little baby wrapped up on this hospital bed, lifeless, just as cute as she can be. I came to find out that the mother was from Franklin, Texas, and just a week prior her house was spared from a tornado that destroyed so many homes. She felt so blessed that they had lived through this horrific storm, only to have this happen.

The husband's out of town. The mother woke up at three o'clock in the morning; the baby wasn't breathing. She did CPR. They get a helicopter, bring her in to McLane, couldn't save her. By the time I got there, the mother is cried out. There's no more fluid in her tear ducts. I try to get some information. She says she's had four miscarriages. She was by herself. She had no one there. And I'm telling you as a judge, to sit there and look her in the eyes, the tears just well up.

Because of "the former cop" in him, Stuart Posey (Victoria County) tends to get more involved in the on-scene investigation of deaths that occur within his jurisdiction than would other JPs. Still, inquests aren't a part of the job he savors.

We see a lot of haunting scenes—scenes that give us nightmares. The most horrific scene as far as being a justice of the peace that I witnessed was a three-year-old who'd been mauled to death by a pit bull. When he went in for the autopsy there was no blood left in his body. That is going to the grave with me.

It's inevitable that an inquest JP in Texas will be most strongly affected by the kinds of deaths that make the evening news. Judge Sharon Fox said that she's seen some "really horrific scenes over the years," but the one that stands out for her was one "particularly gruesome murder."

I really thought I must be on Candid Camera *when I got there because the deputy was telling me, "Well, this happened, then this happened—"*

I thought, you've got to be kidding me. This can't be real. A son and his girlfriend murdered his daddy and they cut him up and put him in a barrel and tried to burn him up. Then they rolled the burning barrel to a different location and burnt body parts fell out along the way.

We got through the whole thing, and then the young man went on trial. It was publicized in the paper, but when our pastor mentioned it, he opened the drawer when I wasn't expecting him to: With this one, the emotion just came flying out.

It isn't always easy for a judge to hold back feelings about a death that results from human recklessness and irresponsibility. Yadi Rodriguez (Hutchinson County) was once put to the test.

I had a little girl that was thrown out of the vehicle. There was no car seat in the car, but her mom was seat-belted in. It made me angry. She was just a perfect little girl and her mom lost control of the car. And the mom, because she was seat-belted in, didn't have a scratch on her. That stuff never goes away. I'm thankful I don't have to do the notifications.

Similarly, Donna Schmidt (Cochran County) was assailed by the mother of a four-year-old, the victim of a fatal traffic accident, for authorizing an autopsy as required by law. It was hard for Schmidt to contain her anger over being criticized for performing her job when the mother hadn't performed *her* job as parent by fastening her child safely into her car seat.

> *I do an inquest and then several hours later I have to perform a wedding. I've learned how to put on that happy face.*
> —Hon. Evelyn Kerbow, Crockett County

Retired JP Suzan Thompson of Matagorda County teaches classes on inquests. The discussion often turns to how to keep depression at bay. She told me that part of handling constant exposure to death is finding the means to walk away from it, learning how to move along with your own life. Yet there will still be times when a judge's response to a particular death won't be appropriate, won't be particularly well thought out, but will, in fact, be elementally human.

One time I got a call to go to the hospital. It was a newborn that hadn't survived. I had no idea why on earth I did this; I'd never done it before and never did it since. I was in the nursery. I just picked up the baby and sat down in the rocking chair. It was the worst thing I could have done. It was probably a maternal instinct. I just had this incredible urge to hold that baby.

I talked to a male judge who had that same desire: Fred Buck (Tom Green County).

I can remember every infant that I've gone to. You walk into the hospital room and it looks like a little baby lying there asleep. You just want to pick them up and hug them. What I've got to keep in mind when I go to one is that it's just a straight shot to heaven when a baby dies.

Donna Wooten (Pecos County) recalled one inquest that nearly "did her in."

This is a little town of three hundred people. I pass this certain house about four times a day. The family had five boys, one after another. There was one little boy I saw all the time. One evening, there was a report of some crazy asshole speeding through town going in excess of one hundred miles an hour on our main road. No one could get him to stop. As the locals were calling the sheriff's department, he crossed the road and drove right inside that family's house. He drove over the five-year-old's head. They called me. I live a minute away. When I got there, the vehicle was still running, the tires were still spinning, and they were restraining the father of the little boy; he was going to get his gun and kill the guy. We knew right away that the driver was high on meth. He was a heavy, long-term user.

The little boy had been camping on his brother's bedroom floor. He was in a sleeping bag and the tire ran over his head and I had to view the body. I've got to put eyes on the victim. I went into the ambulance and it crushed my soul. I don't think anybody is properly trained to deal with this. I was just going through the motions of what I had to do as a justice of the peace. Because that child was under six, it was ordered by law that he have an autopsy. I had to do further damage to the family by submitting his body for an autopsy.

Still, you have to do your job. Judge Wooten told me that she had to remain laser-focused on what the law required from her in spite of an adrenaline level that she described as "off the charts." She said she waited a long time to fill out the death certificate because she was forced by circumstances to put down "accident."

I cried, I cried, I cried, I got sick, I was physically ill over this. As far as I was concerned, it was not an accident. He made the conscious decision to take drugs and drink and then drive a killing machine. After grand jury, I was told I had to put "accident," because it would be years before they had a trial. These people needed a death certificate in order to bury their child.

> ***I'd make a death call and then come home and couldn't turn the light out because if I turned the light out and closed my eyes, that's what I'd see.*** *—Hon. Frieda J. Pressler, Kendall County*

How *do* Texas's coroner-JPs deal with the frequent assault on their own sensibilities, how do they manage the impertinent feelings of empathy for those left behind, the deep wrench of the soul in the most tragic, the most senseless, the most infuriating of deaths, which they are called upon to investigate, to certify, and then to file away with some semblance of bureaucratic dispassion?

Caroline Korzekwa (Karnes County) talked to me about how difficult it is to tend to the particulars of an inquest while managing her own emotional response to what she sees.

It's hard, especially when you know the family. As you're driving over there, you remember that these people are religious people, you've got to make sure you've got the priest there. You've got to make sure that you don't have gawkers and onlookers, and you have to chase these people off. You see some pretty horrible things. You've got to get yourself ready for it. Every time you walk up to a scene, you're picturing the hundreds of others you've already been to.

When I still had my CD player, my daughter made me a personalized CD with all my favorite '80s music. What I'd do is put on my CD and relive the '80s dances and not think about where I was going. When I'd leave the scene, I'd put that music back in just to get my mind off what I'd dealt with. Otherwise, what happens is the scene, the smells, the family—it just gets to you and you end up crying on the way home.

You get the call in the middle of the night. You get the address and you ask, "Who have we got, what have we got?" If you don't know the name, you know it's gonna be a little easier. If you do know the name, you've got to prepare yourself for the family members you're gonna see there. You've got to be able to talk to them. You talk about memories. You spend more time at those and you think, I hope I did a service. I don't want to just walk in there, do my job and get the hell out.

I can remember once when it was our sheriff's brother who'd accidentally got shot by his wife in the back. He was a volunteer fireman. Every fireman in the community was in that hospital hallway. I had to go into the emergency room. I had to call to order the autopsy. I had them on one phone in one hand and I had the organ donor people on the other. I ask, "Where does he need to go first?" I clearly remember them saying, "Well, judge it's your body."

> **On those middle-of-the-night calls—you're not getting any more sleep after that. You lie there and think about what you just saw or witnessed.**—Hon. Gordon Terry, Garza County

Conducting as many inquests as some of the JPs in larger counties do requires walking that line between not depersonalizing a death to the point of dehumanization, but also not investing too heavily in the personhood of the deceased so that you lose your proficiency as a justice of the peace. Rick Hill (Brazos County) learned this the hard way.

What's the one I couldn't shake off? One of the classes in the training center that we taught last year was basically about dealing with the emotional part of death. No matter how tough you think you are, you're gonna have things get to you. I can tell you the one that got to me the most.

My office is literally right next to the A&M campus. A girl was on her way to class, had ear buds in. There was a garbage truck that stopped— they're kind of narrow streets—the garbage truck was going to back up into a cross street and go the other way because they couldn't turn around. Well, the driver couldn't see her. He ran over her, killed her instantly.

I went to that one. It was a Friday. It was a horrible thing. There were kids everywhere. The next day, Saturday, I'm riding my motorcycle. I thought, you know what? I'm gonna stop by there and see, because it kind of affected me. So I turned the corner and I see a police officer there—the officer I had worked with the day before. Kids were writing in chalk on the street. They'd kind of blocked the street off where she'd died. And I went. Well, I needed to find out about her. I went on Facebook and found out that she was a senior at A&M. She had joined an organization that connected kids to the proper faith-based organization they needed to be in depending on their religious beliefs. She'd seen her freshman brother the week before march for the first time in the Fightin' Texas Aggie Band on Kyle Field.

And I realized the mistake I'd made: I'd personalized it. She had a faith, she had a life.

Leslie Ford (Hutchinson County) told me that JPs often form support groups of a sort.

You have to be able to talk to people—fellow judges who understand what you're going through. I've got a few friends I've met at my new judges' school and we call each other all the time. If we're having a tough time with one of our inquests, we'll just call and let it all out. There is a camaraderie that develops with the people on the inquest scene. The officers, sheriff's deputies—whoever is first on the scene—they see everything, too. We're all in it together.

The ones in Hutchinson County, they are all very good about taking care of the judge. You do form a tight bond with them and form friendships. You have your own way of dealing with things. You have to laugh to be able to get through some of this stuff. We make it light when something is dark, and I'm not meaning this in an insensitive manner. It's just a coping mechanism. If you thought about these things all the time, it would drive you mad. You have to find a way to let it go.

What I do is this: When I get home, I get me a Coke Zero and go sit out on my back deck and I just listen to nature. I do have that moment to think about what happened and to take it all in and I say a prayer. I have a German shepherd and he is my sweetheart. He knows when I've had a tough one and he'll come and sit beside me.

> *There are only two JPs in our county. We're both new. We kind of watch out for each other. "Hey, I know that one was bad. Are you all right?"*—Hon. Jon Glenn, Eastland County

Matt Kiely (Caldwell County) has been working with EMS since he was nineteen. He's "seen a lot of dead people," he says. But the 2016 Lockhart hot air balloon crash proved a test even for him.

I learned to cope with it and deal with it, but I'll tell you this: That balloon accident—and it's the best word I can use—it fucked me up. I've gotten better as time's gone on, but I can tell you, in the first month after it happened, my wife was ready to leave me. It was that bad even though we went through the debriefings, we went through all the talks, we went through all of that. To be honest with you, I don't even know what affected me. The only thing I keep going back to is that when I woke up that Saturday morning, the only people that really knew me were the people who supported me getting into this office. Now everybody in the damned world knows who I am.

We've got a great support group of responders that were out there. We call each other and check on each other. We run into each other in town and we sit down and just visit. I think now that it's three years old, we've gotten it past us. We're a part of it now. It's in our makeup now.

But because it's now part of their makeup, part of Judge Kiely's makeup, it never goes away.

> *You just go in there and do your job and you work with the officers— the officers are wonderful to work with. But when you get home at night and everything settles down, you know that's when stuff goes to setting in.*—Hon. Rodney Baker, Bailey County

In the more populous counties of Texas in which justices of the peace
are expected to serve as county coroners, the job tends to eclipse everything else. Inquests take both a physical and mental toll on the judges
who are called to perform this vital duty for the county: paperwork,
logistics, long hours at death scenes, lost sleep. Judge Coleman told me
that going out on death calls can physically wear you down.

One of the judges I'm good friends with had seven deaths this past
weekend. Last week when I was on call, I got a fatality accident at 10:30
at night. I got to the scene. They had transported somebody to the hospital.
As soon as I got home, I got a call that this person had expired. I drove to
the hospital, took care of that. Fifteen minutes after getting into bed, I got
a call that somebody had hung himself. I had to go to that call.

When Judge Coleman got home at 5:30 a.m., it was time to get ready
to go to work—that is, to go and spend the day doing all the *other* things
he was expected to do as one of his county's justices of the peace.

> *My family says to me, "You're always thinking the worst*
> *things that can happen."*
> *And I say, "That's because I see the worst things."*
> —Hon. Sharon Fox, Brazoria County

Everything is relative. There are some judges like Judge Donna
Schmidt, who worked for years in hospice. The job prepared her for
dealing with inquests.

I was with a lot of people when they died, and now I'm there after the
fact. That part is easier for me.

It's also less difficult for Rodney Price (Orange County).

When I was a court-appointed attorney, I represented people accused
of the most detestable crimes. Preparing for trial, I had to look at pictures,
spend the weekend writing jury charges, taking time away from the rest of
my life. Now I can go and look at a dead body for thirty minutes and go
home, say, "Thank you, Lord!" and go to sleep.

How one has lived is often reflected in how one dies, or, rather, the
conditions they find themselves in when that life comes to a close. JPs are
there to shut the book and help to put it away. In doing so, they realize
how many lives will go un-noted, let alone unheralded. Tim Walker

(Lamb County) remarked to me that the vast majority of inquests he's done have been, in a word, sad.

Probably a month in I had an inquest on a gentleman who passed in an assisted living center. They knew that he talked to a child on a regular basis who lived in California, but there was no way to find that person. It was probably by design, but to the common man, that's just not something that enters your mind, departing this life alone. Then you get to those that are very elderly and they choose to be in their homes, where they pass in their sleep, very peaceful, and you just go, "What a way to go!" Live your life the way you want to live it and then go home.

Upon his retirement in 2014, the late George Zimmerman (Midland County) spoke to reporters about how performing over one thousand inquests had given him a troubling look at the fallibility of human beings through bringing to light—as part of his job—the manner in which they died.

Being a JP is like opening an unlabeled can of food in the pantry. You don't know what will hit you. It's a different world you didn't even know existed. The way people treat each other—the crime, abuse, assault, and drugs. You don't realize what all is out there in the dark.[1]

"I see things that we shouldn't see," Judge Coleman told me. "When you're a justice of the peace and you see what we see, life becomes so much more precious. It seems so much more fragile than what we realize."

8

What's Happening in JP Court Is Downright Criminal!

I was a police officer. I've heard everybody's stories. "The reason I was speeding was I needed to go the bathroom real bad." I've heard that for thirty years. Come up with something original and new and I might listen to you.

—HON. RODNEY WALLACE, CHEROKEE COUNTY

IF YOU ARE A Texan (or a visitor to Texas) and are accused of speeding, not carrying liability insurance, running a stop sign, being inebriated and/or conducting yourself in a disorderly manner in public, shoving someone intentionally, trespassing, gambling, jumping bail, leaving a child in an unattended vehicle, texting while driving, shoplifting something worth less than $50, drinking in a car, possessing drug paraphernalia, doing things as a kid the law says you can't do until you're older (such as smoking and drinking), or a whole passel of other forms of illicit, non-felonious behavior—you just might find yourself either in municipal court or justice court (depending upon which peace officer charged you with the offense and where the alleged transgression occurred). There you will be called upon to enter a plea and then either pay for your minor league act of criminality or protest your innocence before judge or jury.

> When I took office in '83, the court costs on a speeding ticket were $6. Now it's $122.10. What they do with the ten cents I haven't figured out.—Hon. Ronnie Davis, Liberty County

106

After they raised the speed limit for the stretch of Interstate 10 between Kerr County and El Paso County to 80 mph, Donna Wooten (Pecos County) said that even with this generous new speed limit, her court still saw its share of speeding ticket filings. What's the highest she can remember? 132 mph. A Yamaha motorcycle, whose operator most definitely did not want to get stopped, was clocked at this speed for a span of one hundred miles.*

> *One day I had this guy with a ticket for speeding who said he couldn't have been going the ninety-five miles an hour that they clocked him at because he had an old car and it vibrated when he hit ninety.* —Hon. Patricia Ott, Williamson County

A majority of the Class C misdemeanors that get filed in justice court relate to traffic offenses. Russell Johnson (Coke County) predicts that if you drive long enough in the state of Texas—he doesn't care how good a driver you are—you are destined to get a ticket.

But there are a good many other Class Cs that have nothing to do with vehicular misbehavior, and their variety can add a little spice and levity to the ho-hum of Class C adjudication drudgery.

One misdemeanor that doesn't ordinarily make it all the way to trial is littering. But Jeff Monk (Johnson County) related one of the most dramatic littering cases he'd ever heard (or heard *about*). The defendant had been charged with littering . . . dead chickens. The next-door neighbor's dog had gotten into his and his wife's yard and killed their chickens. His wife was upset because these were her pets, Monk said, her *babies*. Now her babies were dead and she wanted to show the owner of the homicidal dog what the animal had done, but it wasn't the wife who got caught in the act. It was the husband, who had flung one over the fence, presumably to show loving solidarity with his grief-stricken wife.

So we're in this criminal case and there's a bench trial. The prosecutor's sitting there and we're all rocking and rolling. You'd think we were in district court and this was a capital murder case. The state was calling the state's witnesses: the officer who went out and took the report, the lady who had all the chickens thrown in her yard. The defendant came up and said, "I just threw one chicken."

Then they got the wife on the stand, and it was a Perry Mason *moment. She was in tears. "He* didn't *throw the chickens in the yard. I threw the chickens in the yard. He's not responsible!"*

I said, "Ma'am, at this time I have to inform you that you have the right to remain silent." I read her her rights, and I looked at the state prosecutor and I said, "Do you want to pursue charges on this lady?" Because she'd now confessed to a Class C misdemeanor in open court. The state declined to pursue charges at that time. I found the husband guilty.

Judge Tommy Ramirez's precinct in Medina County is one of the highest revenue-generating precincts in the state of Texas for a couple of reasons. A weigh station is located there. According to Ramirez, truckers and the trucking companies they work for get cited for "a boatload of violations": for being overloaded, for flat tires, low tires, lights that aren't working, brake assemblies that are out of adjustment, and "everything in between." It isn't the sexiest part of what a justice court does, but it does bring in the fines. Also, since Interstate 35 runs through his precinct, he has to deal with a lot of drivers speeding back and forth between San Antonio and Laredo. In Precinct 4 of Medina County, chirps and sirens beget reverberating cha-chings in the justice court of divine little Devine, Texas.

> *The guy called about his ticket and I just asked him,*
> *"Did you have a medical emergency?"*
> *"Well, judge, I had my head up my you-know-what."*
> *Well, I guess that would qualify as a medical emergency.*
> —Hon. Gordon Terry, Garza County

Are all Class C misdemeanors equally wrong? Perhaps in the eyes of the law—or else they'd be classed differently. But they're not equal in the eyes of certain JPs. K. T. Musselman (Williamson County) is just one of many JPs who exercise discretion based on their own belief system. He believes that it even overrides one's political party affiliation, and that voters would do better to vote for candidates based on their espoused principles and values than on which party they belong to.

There are things that Republican and Democratic judges do that party affiliation doesn't really play into, especially when you come down to values issues. Are you going to be high or low when you're setting your bond? That's where you see judicial discretion. I know myself well enough to know if we ever have cases where animals are being abused, that's a real sticking point for me and I'll probably be tending more toward the maximum on fines.

When it comes to charges involving marijuana possession, Mussel-man told me that because pot is "legal in half the country," it hurts him that "this person is going to get a fine for something that half the country doesn't have to deal with." So he typically lowers fines on charges involving the possession of marijuana-related paraphernalia.

For Jeff Wentworth (Bexar County), there's a special kind of motorist who gets his goat.

I give lectures on a pretty regular basis to people who come up to the bench having been cited by a deputy sheriff or state trooper for speeding in a school zone or a construction zone. I explain to them that those are the two most serious offenses I hear in my court because you can actually kill or injure a construction worker or a kid.

Criminal defendants in Texas justice courts often annoy the state's JPs. They either don't make nice, or they make stupid, or they just simply get on the judge's nerves. JPs see smart criminal defendants and they see boneheaded defendants who might justify the theory of reverse evolution. Judge Daniel gave me the perfect example of the former, and Judge McIntosh presented the latter.

Judge Randy Daniel (Henderson County): *I'd just finished up my magistrations for the day. The deputies brought in a young woman, and they came over to me and said, "Judge, we've arrested this girl for public intoxication, and we were wondering if you could magistrate her this morning."*

So they finish up booking her, and I'm sitting there and what's going through my mind is this: What am I going to do here? Is there any way I can have any fun with this? Which was probably the wrong way to think.

When they brought her up to me, I said, "Ma'am, I understand they brought you in for public intoxication. I need to know if you can under-

stand the warnings I'm giving you." I said, "Can you count backwards from ten to zero?"

"10–9–8–7–6–5–4–3–2–1."

"Good. Now, can you recite the preamble to the United States Constitution?"

"We the people of the United States, in order to form a more perfect union . . ."

The young woman recited the *entire* preamble. Judge Daniel cut her loose, while scraping that egg off his face.

Judge Bobby McIntosh (Uvalde County): *I had a fellow come all the way from Houston to contest his traffic ticket. He wanted his day in court, he wanted his trial. We had a bench trial. As we worked through it, his contention was that the officer brought a dope dog that ran around the vehicle and indicated that there were narcotics somewhere in the gas tank area. The deputy stated that nothing was found. The defendant's whole defense for the speeding ticket was that because the dog malfunctioned, so to speak, the radar likely malfunctioned as well.*

> *I have a quote on the bulletin board in my chambers, and this is true across the state of Texas: "Common sense is not particularly common."—Hon. Randy Daniel, Henderson County*

JPs are sticklers about defendants entering a plea on their charges. There is a reason for this, which Stan G. Mahler (Young County) illustrates with a predicament in which he once found himself. A defendant came in and asked for a trial. At the same time, he admitted to what he had done. Judge Mahler had to hand the case over to another judge. Mahler told me, "A lot of people want to go to trial because they want to present their side of the story." But "not guilty" means you didn't do it; it doesn't mean, "I know I'm guilty and now *you* know I'm guilty, but let's pretend like I didn't just say that, because I'd like my day in court. *Your* court."

How do you *unhear* that?

Sharon Maxey (Falls County) shared with me one of the hardest parts of being a JP: making defendants she sees in court understand that ignorance isn't a defense when it comes to the law. This also goes for garden-variety stupidity. Carl Davis (Anderson County) told me about a particular case filed by a game warden in his county.

A guy from Dallas killed a deer, and the antlers on the deer weren't long enough. They had to be so many inches. He wanted a jury trial. After the state presented its case, he got on the witness stand himself. He said, "This deer is the same size as the one I killed around Dallas. I know because I've got that one in my freezer and the antlers on that one aren't as long as the ones here." So they got a warrant, went to his house in Dallas, and charged him for the ones in Dallas, too.

—⁂—

Alcohol and drug abuse: the twin banes of a JP's professional existence. There isn't a single Texas justice of the peace who hasn't had to deal with fallout from these two statewide epidemics.

Alcohol—or, more narrowly, the abuse thereof—impacts a justice court beyond the simple filing of minor in possession or public intoxication misdemeanor charges. Magistrate JPs set bond and read rights to those in their county who get intoxicated and place themselves behind the wheel of a motor vehicle. Some Texas JPs are allowed by law to sign a warrant for a forced blood draw to determine the level of inebriation in a DWI pick-up when the suspect refuses to submit to giving a breath or blood specimen.**

Donna Schmidt (Cochran County) signs them. She doesn't necessarily like having to deal with them, though.

Most of the people I see are really belligerent: "You ain't gettin' any blood out of me!" I make sure they understand that since I'm here, they're going to lose their license for six months because they aren't cooperating. "I can't lose my license!"

"Well, you just did, because you aren't cooperating."

I had one gentleman who was like: "You can't sign THAT! YOU CAN'T SIGN THAT!"

I said, "Give me one good reason why I can't."

He said, "Ummm, I'm Muslim."

I said, "You're no more Muslim than I am. Besides, if you were Muslim you wouldn't be out at two o'clock in the morning driving under the influence!"

Judge Schmidt is dead serious when it comes to dealing with people who drive drunk in her county. She makes the DWI defendants she magistrates get an interlock device as a bond condition, "because I know enough people in this town and I don't want this person driving around drunk and killing one of my friends or one of my family members!" She told me she's pretty sure that for every intoxicated driver in her county who gets stopped, there are probably seven more out there who don't.

The stats agree with Judge Schmidt. With sad and disturbing consistency, Texas tops the list each year for the number of alcohol-related traffic fatalities. In 2018, 1,439 people lost their lives in the state at the hands of a drunk driver, including, at times, the driver himself. (California, a state with over ten million more people, placed second, with 1,069 fatalities.) And there was only one state—Montana—that surpassed Texas that year in the percentage of its highway deaths that were related to drunk driving—43 percent to 40 percent. An even more unsettling way to look at this: Nearly 14 percent of the nation's 10,511 alcohol-related traffic deaths in that year took place in the Lone Star state, and 2018 wasn't an aberration.[1]

Although drunk driving in Texas should be no laughing matter, there are times when the absurdity in dealing with intoxicated individuals is unavoidable. Lex Jones (Marion County) shared the following:

A group of us had put together a rescue dive team for Lake O' the Pines. In the county below us somebody had thrown guns off one of the bridges, and we found them. As we were walking up the steep hill that comes up to the bridge, there's three of us, all wearing black wetsuits and toting all our heavy gear and fins. One of the officers is a huge guy.

Well, a car comes through there and a fireman who's flagging cars waves at him to slow down. He speeds up instead, goes flying through there. The fireman radioed the next fireman to get the driver to slow down. When the driver reached the second fireman, that fireman threw a cup of water on the windshield. The guy jumps out of the car and he's going to beat up the fireman. The two deputies and I are standing on the side of the road with all this scuba gear on, watching. This guy is stumbling, cussing the fireman. The big deputy walks over and helps the guy up and tries to give him a sobriety test but the guy's so drunk he can't even walk. The deputy just carries him over to the patrol car and takes him to the jail for DWI. Well, guess who magistrated him the next morning?

He's sitting at the end of the row of guys across from where I'm sitting. When I get to him, he's bent over, rubbing his face with his hands. He looks up at me. "I'm never drinking again."

I said, "What's wrong?"

"Judge, I got arrested by frog *men! And I think* you *was one of 'em!"*

As county magistrate, a JP will often find herself setting bond on individuals for whom the situation would have been markedly different if alcoholic intemperance weren't a superseding factor. Protective orders must be considered if, for example, a wife fears that her husband, who has been arrested for intoxication-implicated misconduct, poses an ongoing threat to her and her children.

> *I see people my age at the jail. They don't have teeth. They look like they're eighty years old. It's just so scary to me. I try to tell my kids: all it takes is one time with meth, because it's such an addictive drug.*
> —Hon. Kim Redman, Wise County

Coryell County, where John Guinn serves as JP, is home to several prisons. Part of Fort Hood, the most populous US military installation in the world, is also located there. I asked Judge Guinn if the prisons and the military post have an impact on his job as JP. He told me that he is actually magistrating fewer people on DWI charges than he was fifteen years ago, but that drug charges have skyrocketed. Methamphetamine use, he said, has become a bigger and bigger problem in his county, just as it has all over the state.

Meth is one thing, but as we heard from Judge Musselman, pot is a different animal. While most JPs don't want to see Texas go the way of Colorado and California, there is a happy medium to be found, as Jon W. Johnson (Smith County) explains:

I look at the big picture. When you're a judge, when you're doing an official duty, you try not to let any personal feelings get in, but it's hard not to with marijuana when you realize that, but for Texas, some of these people wouldn't have spent the last twenty years in a jail simply for having less than an ounce of marijuana. Anything less than two ounces is a Class B, which is an arrestable offense. If they don't have money and family, I might give them a PR bond. I don't think the sheriff wants to waste jail space and the cost of jailing someone over a misdemeanor marijuana charge. There have been bills to legalize marijuana, but more bills to make it a Class C misdemeanor like shoplifting: you get a ticket and come to court and pay a fine. I think a lot of the JPs in the state are against decriminalizing it, but by making it a Class C misdemeanor that we could deal with in our court, a person could just pay a fine and be done with it, like open container. Right now, if you have a bong, you get a ticket. If you've got marijuana, they'll put you in a squad car and take you to jail.

Because US Route 84 comes down through Bailey County from Pagosa Springs, Colorado, Judge Rodney Baker says he sees more than his share of drug charges—both the Class C drug paraphernalia tickets that get filed in his court and the higher-class drug possession charges that he deals with in his magistration duties. More than one West Texas JP talked to me about having to set bond on defendants caught bringing legally purchased Colorado pot into Texas, some who'd been holding their breath that they wouldn't get caught with their reefer contraband, others who were literally oblivious to the fact that legal Colorado pot becomes *illegal* Texas pot once it gets transported across the state line, regardless of the amount.***

> *I had a district attorney always calling me and telling me I was setting the bonds too low. Then he went into private practice and started calling me and telling me I was setting the bonds too high.*
> —Hon. Ronnie Davis, Liberty County

Magistration is one of the hardest parts of a JP's duties to characterize. When you read someone their rights and set their bond, you never know if the defendant is going to throw you a curveball. Sheron Collins (Hale County) shared her favorite story:

I was magistrating a gentleman on a cattle charge who asked for a court-appointed attorney, so I started to fill out the paperwork. I've got it memorized. "Are you employed?"

He didn't say anything. He just got kind of quiet. I looked up at him. He puts his arms out. "Judge. I steal cattle for a living."

"I don't know what the prosecutor's gonna do to you, but I'm gonna let him know that you're the most honest man I ever met in my entire life!"

Sherri LeNoir (Limestone County) found herself in a significantly more awkward situation when it came to a particular gentleman she was magistrating.

My son-in-law and my daughter moved back to our county. When they did, the jail was brand new, and he went to work there. One day they bring a guy in, I arraign him, read him his rights, tell him what the charge is, and that kind of thing. As I'm gathering my stuff up to go, my son-in-law, Brian, says, "You've got one more."

I said, "Bring him in."

He said, "I can't."

I said, "Why not?"

He said, "He's in the holding tank and he's naked."

"He's what?"

"He's naked." The guy had a blanket—a suicide blanket. When they do that, they take away all your clothes and those blankets are supposed to be made so the person can't rip them up and hurt themselves. He just chose not to use it.

Of course, Brian thinks this is funny. I said, "Ok, well, I guess we'll walk down there and we'll open the window and I'll talk to him." So that's what we did: I waited until Brian had brought him all the way up to the door so all I could see was his face through the little peep hole, but then, of course, we had to open up the bottom part where they sign, and I didn't want to see him there.

> *Nearly every time I magistrate people, they're crying. I don't take that lightly. I know smart people do dumb things.*
> —Hon. Pam Mason, Donley County

When Kerry Crews (Hunt County) performs his duties as magistrate, he has no difficulty looking over probable cause affidavits; as a former police chief, he used to train his officers in how to write them. Similarly,

Randy Ellisor (San Jacinto County), because of his long time in law enforcement, holds the officers and deputies who come before him to a high standard. Former deputy sheriff Trisher Ford (Tyler County) does, too:

I come from a small department, so nine times out of ten I'm gonna know this officer. I hold them to a "if it's not in that report, then it didn't happen" kind of standard. I can understand you not putting something in the report and forgetting about it, and I'm not saying you're lying whatsoever, but that's the difference between criminals and the good guys: we go by the rules.

After two decades in law enforcement working with border patrol, the state police, and the Victoria County Sheriff's Office, Stuart Posey understands the reasons for magistration, but he says a lot of his law enforcement colleagues look at this judicial proceeding in entirely the wrong way.

In law enforcement you have this mindset that when someone gets arrested you want the highest bond possible, but, of course, once I became a judge I had to be very neutral. You can't treat setting a bond as punishment.

> *By the time we get there, the damage has been done and the only thing to do is to help them. One of a magistrate's duties is to try and not hurt them any more than they've already hurt themselves.*
> —Hon. Pam Mason, Donley County

I asked Mike Towers (Bandera County) why, given that he had previously done quite well in the tech boom and was financially comfortable, he would want to put up with all the *Sturm und Drang* of being a Texas JP—a job that in Towers's case, included spending a lot of time at the jail.

Well, the honest answer to that, and I know this sounds corny, but the reason I first became a peace officer was because I could contribute to the community. When I'm at the jail magistrating, 999 out of the 1,000 people I deal with are good enough people. They're just having a bad day. They had too much to drink or they had a fight with their wife, or they didn't take their meds, or they took somebody else's meds, or whatever, okay. Every once in a while, I run across some sure-enough evil turd who needs to be in the penitentiary. (That's a highly technical law enforcement term.) The bottom line is that those people are lost. There's nothing that I or anyone else can do for them. But they're the exception. The rule is to try to help people in the community that are having a little bit of trouble. And to the extent that we can *help them, that gives me a great deal of professional satisfaction.*

Among the things that the JPs I spoke with opened up about the most were their magistration responsibilities. Not all JPs magistrate. In some counties, this job falls to municipal judges, or, in the most populous counties, there are judges who are hired expressly to read rights and set bail. But for justices of the peace who do magistrate, the job is taken very seriously.

Jon W. Johnson (Smith County): *Every fifth week, starting Monday through Sunday I start my day at the county jail at eight o'clock, and then I'm usually out of there at ten. I see around fifteen to twenty people who have been newly arrested overnight, and I tell you that for a JP, it's pretty fascinating. In my courtroom, all I really see are Class C misdemeanors. You set punishment on these by fine only. But when I'm magistrating, my whole job is* not *to decide guilt or innocence, but to advise them of their federal constitutional rights, set a bond, and notify them of any special conditions if they bail out of jail. JPs in Texas can magistrate all the way up to capital murder.*

Billy S. Ball (Angelina County): *My office is in the jail complex, so I handle all the magistration and I issue the majority of the warrants. I do bond reductions, bond revocations, EPOs, the list goes on.*

When I magistrate, I'm not a cookie cutter. I view every case on its individual merits. I have a system I use. Are you gonna show up for your hearings? Are you a threat to the community or to a particular person? I'm not here to make a big bond just because you pissed off some police officer. I am a proponent of bond conditions. I started with six and I'm up to about thirty one. Even the district courts use my bond conditions. Have to report to probation as soon as they get out of jail, can't possess or consume alcohol or drugs, need to get tested, and if there were children involved, I don't let them go to places where children congregate. A lot of my bond conditions have to do with protecting the community. My goal isn't to set some high bond and impress anybody. I'm way past the day of impressing.

Billy Hefner (Colorado County): *Magistration is at the total discretion of the judge involved, and there are two things to consider: you've got to protect the public and you've got to make sure the person shows back up for court. I have to review all the information and make my judgment. If it's non-violent or close to a civil case, you don't have to set up as high a bond. Assault with a deadly weapon, that's a different situation. You've got to go through bond conditions and protective orders—you've got to protect the individual's family. Most often it's a husband and wife that got into it or a boyfriend and girlfriend that got into it, and obviously one or both of them were drinking or whatever. At the same time, you need to set a high enough bond that it won't come back to bite you.*

As the only justice of the peace in Clay County, John W. Swenson Jr. told me that being on call seven days a week can be a real grind. It's been five years since he's had a vacation, but he feels uneasy about leaving. He has forty-eight hours to magistrate someone who has been arrested, but he hates to see anyone sit in jail for longer than they should, particularly those who get picked up on certain misdemeanors, like driving with an invalid license. He asks the jail to call him if they've brought in anyone who is a good candidate for ready release, especially if they really need to be at work the next morning.

Where in the past a good many traditionally minded Texas JPs were loath to give up their visits to the local county jail to execute their duties as magistrate, safety concerns related to the COVID-19 pandemic required that even the most technology-averse JP embrace off-site video magistration for the short term. The upshot is that most of the judges I spoke with during my 2020 check-in now believe that this temporary operational exigency will be made permanent in a majority of Texas justice courts, even post pandemic, and that in-person magistration may now be largely a thing of the past.

As magistrates, JPs also sign search and arrest warrants. When I spoke with Clyde Black (Houston County), he pointed out that even though the Texas justice court adjudicates only the lowest class of misdemeanors, because justices of the peace can be called on to sign certain important criminal warrants, they participate in the earliest phase of bringing a guilty defendant to justice—or, conversely, protecting the rights of someone in danger of being falsely arrested. Ironically, a serious felony that will eventually be heard in district court might have the "lowly" justice of the peace participating in the launch of its trajectory.

When law enforcement comes to me for warrants, there's a great opportunity there for a judge to review those criminal cases and make sure that they're good cases. I try to ensure that there's good probable cause before I take somebody's freedom away from them on a warrant.

In the rural areas—and I don't want this to sound negative—occasionally law enforcement hasn't had quite the experience and training as some of the larger departments, and sometimes we'll find that the reasons for wanting to arrest somebody don't necessarily measure up to the needed requirements. I think it helps law enforcement to point this out, and actually protects the citizens, which we're supposed to do.

JPs hold peace bond hearings, which can result in placing someone under bond for a specified period of time in hopes of preventing a specified offense against person or property. Magistrate JPs can also sign an emergency protective order (EPO) when an arrested defendant poses an ongoing threat to his alleged victim(s). A justice of the peace must also decide if an order should be amended in the event the alleged victim (frequently a spouse) resolves to forgive and forget because "he'll never do this again. He promised." Although peace bonds aren't signed by JPs with nearly the frequency they were when I clerked in the 1980s, I have quite a few memories of my JP reading the riot act to wives and girlfriends who were struck with a wave of exonerative feeling for their contrite significant others and entreated the judge to remove the peace bond.

On rare occasions, things don't even reach the point of putting the peace bond in place before one or both parties (sometimes both are put under bond) decide to forgive and forget. Perhaps the most striking example of spontaneous comity in the middle of a peace bond hearing was related to me by former JP John Payton (Collin County).

We take a fifteen minute recess. I come back and I get on the bench and ask the bailiff, "Where's the couple?"

He says, "I can't find them."

I say, "What do you mean you can't find them? Go see if they're outside."

He says, "Sure. Maybe they're in their car."

Sure enough, they're in their car. They're having sex. The constable yanks them out of the car and takes them into the courtroom. And I say, "The case is dismissed. Don't file a peace bond in my court ever again."

Texas JPs are even on occasion called on to untangle the consequences of criminality that affect their court only indirectly. For example, it is part of a JP's job to determine ownership of seized stolen property located in his county. Judge Hefner told me that when a large theft ring in Houston was broken up, it fell to him to decide how the stolen farm equipment that had been stashed in Colorado County would be distributed and disposed. Sometimes it's a complicated business if an insurance company has already made a payout to the original owner. Maybe that owner wants the late model hay baler back, but now has to reimburse the insurance company for the claim it paid out. (Where's that darned equipment depreciation schedule?)

How does crime in a JP's precinct today compare with the level of criminal activity that took place in decades past? Jackie Miller Jr. (Ellis County) thinks that things are much worse now than they used to be.

We have more heinous crimes now. There wasn't a methamphetamine problem back in the early '90s, as we have now. You didn't have as many child molestations. We even have MS-13 in the Metroplex. They murdered a young man about five or six years ago.

No justice court in Texas is left unaffected by that disturbing tendency in the human animal—even a human animal that speaks with a Texas twang—to be bad, and sometimes to be bad in ways that keep JPs up at night. Several judges told me during the COVID-19 pandemic that they were witnessing troubling increases in crime in their communities. One of these judges was George Trigo, who serves in La Salle County.

We are seeing a lot of family violence and are issuing more emergency protective orders. We have been in lockdowns and/or quarantines on several occasions and this puts additional stress on individuals. We've had virtual schools, so with children not being able to attend school, they remain at home, and some parents are unable to work, thereby causing more stress. The number of children who are abused has increased throughout the state.

pushes responsibilities onto the schools even before it gets to the courts, which I have no problem with, but once it gets to the court, we're now very limited in what our sanctions can be. The judges are restricted from making good decisions that will benefit the next generation. Was the law abused by some courts? Yes. I will not deny that. But what I did when I first started hearing these cases was I thought about standing in the court myself—standing before that JP who made a difference in my life. I want to make that same difference in somebody else's life.

> **When they first changed the failure to attend school law
> I said, well, you took out my teeth and gave me false teeth.**
> —Hon. James R. DePiazza, Denton County

When the law changed, Tisha Sanchez, a JP court clerk at the time, said that the county attorney for Palo Pinto County stopped handling truancy cases.

It really hurt the schools as far as attendance. He said, "I'm not a civil attorney." No truancy cases were filed for two years.

When I got into office, we got a new county attorney and a new county judge; I got with them and the school superintendent and I said, "I want to get this back."

Sanchez said she thought everyone was going to throw a party because finally they could deal with this problem.

Talyna Carlson (Gregg County) finds that the change in the law prevents her from seeing students as often as she used to. The old system, despite its shortcomings, brought the kids into her courtroom so she could work with them.

I was standing at the Clinique counter in Longview, and this big woman said, "Are you that judge from Kilgore?"

I was thinking, I'm fixing to get beat up, but I said, "Yes, ma'am."

"Well, I'd like to tell you that if you hadn't been so tough, my grandson would have never graduated from high school. Can I hug your neck?"

When they changed the laws and I couldn't see the kids anymore, I couldn't ask the boys, "What's your dream truck? What color is it? What kind of wheels do you want on it?"

She misses that.

As does Sherri LeNoir (Limestone County).

Because I used to be a teacher, I took care of all the truancy cases here in Groesbeck. That allowed me to work with the school again. I was used to dealing with the administrators and students and teachers, so it worked out really good. Then the law changed, and schools had this list of things they had to do first before they could file. Then when they did *file with us, we were just a pass-through; it would go to the county attorney's office, they would look at the case and they would decide whether or not they had all the necessary paperwork on their end, and* then *it came back to us. Once all that happened, it pretty much tied our hands. We went from having eighty cases a year to possibly two or three. It tied the school's hands too. I didn't like that at all.*

> **The bottom line is that we're not a counseling agency. We're not supposed to be their parent. We are supposed to be the court holding them to accountability. If you have no way of holding them accountable, what is the purpose of putting them in the court?**—Hon. Patricia Ott, Williamson County

We Shouldn't Be Sending Kids to Jail for Not Attending Class

"The justice court shouldn't be the first step for failure to attend," Louie Ditta (Harris County) told me. "The first step shouldn't be, 'This child isn't going to school; let's put him before a judge.'"

As a former assistant high school principal and elementary school principal, Rick Hill (Brazos County) was familiar with the justice court's role in keeping kids in school; he'd made numerous appearances in his predecessor's court when he was working as an educator and school administrator.

Coming from my education background, I was glad they decriminalized it. It was not about making the kids criminals; it was about getting them educated. A lot of judges—they feel like once they decriminalized it, they took away everything we could do. But there are lots of things we can do. We can order them to counseling. We still have tools in our toolbox. More often, it's not criminal activity that is at issue. There's just something going on in their lives. Maybe this is a kid for whom going to school just isn't their thing. I get kids that are already on their own, kids that are working, kids that are parents. To me, it's all about working with the resources you have in the community to get them support.

Sonia Guerrero-Perez (Dimmit County) is quite comfortable with the new standard. It isn't as if she hadn't already been devising her own ways to help kids stay in school. She even started a program with the local school district to bolster school attendance.

We created a task force to help our young individuals and encourage them to stay in school and graduate. Everyone seems to think that truancy is a school district issue, but in my view, it's a county issue, because maybe that child isn't in school because of trouble he's having at home. There might be things we don't even know that he's dealing with: mental health issues, abuse, drugs. He could be breaking into my home or somebody else's home. It has to be an issue for everyone. We all need to care about it. I feel that being part of the conversation with parents during orientation and registration about the importance of sending their children to school is helpful. Children should be in school not just because the law says they have to, but because they benefit from getting an education.

I love being able to go and do career day with the younger children. The older children at the junior high level can come and sit in during a trial or a hearing so they can see what it is that we actually do. I actually hold a mock court. We have a plaintiff and a defendant and the students can ask questions.

Stephanie Frietze (El Paso County) told me that it's been the successes that have colored her own views on the truancy-related responsibilities that JPs have.

I tell the kids, "You need to graduate and come back and we'll take a picture together and celebrate." And some of the kids do come back.

"Look, judge!" they'll say, "I got my diploma."

"Give me a high five!"

In 2008, David Cobos (Midland County) received national attention for his innovative approaches to getting kids in his county to stop skipping school. Through his Justice Court Alternative Sentencing Program, Cobos became the first JP in Texas to use global positioning technology to track the whereabouts of teens who refused to go to class. The program involved the use of GPS ankle monitors, and, in spite of criticism by the American Civil Liberties Union of similar programs as invasions of privacy, this and other creative steps taken in the same direction raised school attendance and cut Midland County's juvenile detention rate in half.[1]

Regardless of whether Texas truancy laws have changed for the better or for the worse, Larry Flores (Frio County) has found a variety of ways to make an impact on the children in his precinct. He knows kids. He used to be a schoolteacher, but even his background as a police officer gives him an advantage in working with kids.

This is a small town. We're very limited in resources. What helps me a lot is the experience I had as a teacher, so I understand more or less where the student is coming from. Also, most of the parents are ex-students, so I know the family's background. The parents know who I am, so we try to work together as much as possible out of respect.

Most of the kids are very good kids, but sometimes the school system doesn't have the resources to keep them engaged in school. They lose interest, so I try to motivate them—get them into band or playing football.

Michael Jones Jr. (Dallas County) asks the kids he sees for truancy to write an essay, which gets them thinking about how to change their situation and how to improve their chances for a promising future.

Tell me how you're going to get up on time, get to school on time. Tell me what you're going to do when you get out of school. Are you going to be a doctor? How do you become a doctor? You have a higher chance of achieving a goal if you put your mind to it. The ones who are undecided, I have them fill out a job application.

Judge Flores looks for ways to encourage kids and keep them involved. In particular, he decries the school shootings we've seen over the last twenty-five years, and wonders about the things that could have been done to keep the perpetrators from reaching a point of such violent hostility toward everyone around them.

I want this kid to walk out of here and respect that we're here to help him, to walk out of my court at least with a smile. If I have to spend all day on truancy, I'll do it. That's my personal philosophy in handling the kids. Like I say, when I see them out on the street or in school, I just want to shake their hands and maybe hug them, and say, "You're doing a good job."

Judge Flores has found that now that he's a judge—having once been a police officer—he can take those experiences when he visits classrooms and engage the students in personal ways. He still teaches driver's ed, where he often talks about what he's seen as an inquest judge, opening their eyes to the real-world consequences of the choices they make as they move into adulthood (most dramatically on the county's roadways). He tells the kids that his biggest fear as a justice of the peace is having to go out at two in the morning to certify the death of one of his students.

There are other forms of juvenile misbehavior and law-breaking that can place an adolescent before a justice of the peace. While Texas's juvenile courts have jurisdiction over kids who violate most state laws—they hear those cases in which delinquent conduct is at issue or in which the child is potentially in need of supervision—there are still areas of the law in which JPs are actively involved in the welfare of the state's kids. Texas's justice courts handle fine-only misdemeanors that can involve kids, some of which are offenses unique to adolescents. For example, JPs adjudicate juvenile alcohol offenses, tobacco offenses, disorderly conduct cases, and cases involving graffiti vandalism.

What keeps me up at night? I have teenagers.—Hon. Jon Glenn, *Eastland County*

Like Judge Flores, Katy Marlow worked as a teacher (for eighteen years). She also drove the school bus and did a lot of other school-related jobs in Foard, one of Texas's smallest counties. She places a lot of importance on dealing with juvenile crime.

I know most of the kids from the school. I assure them that we all do things wrong. Sometimes their minds just don't work and they don't comprehend things as fast as they should. If I have to magistrate them, they start crying because they feel like they've disappointed me.

Yadi Rodriguez (Hutchinson County) is heavily invested in the kids she sees in her court. She's gone above and beyond with some of the children she sees, on occasion buying them clothes and groceries. "I will continue to do that so they can continue to go to school."

I counsel kids that have gotten into trouble. One day a week I get them to come by after school. You just get them in there and you shut the door and you say, "Tell me what's on your mind."
—Hon. Rodney Baker, Bailey County

"There are certain things that stick with you," Connie Hickman (Navarro County) told me.

I had a girl come in here yesterday. These kids come back here when they're grown and they say, "You're the only reason I graduated." Kids who I found out weren't going to school because they couldn't see. They couldn't afford glasses. So I made arrangements for them to get glasses. Girls that didn't have proper underwear, who were made fun of because they didn't have bras and things. I had access to ways to help them with their problems. Those kinds of things have meant so much to me. Now I'm seeing their children, their grandchildren!

Olivia Neu works with a lot of kids in her precinct in Cooke County.

I had a little girl one time whose dad appeared with her and it was a sad situation. I ended up trying to get her into a better situation. She came back to see me after her case had resolved. I brought her into my office, and she shared with me some personal triumphs she'd had. When she got up to leave, she said, "Can I give you a hug?" I can tell when it's a kid getting in trouble because they don't know any better and need guidance.

Not that there aren't times when the laws of the state of Texas are either creatively construed or ignored altogether in applying the proverbial—and sometimes literal—hickory stick to misbehaving youths. A justice of the peace in Montgomery County, Texas, was publicly reprimanded by the State Commission on Judicial Conduct in March of 2002 for ordering the foster parent of an unruly child in his care to give the boy "a good butt-dusting."

The judge wasn't merely making a suggestion. Even though the foster parent had been instructed that he wasn't allowed to paddle the child, the judge indicated that it was perfectly all right to do so if the parent had the judge's permission, and then he retrieved an "eighteen- to twenty-four-inch" paddle from his chambers with "holes bored into the flatter end" and a special grip on the handle. After being given the paddle, the foster father swatted the boy's buttocks three times in the presence of the judge and court personnel. He stated that he paddled the child because he feared the judge would throw him in jail for contempt if he refused the order.

A witness to the hearing stated that this wasn't the first time a child had been paddled in this judge's courtroom. The judge defended his actions by saying, "[The foster child] doesn't understand any other punishment but corporal punishment. That was the way I was raised and you were raised, and we were much better kids than the current generation."[2]

Juvenile justice isn't just about juveniles. It's also about the parents of those children, what they've done—or haven't done—to their detriment, and how they can do better by their kids. Donna Wessels (Wharton County) likes to show the young people who come into her courtroom pictures of her own kids.

I have pictures of them in college in their graduation robes; I show those pictures and I say, "This is what I'm most proud of: my kids finished college." I try to impress on the children I see how important it is to go to school, to have a chance in life. Of course, so many of the problems come from the parents. They're too lazy to get the child to school, or something else is happening at home.

And there are the rare times that a judge might be a very recent juvenile himself! Consider former Collin County JP John Payton, who became judge at the age of eighteen. Payton attributed his decision to run for the office at such a young age to what he went through as a child, growing up in an environment of fear and abuse. When he took office, he sought to be a champion for kids faced with an array of challenges that often collided with their ability to stay in school.

I was at risk. This is what these at-risk kids want—not someone to sympathize with them but somebody to empathize with them. I needed somebody to motivate me, keep me straight, keep me moving forward. These kids' stories were no worse than my story. And I could relate to them. I could apply a very compassionate tough-love approach, knowing that holding them accountable was going to make them successful, because it's what made me *successful.*

Kids want expectations. When they start becoming trouble, that's when they need those expectations more than anything else. Instead, we're giving them negativity. They don't want to feel that you're gonna beat them down over it. My success rate was 98.8 percent. I saw over ninety-seven thousand kids. I loved these kids. They were amazing. Kids are *amazing. It's adults who are screwed up.*

Payton created a community service program that allowed him to work alongside the students himself. Together they built fourteen houses for Habitat for Humanity.

That's something that all Texas JPs have in common: once upon a time, they were all kids. Fred Buck (Tom Green County) takes what he remembers about his own youth to the bench with him every day.

My dad died when I was fifteen. I never got in trouble . . . because I never got caught. I never hurt anybody, never stole anything, but I drank a lot of beer and I raised a lot of hell. There are so many people that gave me so many second chances.

Jon Glenn (Eastland County) gives kids second chances, but he also gives them a straight slice of what the real world is like. Actions have consequences, which can impact a teen's whole future.

I had one come in—he had the trifecta: speeding, no license, and drug paraphernalia. I called him and his mom into my office and we talked and I came to find out: stupid sixteen-year-old kid. Hormones. Broke up with his girlfriend and wasn't thinking. I used to be a drill sergeant. I treated him like a basic trainee and broke him down and built him back up. I said, "One thing you didn't think about: What if I was on that road and you hit me, with my wife and my kids in the car? You'd be facing the pen for manslaughter."

Keeping kids safe and on the right path applies to his own daughter and stepchildren as well.

I walked into my office one day, looked down at the magistrate's form, and said, "I can't magistrate this one, because I'm related." One of my stepkids. Now he's gotten himself straight. I've also got stepdaughters and my own daughter. I basically told all the law enforcement in the county that if the first thing that comes out of their mouths is, "Do you know who my dad/stepdad is?" then charge them with resisting arrest!

Texas JPs see kids in their courtrooms for a lot of reasons, and often those reasons have to do with messing up, needing to be straightened out, to be put on the right path. But JPs also see kids *outside* their courtrooms . . . being put into body bags. As noted in chapter seven, "I'm Blessed That I Don't Dream about Them," one of the hardest things a Texas justice of the peace has to do is sign a death certificate for a teen who's chosen to end his or her life. I spoke with a judge who hadn't been on the job for very long when she came face-to-face with both the reality of teen suicide and the harrowing consequences of anti-gay bullying.

I had a sixteen-year-old a couple of weeks ago who shot himself. Suicide. That was one of my worst. He left a suicide note. Basically, he was being bullied, not only by friends but also by his parents. To read that suicide note and what he told his dad, I can't imagine what that would be like for a parent. He was gay and his dad constantly told him he was going to hell. In his note he wrote, "You know, Dad, you're probably right. I probably wouldn't have amounted to anything. But I do know one thing: I will see you in hell."

The last word in this chapter goes to Fernando Villarreal (McLennan County), who speaks for a lot of his colleagues when it comes to juvenile justice.

People ask, "Why do you do it?" Because I can make a difference. We're on the front lines, because generally when a student starts messing up and having to deal with the law, he's gonna become a statistic in the judicial system: school drop-out, low wages, prison, and what have you. So we see ourselves collectively trying to prevent these things from happening in the future. If we can make a difference here, we can help both the individual family and society. We can help people go on to have a productive life. That's one of the things that keeps me going.

10

Gettin' Hitched

People are in a good mood and happy to see me; that's the exact opposite of most of my courtroom meetings. Tears of joy vs. tears of loss.

—HON. JEFF WILLIAMS, HARRIS COUNTY

People who can't afford a wedding in a church or can't afford a big venue or don't have a church home, they need to have a place to have a nice honorable service. It's a service that the justice court has always provided, and I think that's a good thing.

—HON. TIM BRYAN, GREGG COUNTY

ASK THE MAN OR woman on the street what a justice of the peace does and the first thing you'll probably hear is, "Don't they perform weddings?"

Or is that something you only see in the old movies?

Yes, old movies are certainly a good place to spot a marryin' JP—usually an older gentleman with a wife at the parlor spinet, her fingers twitching to play "Here Comes the Bride" and, sometimes, "I Love You Truly."

But real-life Texas JPs have swapped doily-filled front parlors for the local VFW hall and country club gazebo. They perform weddings in city parks and state parks, on lake docks, beneath the sinuous boughs of ancient live oaks, on Texas waterways in bass boats and on riverboats, squeezed into hot air balloon baskets, upon the brows of rolling hills carpeted in bluebonnets, and, I've even heard, within their very own courtrooms.

Jeff Williams (Harris County) says that weddings are probably the best part of being a justice of the peace.

We've had people dressed up in full wedding gown, trail, veil, and tux. Others come in wearing T-shirts and flip-flops. There are mail-order brides who speak not a word of English and their American spouses who speak not a word of their language. Somehow, love finds a way.

I like to have folks give wedding vows and exchange rings. Sometimes they drop the rings and have to go scrambling for them across the floor, and once, little junior came running up from behind me to hug his mom and I tripped over him and did a somersault into a stuffed chair to avoid mashing the little one into the floor. I was told I had the moves of a great running back!

Sylvia Holmes said the thing she was most unprepared for when she became a JP in Travis County was performing weddings.

Nowhere in judge college do they teach you about weddings. They just say, "You're gonna marry people." That is literally what they told us. I started on January 2 and then on January 4, one of my clerks said, "Hey judge, we got a walk-in wedding."

"We've got a what?"

I'd defeated an incumbent, I'd taken the bar exam, I've jumped out of a plane, yet I'm scared to marry someone. I didn't know what to do.

Judge Holmes quickly learned what to do. When I talked to her after only eight months on the job, she said she'd already married one hundred couples.

After speaking to quite a few Texas JPs about bringing couples together in matrimony, I've developed a theory that I certainly didn't anticipate: grooms cry more than brides. Two judges told me this, so I decided to check in with some others. I asked them flat out to weigh in on my unusual theory, given their own observations.

Nearly every one of them agreed.

Donna Wessels (Wharton County) subscribes to the "tearful groom theory" through personal experience:

I married this gangster kind of guy, sagging pants, all tatted up, and they'd written their own vows. And he cried. I like to take a picture with the people I marry, and he was like, "This is private, right? You're not gonna tell people that I cried, right?" Afterward, he wore his sunglasses, I guess so that nobody could tell he'd been crying.

J. R. Hoyne in Kerr County says that for some of the ceremonies he has officiated, he's sobbed right along with the groom.

There has been more than one occasion like that. You get these guys—they repeat their vows and tears come to their eyes because of the ceremony and the person who's with them who's so important to them. I've felt that same kind of emotion because I cried at my *wedding. When the guys and sometimes the gals get choked up, it's very moving. Weddings for us JPs are opportunities to be part of somebody's life, and I always express to the folks getting married what a privilege and an honor it is.*

Crying grooms? That's nothing! Let me tell you about fainting grooms. Would you know anything about that over in Harris County, Louie Ditta?

I had a groom that fainted, and they had to catch him. When they were putting him in the back of the ambulance, somebody asked if the wedding was finished, and I said, "I now pronounce you husband and wife," as it was pulling away.

I've had close to ten people in weddings who've fainted. They say if you're nervous and you lock your knees, that's when it happens.

Texas JPs, who have seen it all when it comes to the wacky, wonderful world of Lone Star knot-tying, are usually good at holding it together, keeping those chuckles and chortles firmly tamped down.

Except for those times when they can't.

I could write a second book filled with all the nutty, off-the-wall wedding stories I had the good fortune to hear. Here are some of my favorites:

Charlie Hodgkins Jr. (Palo Pinto County): *It was about two or three months after I came into office that a lady came to the back door of my house. She comes in and this guy's with her, and they're both really drunk, and she says, "We want to get married."*

I said, "Let me take a shower and shave and then I'll meet you at city hall."

"No, no, we want to get married right now."

I said, "Okay, I'll be at city hall in about five minutes."

This was Hodgkins's very first wedding. He called a fellow JP, who directed him to the "blue book," where he'd find the ceremony.

He couldn't find the ceremony.

I looked where he told me it was supposed to be, and it wasn't there. I looked through the table of contents, and it wasn't there. This gal, she kept going, "We've got to get married! We've got to get married!"

The guy says, "Well, we can come back."

But she was like, "We have to get married!"

Finally, she said, "Give me that book! I've been married by a JP three times."

And I swear to God, she turned right to the spot in the blue book! I married them, and they stayed married about six months.

Since then I've realized that it doesn't matter what you say, just so long as you sign that marriage certificate.

Mark Holt (Walker County): *One of the most fun weddings I did was for an officer. He's a great guy. He came down the aisle and you could tell he'd been crying because of this spectacular day. Then the bride walks down the aisle with her dad. She comes from a little rougher side of the tracks, and her dad's belt is broken on the tux and he's trying to hold it up while he's walking her down. I start the ceremony and the groom and bride start whispering to each other and I'm like, What are they doing? All of a sudden, he holds out the napkin he's been using to dab his eyes and she spits her gum into it. I could not stop laughing.*

> *It was like a swamp with all the cypress trees. They'd built a deck with pallets and two-by-fours. The bride's kind of heavy. She steps up on the platform and crushes it. I did the ceremony with people standing in the mud and the rain, and everybody just had to wade out.*
> —Hon. Lex Jones, Marion County

Ronnie Webb (Somervell County): Judge Webb recalled a wedding he performed at Rough Creek Lodge for a surgeon and doctor from Baylor hospital in Dallas. Prior to the wedding, the groom hashed out his plans with the judge.

The plans involved a horse . . . a big, black horse.

The groom told me, "I'm gonna be staged out in the woods, and when I hear the 'William Tell Overture,' I'm gonna come in on this horse."

The day of the wedding, I was on this rock extension into the lake. One hundred fifty people were all facing the lake. She walks down the aisle, and I said, "Who gives this bride away?"

Her son said, "I do."

Then I said, "It appears that the groom is late," and everybody is giggling because they know he's always late. Nobody knew about the horse. Then the organist goes into the "William Tell Overture."

That's the cue for the galloping appearance of the Lone Ranger, MD!

I said, "Well, sir. It's nice of you to make the wedding."

At the end of the ceremony, after I said, "You may kiss your bride," they had a fireworks display right over the lake. He got back on the horse and she got on it with him. Her son had to give her a push to get her up there, and then she started sliding off as they . . .

. . . rode off into the sunset, otherwise known as the wedding reception.

> **I did one wedding where they had a horse walk down the aisle with them. When I got to the part where I asked if anyone objected to the couple being married, the horse neighed.**—Hon. Mark Russo, Rockwall County

Bill Price (Coryell County): *We used to have a hometown radio station. They had a promo every year where they would give away a wedding, and the first year they did it, they had a guy who flew a little Cessna, so the wedding is gonna be done on the airplane. They called me and I said, "Sure. I love to fly. I'd be happy to do that."*

Well, I got out of bed that morning and I went straight to the floor. My back went out. I self-medicated. I called my wife and she took me to the doctor and he medicated me a little more, and by the time I got to the airport I was as high as could be. The last thing my wife said when I got on that airplane was, "Now, Bill, you marry them. You don't read them their rights."

> **I love weddings. It helps me get through the inquests to know that love does go on. I've married two people who have lost their spouses. That gives me fulfillment and joy.**—Hon. Teri Nunley, Kendall County

Debra Ravel (Travis County): *There was that wedding I performed at Hippie Hollow. The groom was paying homage to his Native American roots. His bride had a lovely dress on with fringe and beading and she looked very put together. But he couldn't find the proper costume, so he made his own. It looked like a kind of loin cloth. He sewed it with leather on the sides, only it wasn't long enough. They were facing me on a high hill on a windy day and I said, "Do you take . . ." and I looked down and he was either very excited or very frightened. About half the ceremony it was like that. I thought, If I can get through this wedding without losing it, I can get through anything.*

> **I had two who met online gaming. I changed their vows to "for higher score or lower score."**—Hon. Mark Russo, Rockwall County

Suzan Thompson (Matagorda County): *I remember one weekend years and years ago, I'd scheduled three weddings: one for Friday night, one for Saturday morning, and one for Saturday evening. On Sunday, at my home office, I got a call from the lady who I married Friday night. She was like, "Is there any way you can not turn that license in?"*

I said, "Ma'am, that's against the law. What's the problem?"

She said, "I just don't think this is going to work out."

A couple of hours later, the groom from the second wedding calls, and he said, "This is not going to work out."

I said, "How do you know this isn't going to work out?"

"I'm just telling you right now, this is not going to work out."

I said, "I can't give you the license. That's illegal. I married you and that's just the way it's gonna be."

After that one hung up . . . I left the house.

John Payton (Collin County): *I had a fun wedding where everybody in the wedding party was dressed up like in western days. The girls were all in can-can dresses and the men were all in trench coats with bolo ties and cowboy hats, and we all had old Colt .45 six-shooters on our hips and they had wax bullets in them. The people coming to the wedding had no idea. It was pretty funny when the couple came down the aisle and I*

asked if there was anybody here "wishin' to contest this here weddin'?"
The bride and the groom ducked, and I pulled out my gun and pointed
it at the crowd. They all jumped for cover and I started unloading these
wax bullets from my gun, and, of course, they sound like real bullets and
there's black smoke coming out. It was something to behold. I got called
Judge Roy Bean after that.

> **I sometimes get a groom who will say "awfully wedded wife."**
> —*a whole passel of Texas JPs*

Dale Ramsey has performed a lot of wedding ceremonies over the
thirty years he's been one of Briscoe County's two justices of the peace,
and quite a few of them out of doors. He remembers one that he performed on a ranch.

They had a pet deer. When the bride and the groom and everybody
came down the aisle, the deer was right behind them, then he kind of just
moseyed off on his own.

Ramsey has had some weddings in which he wished he could have
told the couple "not to do it."

Jo Rita Henard (Collingsworth County) has found herself similarly
conflicted. It took only a few hours for her concerns to be validated. She
told me she married an eighty-year-old man and a twenty-five-year-
old "floozy-looking woman." The man phoned Judge Henard the next
morning wanting a divorce because his bride had cleaned out his safe
and then vamoosed.

My favorite May/December wedding story comes from Shanna J.
Gates (Frio County):

I was asked to perform a ceremony for a couple in their home. I hadn't
met with them personally, just by phone to make sure they had their
license and that it was valid. Upon entering the home, I see an older
gentleman in a wheelchair, eighty-plus years old, dressed in a suit with
a boutonniere. I thought he was probably the grandfather of the bride or
groom. In walks the young lady—mid-twenties—in a white dress, appar-
ently the bride. I'm waiting on the groom to show up and, lo and behold,
it's the old gentleman in the wheelchair! He laughs and tells me he "likes
the young ones," and to make the wedding a quick one 'cuz he's ready to

consummate the marriage as soon as he gets rid of the company. I about died with disbelief. I thought for sure I'd be back to hold an inquest.

And then there are your December/December weddings.

Rodney Wallace (Cherokee County) married a ninety-year-old groom to an eighty-nine-year-old bride.

The man comes in my office and he says, "Wonder if you can marry me and this ol' gal I've been a-goin' with?"

"How'd y'all meet?"

"Dancin.'" They'd met down in Rusk at the VFW. "There's no turnin' back," the man said. "We's in love."

Then for Benjamin Collins Sr. (Jefferson County), it was the other way around:

He was eighty-nine and she was ninety. They had been high school sweethearts. They both married other people. They met at a bereavement group and fell back in love.

Not every wedding performed by a Texas JP is bathed in sweetness and light. Andrew Cable (Hays County) performed a ceremony in which a clash of cultures escalated into an exercise in fierce religious brinksmanship. Cable was set to marry "a red-headed, white-skinned American kid" to a young Lebanese woman. A major difference of opinion about a certain veil sent the bride fleeing to the dressing room, where she commenced to taking off her wedding gown. The question was whether or not the groom would be allowed to lift the bride's veil at the end of the ceremony and kiss her.

Well, the Muslim religion says absolutely not. The American husband-to-be said, "Yes, I am."

My wife went into the dressing room and told the bride, "You've got five minutes and then the judge is leaving."

I went and talked to the red-headed kid, who was being a real turd, and said, "Let me tell you something, buddy. You need to do what they ask you to do and get this done. If you have issues, it needs to be between you and your wife."

Long story short, we start the ceremony. It's been two hours since the wedding was supposed to start. The harpist is gone. It's dark, and the photographer can't take pictures. At the end of the ceremony he lifts that veil, and even though I told him not to, he kisses her anyway, and, oh my gosh, I thought there was going to be a hanging!

It goes without saying that there are JPs—I'm not naming names—who make quite a bit of scratch gathering together the dearly beloved, eliciting those all-important "I do's," and then pronouncing couples "husband and wife." ("*Man* and wife" went out with rotary phones, and please feel free to replace *husband* with *wife* and *wife* with *husband* as needed.) The money they make is theirs. Texas JPs don't have to share a cent of it with the county. (Or with the clerks who schedule their ceremonies; only one JP, Shane Brassell [Hill County], told me that back when he was still doing weddings, he'd set part of his fees aside and give them to his clerk as a Christmas bonus.) It has been confided to me by a couple of "you didn't hear it from me" judges that some big city JPs have been known to run for the office *just* for the wedding fees.

Of course, payment doesn't have to be in money. Rodney Wallace (Cherokee County) once married a couple on a Carnival cruise ship before it reached international waters for the elaborate sum of a bucket of beer.

Judge Wallace shared a conversation he once had with some of his fellow JPs about a particular form of wedding officiating remuneration known as cold, hard cash:

I was in a judge's conference down in Austin. You learn more sitting around the bar with a bunch of judges than you do in class. There were about fifteen to twenty of us sitting around in a circle, and the subject of weddings came up. We all got to talking about it. "What'd you think about what the Supreme Court did?"

This one judge from South Texas on the coast, he said, "Let me tell you something, judges. We're performing a civil ceremony. I was raised a devout Catholic. But I still do weddings. Let me tell you why. I get $250 to do a sunrise wedding on the beach. I get $250 to do a sunset wedding. I make $1,000, $2,000 a week doing weddings. If the Supreme Court says two dogs can get married, I'm doing it."*

I feel like doing the wedding for free is my gift to them.
—Hon. Katy Marlow, Foard County

Then again, there are JPs who don't charge anything at all. Sometimes judges will go gratis on special days. In Hidalgo County, two JPs who share the same last name hold wedding marathons on Valentine's Day, opening their doors for the whole day for free hitch-ups. On February 14, 2020, Jason Pena united fourteen couples, Juan Jose Peña Jr., thirty-four. Judge Peña told me that some couples walked in alone, whereas others were accompanied by a large, happy entourage of families and friends, everyone dressed up and festive.

If you want to get hitched during office hours in Washington County, Judge Douglas Zwiener is happy to do it for no charge. I cynically reminded him of all the discretionary income he was losing because of this arrangement. His response: "I lost that when I had a teenager."

Other Texas JPs charge and then turn the fee into a wedding gift, like Benjamin Collins Sr. in Jefferson County.

We charge a fee when they come in, but I'm kind of old-fashioned. I give that money right back to them as a gift from my family to theirs. When you go to a wedding, you're supposed to bring a gift, and like I tell them, use this to go to dinner, start a college fund, whatever you choose to do with it. God has blessed me with this position, so it's only right that I bless others. Seeing two people in love, the smile on their faces—it's all worth it.

I've only had one where I kept the money, because he was rude. He came in, "How long's it gonna be? What took you so long?" I was thinking, really? We went to lunch on him.

Beth Smith (Hays County) has a special reason for loving to do weddings. She donates all the money she makes marrying people to charity. She says sometimes it's a child cancer fundraiser, or the food bank, or the local women's center. She also hasn't raised her price in over twenty years. It's still $50, just like it was the day she came into office. Weddings, she says, are the highlight of her day.

They're special for Cameron County JP Sallie Gonzalez, as well. She's one of the few judges who is willing to meet couples at the port of entry on the Progreso-Neuvo Progreso International Bridge, where she has joined Texans and Mexicans in matrimony for nearly thirty years. "To me, it's an honor," she said. "My father was from Mexico and my mother was from the United States, and they were married sixty years."

> *I've married people on the pitcher's mound, on the beach when they were damned near naked. I've married them in my front yard, in my back yard, in my living room. I've married people at my wife's convenience store when I was trying to eat lunch. I married a couple where they went straight to the hospital to have the baby.*
> —Hon. Charlie Hodgkins Jr., Palo Pinto County

Brenda Dominy probably holds the record for officiating the best-attended wedding ceremony held in Cherokee County. She performed the wedding in the winners' circle of the county's dirt racetrack, joining a wrecker driver to his heart companion. The entire ceremony took place during intermission, everyone at the races that night serving as witnesses.

> *I did a wedding where everybody was in the swimming pool. They invited me to get in with them and I said, "If I did that, I'd be distracted by watching out for the man with the patch and one leg and harpoon in his hand."*—Hon. Bill Price, Coryell County

Inevitably, there will be times when JPs will—as my grandmother used to say—just get the devil in them. Sonia Guerrero-Perez (Dimmit County) likes to tease the grooms she's marrying. Right before the ceremony, when it's just the groom and her standing up front, she'll look at him with theatrical solemnity and say, "It's your last chance to run." She says it takes the nervousness away. Julie Sanchez (Hudspeth County) has her own fun with the couples she marries. She informs them that the judge is giving them a life sentence. Andrew Garcia Jr. (Lampasas County) contributes to the festivities in this way:

Sometimes I say, "I just want to do one last thing," and I ask the lady to "put your ring finger on my hand," and I'll say to him, "You put your hand on top of hers." Then I say, "Look deep into the eyes of your husband-to-be, and say, 'I love you dearly, John.'" So she'll say it. "Okay, John. You look deeply into Jane's eyes and say, 'I love you dearly, Jane.'" And he'll say it. Then I'll say, "Now remember, John, that's the last time you'll have the upper hand and the last word."

> *I did one at a church in which I figured out pretty quickly why the preacher wouldn't do the wedding. These people were heathens. Somebody had to tell the father to take off his cowboy hat and mirrored sunglasses before he walked the bride down the aisle.*
> —Hon. Bill Price, Coryell County

Stuart Posey (Victoria County) used to perform prison proxy weddings in which someone would stand in for the incarcerated groom during the ceremony. "You'd perform the ceremony," Posey told me, "and then maybe a month later they'd be wanting to come in and get an annulment."

Even before the law changed in 2013 to no longer permit them, Mark Holt (Walker County) didn't do prison proxy weddings. It didn't matter that the Huntsville Unit was in his county.

"I'm not marrying somebody in prison to somebody that's not. You never know if it's a scam. I'm a little jaded on trusting people. I try to keep myself out of trouble."

When the law once again allowed inmates to marry in 2015—this time within the prison compound itself—those judges who wished to conduct wedding ceremonies between the incarcerated and the non-incarcerated were instructed that they had to undergo a process that Joe Martinez (Gray County) characterized as "a little involved."

You have to meet with the person outside the prison at a specified time. Then you go in there and get all checked in and they take you to, like, a day-room. They bring the guy out. Everybody—the warden and the assistant warden—they're all in kind of a circle around him like they're trying to make sure he doesn't get away. I went ahead and did the ceremony. Then they said, "Okay. That's it. JP, you gotta go. We're done here."

It was odd.

In some cultures, a wedding celebration can last several days. There was at least one wedding in the state of Texas that took things to the op-

posite extreme—it lasted no more than several seconds. Cyndi Poulton
(Jackson County) performed it.

*One of my old sergeants came in with his bride-to-be and said, "Look,
we've been planning this with too many hands in the jar. They want to
make it bigger than what it needs to be. This is our second rodeo and we're
tired of it. Can you marry us?"*

"Sure. You want to do it today?"

"If you want."

I looked at her and I said, "Do you want to marry him?"

"Yeah."

"Do you want to marry her?"

"Yeah."

"Good. Godspeed."

Occasionally, a Texas justice of the peace will marry couples not of the
human species. In 1996, Mike Nelson (Galveston County) officiated the
wedding of Bonnie and Shorty at the Bayou Wildlife Zoo near Dickin-
son, Texas. The couple were endangered white rhinoceroses. Bonnie was
dressed as bride and Shorty as groom until Shorty made it known that
he didn't like the top hat, and so the roles were reversed.

And then you've got your rustic love matches that range from the
pastorally bucolic to the extra-crispy country-fried. A West Texas JP told
me confidentially, "We live in a community that's more rural. Most of
the weddings are rural, kind of western. I don't want to put this in the
wrong context, but I do a lot of *redneck weddings*."

Susan Moore (Goliad County) was comfortable conveying something
similar when she told me about a downhome wedding she performed.
It was held outdoors. The bridesmaids were covered in tattoos, the ceremony took place under a tree, hay bales were used for seating, and the
music—stopped and started as needed—emanated from a pickup's CD
player.

*I had a gentleman come in to get married wearing a wife-beater
T-shirt. He considered himself dressed up.*—Hon. Shawnee Bass,
Erath County

For Sara Canady (Wilson County), it was all about the beans:

One time I was doing a wedding out in the county and it was pretty hot.
"Well, where do you want to do this?"

"Out here by the barn."

I'm looking at my watch and I'm like, "There's the bride and there's the
groom. Why can't we—?"

"We have to wait for Aunt May-ree."

"Why?"

"Because Aunt May-ree's bringing the beans."

"Well, where does Aunt May-ree live?"

"Right over yonder."

"Can you call her?"

"She don't have a cell phone."

"Well, are the beans ready yet?"

"She's comin'! She's comin'!"

Then the cows start mooing.

Judge Canady kept looking at her watch. There was another event she
would soon have to leave for. Made no difference. There wasn't going to
be a wedding until Aunt May-ree arrived.

You see, she was bringing the beans.

Sometimes brides don't show. Judge John Payton (Collin County)
had one of those.

I was supposed to do one at the Dallas Arboretum. It was in the sunken
garden—the sunken woman's garden, and a beautiful setting. Very expen-
sive. They had about four hundred guests, and everybody's there except
for the bride. We wait and wait. I finally tell the groom that I've got to go.
I've got another wedding, and it's been two hours now, and no bride. He
says, "Let me call her one more time." I'm standing there, he's got her on
speaker, and she picks up. She sounds like she's three sheets to the wind. He
asks where she is. Well, she and the limo driver decided that they wanted
to go to Vegas. She decided she didn't want to get married after all. The
bride's parents easily spent $25,000.

More typically, it's the grooms who get the cold feet. Judge Beth Smith
had to deal with an icy-toed groom on one uncomfortable occasion. The
bride's friends didn't seem very upset; they hadn't wanted her to marry
him anyway.

They were telling me, "We hope he doesn't show up."

The bride said, "This happens, right? Grooms are sometimes late?"

I said, "Well, sometimes they are."

I didn't want to say that grooms don't usually leave their brides hanging for forty-five minutes. But when it got to be forty-five minutes, the bride's friends realized that they could track his phone and they found him at a bar in Round Rock. By now, it's time for me to leave. I had her wedding license, so I gave it back to her.

The woman called me about six weeks later: "We went ahead and got married the next week." Well, bless her heart. I'm pretty sure this one isn't going to last.

Fernando Villarreal (McLennan County) has had four scheduled weddings where the groom didn't show. There's a tradition in the Mexican American community to invite the judge to stay for the wedding dinner and reception. In one case, after the groom never appeared, the family pretty much shrugged it off: "Well, okay. Let's all eat."

Villarreal wasn't the only JP to tell me that he enjoys performing weddings for Mexican American couples because of the high regard with which the officiant is traditionally treated. Michael York (Lee County) looks forward to these weddings too . . . and to the requisite banquet.

Sometimes the cup of nuptial good feeling runneth over. Other times, not so much. Judge Donna Wessels was unsure about a couple she married only a week before she talked to me.

I got to the part in the ceremony where you pause and let them say their vows. Earlier, I'd asked them if they'd finished writing their vows.

He said, "I did."

And she went, "I didn't."

So, when it comes time, he says his and they're real nice and sentimental and gushy and all that stuff, and he even says he's willing to die for her.

After he was done, I turned to her and said, "Do you have anything to say?"

And she's like, "I'm good."

"Well, at least say, 'I love you.' Say something."

"I'm good. I'm good."

Like her colleague Judge Smith, Wessels doesn't have a good feeling about the potential longevity of this marriage either.

I asked quite a few JPs, both those still performing weddings and those who did so in the past, to reminisce a little about extra-special ceremonies they conducted over the years. David Sellers (Runnels County) related one that particularly moved him:

There was a woman that wanted to get married as soon as possible due to her father's illness. I performed the brief service on the sidewalk under a shade tree. That frail man crying while his daughter was getting married was one of my best memories.

During the last quarter-century of the previous millennium when Sarah Miller served in Erath County as justice of the peace, she performed 1,700 weddings. She still remembers her very first, back in 1975:

I hadn't been in office two weeks when this couple called me and said they were driving through Erath County on the way to somewhere else and they wanted to stop and get married. I said, "But let me tell you: I've never done a wedding before."

They said, "We don't care. We've been married before. We'll help you." And they did. They came in and that broke the ice and I was fine after that.

On another occasion the jail administrator tried to prevent Miller from marrying anyone in his custody. She wasn't having any of that:

We built a new jail and the jail administrator said, "There's not gonna be any weddings in this jail."

I'd been going to the jail and doing weddings. This couple called me and he was in jail and he said, "My girlfriend's fixing to have my baby, and I want to give it a name. I want to get married." So the girlfriend went down and got the license.

I said okay, "We'll call the jail." One of the jailers was in on it with me. He got the groom on the phone on my office intercom and I had her in my office and we did the wedding.

The jail administrator just threw his hands up and said, "I give up."

Judge Janae Holland (Wood County) gives silver dollars to the couples she marries.

I also have a nice certificate that I make. I tell the bride and groom that the coin should remind you of this day—the happiest day of your life. Things are going to get hard, so when you look at this coin, you remember this day.

Judge Stacy Spurlock (Jack County) takes a picture. She tells the couple, "This is for when you're old and you're sitting on your porch and you can't remember who married you."

Once the ceremony is over and the judge has signed the wedding license, then stick a fork in it, folks, the deed is done. It doesn't matter if the license has yet to be filed with the appropriate county clerk. JPs can't annul and they can't divorce, even if, in the case of a wedding that Ciro Rodriguez (Bexar County) officiated, the bride finds out after the knot has been tied that her new husband "had killed somebody." At least there was some advance warning for another wedding Judge Rodriguez officiated. When he asked the attendees if anybody had any advice or recommendations for the bride and groom, one of the bride's old boyfriends yelled out, "Don't get married!"

Chuck Ruckel (Collin County) had a stickier post-ceremony regret situation on his hands. The couple were both medical doctors. In this case, they got married, decided shortly thereafter that they didn't want to be married, then reversed course again.

They both had very busy schedules and wanted a Saturday wedding at a particular time. I had other things planned for the weekend they wanted, so my clerk told them no. They insisted that they could only marry on that weekend and at that time and were willing to pay two or three times my normal rate. I relented and scheduled the wedding on their desired Saturday. The wedding went beautifully, but at the end they asked if they could deliver the wedding license personally to McKinney for filing. I'm in Plano and normally do not allow this, as I'm responsible for the proper filing in McKinney. They insisted that they needed a certified copy of the license on Monday, and, as medical doctors, would guarantee that it would be done properly. Again, I relented and allowed them to take the license with them. After all, they'd paid me far more than my usual fee!

Several days later, they called to schedule their wedding again. When we asked why, we were told that on the way to McKinney to register the license they'd gotten into a nasty argument. The husband ripped the marriage license into small pieces and tossed it out the car window. His form of divorce, I guess! Of course, they had now reconciled and wanted a new ceremony.

This time I charged them twice what the first one had cost!

Sometimes, you'll have one where there might be one hundred fifty people. You don't want it to be, "You take her, and you take him." You want to give them a little extra.—Hon. Ronnie Webb, Somervell County

Then there are those judges who do weddings, but don't necessarily *like* doing weddings, just like JPs don't generally *like* doing inquests. Scott Shinn (Van Zandt County) actually prefers inquests to weddings.

To be honest with you, an inquest is easier than a wedding. When you get to an inquest, you're the judge and you have a job to do and it's well defined what your job is. When you show up to do a wedding sometimes you don't know the bride or the groom. You can't get things moving along, you're just at their mercy when they finally decide they want to walk up to the front. For me, that's difficult. You're not in charge of the ceremony and you don't have any authority unless they commit a crime in front of you and you choose to deal with that.

> **In the first six months of my term I had more weddings than deaths. I brought more people together than I saw put in the ground.**
> —Hon. Kerry Crews, Hunt County

I'll let judges Ott and Garcia pronounce this chapter *finis*.

Patricia Ott (Williamson County): *It's disheartening to be at a party and have someone say, "You married me."*
"How are y'all doing?"
"We're divorced."

Andrew Garcia Jr. (Lampasas County): *I did one where everything was black—black wedding rings, black eye shadow, black nose ring. It was kind of eerie. They didn't want a prayer.*

Well, of course not.

NOTE

*In the following chapter I take up the impact that the 2015 Supreme Court ruling on same-sex marriage has had on Texas's justices of the peace.

11

To Hitch or Not to Hitch

Look, I just do the wedding. I don't go on the honeymoon.

—HON. BILL PRICE, CORYELL COUNTY

JUDGE BILL PRICE DOES a lot of gay weddings.

I think it's because I'm not discouraging. I told these other judges, "If you don't want to do the wedding, tell them to come down and see Judge Price. He's got a ceremony that he's crafted for this situation and he'll be happy to do your wedding and take your money."

A lot of Texas JPs agree with Judge Price, but a good number don't. It is for this reason that this second group (sometimes in all-county solidarity) has decided to adhere to the state attorney general's opinion on the 2015 *Obergefell v. Hodges* Supreme Court ruling and not perform *any* weddings. They are guided by their strong religious faith and what they believe is a sacrosanct pillar of that faith: that the institution of marriage should be a sacred union between a man and a woman. Their decision is—at its core—a willing act of allegiance to their faith and to the principle upon which they firmly stand.

Well, upon which some JPs firmly stand. Others struggle.

Still other Texas JPs of deep Christian faith have wrestled with the issue and ultimately decided to carry on. This group of judges, many of whom find gay marriage personally objectionable, will continue to marry people—both straight and gay—because it's now legal. As one judge told me: "It's the law and I'm going to follow the law."

There is yet one last subset of religiously grounded judges who told me that they've experienced a realignment in their hearts. Not only do they perform gay marriages, they have come to believe that their own faith has been strengthened because of what they now perceive as an opportunity for demonstrating practicable accordance with their understanding of the expansiveness of God's love. They tell me that this realignment has, in interesting and powerful ways, altered who they are and their understanding of the potency of love.

Jeff Monk (Johnson County) explained the journey he took:

The biggest decision I had to make was whether I was going to do any more weddings after the Supreme Court same-sex marriage ruling. I knew from my faith growing up what the Bible teaches. So when the decision came down, I was going to keep my word: I'm not going to do weddings. Then I talked to a pastor friend of mine and I expressed my torment: I'm not an ordained minister. I have a job that I'm elected to do, and that job has to be equal to all persons. I'm in a position where I can minister to people that you can't. And then I was reminded of John 3:17: "Christ did not come to judge the world but to save the world." Here I am judging people, and yet I'm not doing what Christ commanded us to do, that is to love and share his faith. I stepped back and I decided, you know what? I'll do same-sex weddings. And I've probably received more blessings in the long run from some of the couples I've married because they've come up afterward and said, "We understand your belief. But I have more respect for you now than I ever had before because you showed love to me like nobody ever has."

Some of those people have become good friends.

> *One of the JPs I taught in school—she asked me if I was going to do gay weddings, and I said yes, and she said, "Well, you're gonna burn in hell."*—Hon. Debbie Horn, Potter County

One of the difficulties I had in preparing this chapter was presenting as objectively as possible the arguments both for and against continuing to perform weddings following the landmark 2015 ruling. Texas judges who still perform weddings, both those who do so with a grumble of reluctance and those who enthusiastically celebrate the extension of the civil right of marriage to same-sex couples, have crafted arguments for their side that are well articulated and filled with thought-provoking nuance. Those who oppose gay marriage on the grounds that marriage is a sacred religious institution that follows the directives of scripture have rarely ventured much farther than a simple, unambiguous statement of religious principle.

In the case of Lubbock County JP Jim Hansen, his statement was a public one, released on June 26, 2015. Judge Hansen addressed, unequivocally, his decision to stop performing weddings. He spoke for a lot of other judges from whom I got the sense that no further explanation was needed:

My understanding of the Supreme Court decision regarding same-sex marriage is that I have two options. I can either perform all weddings, including same-sex marriages, or I can no longer perform any weddings. The statutes say a Justice of the Peace may perform marriages, it does not say shall. For personal religious reasons, I have decided to no longer perform wedding ceremonies effective immediately. Upon announcing this decision, I also wish to share that I have no anger, fear, or hatred toward any person or party. I am simply guaranteed my religious rights as guaranteed under the United States Constitution.[1]

It's a fault line between JPs that may some day in retrospection receive the close examination it deserves. For the time being, I can only offer the thoughts and opinions of those judges who chose to speak candidly about an issue that continues to divide practitioners of the profession.

One of those JPs who sits squarely in Judge Monk's camp is Benjamin Collins Sr. (Jefferson County). He notes that the question goes to the fundamental reason people get married.

You see two people in love, it's a blessing. I've done, so far, over one hundred weddings since I came into office in January. When I started campaigning, that was one of the things they asked me: "Are you gonna do weddings?" I thought all JPs did weddings! When I was growing up, if you didn't want a big church wedding, you went and had a JP do the wedding. When it comes to same-sex weddings, I was like, well, everybody has a right to be happy, regardless of who they choose to be with. If they're in love, who am I to judge? With all the bad things we see—all the homicides, the suicides, all the death I see—to see two people in love . . .

It wasn't that many years ago that interracial marriages were illegal.

Even after interracial marriages became legal, there were still JPs like Eldon Sheffield (Tarrant County) who told the press in 1983, "When I perform a marriage, I want it to last. If the good Lord intended us to mix up like that, he would have made us all the same color." As you can probably guess, Sheffield got himself sideways with both the ACLU and the Dallas chapter of the NAACP. But the judge just shrugged it off. "I don't mind them getting married. I just don't want to be a party to it."[2]

There are differences, some JPs say, between one of their number refusing to marry a couple of different races and those who refuse to marry couples of the same gender. They say it's apples and oranges.

Other judges might respond, "It's more like McIntoshes and Granny Smiths."

Wayne L. Mack (Montgomery County) embraces his strong religious faith every day. He also marries same-sex couples. He comes at it from an interesting direction: Why is government involved in marriage anyway?

I'm very devout in my faith and I also view when I put that robe on, I'm not a Christian judge, I am the judge in that courtroom, and whether I have faith or don't have faith, how I live my life and how I treat people has an impact. I've been in leadership in our community for many years. I've felt for many years that government should have been out of the marrying business decades ago. They should have created civil unions. It's not government's role to tell people who they can love or what they can do in their bedroom. I have very strong views about all kinds of things that God refers to as sin but that's God's place, not Wayne's place. My place is to love everybody the way that God loves me. I feel when I put the robe on, I'm not a Christian judge, I'm a judge.

Standing up to the US Supreme Court and your own state's attorney general by refusing to perform same-sex weddings while continuing to marry opposite-sex couples can prove a professional complication. In the case of a JP in McLennan County, the result was a public warning by the State Commission on Judicial Conduct, but not necessarily for the act of defiance itself. The judge, who asked her staff to give inquiring same-sex couples a statement explaining her decision not to marry them due to religious conscience, was called to task for testifying before the Commission that she would recuse herself from any case in which a party doubted her impartiality on the basis of her stance on gay marriage. It was the idea that doubts might be raised about her capacity to act impartially before a gay litigant or court petitioner that became the fly in the unguent. (Canon 4A[1] of the Texas Code of Judicial Conduct states that "a judge shall conduct all of the judge's extra-judicial activities so that they do not cast reasonable doubt on the judge's capacity to act impartially as a judge.")[3]

And yet this is the linchpin of the argument made by Connie Hickman (Navarro County) about fairness or the *perception* of fairness as demonstrated toward members of the LGBTQ* community when they find themselves standing before a justice of the peace.

When these conversations first started, I just stood up and made my opinion known. We do things every day here that morally in my soul I don't think are right. Morally, I shouldn't be putting a brand-new mother and a baby out on the street for eviction, but the law requires me to do that if the plaintiff has followed the law. Do I like to do that? In my heart, no. But I swore and took an oath to be a judge and if I'm gonna be a judge, I can't segregate different groups of people from one another. It's my opinion, if you take a stand against performing a wedding for a certain party, then you should never preside over a case that includes that party. People come into the court—there's family violence, they have eviction issues, they have small claims issues. I don't think you can be fair and impartial to a group that you've taken a stand against as a judge. You can't pick and choose when you want to be a judge. I think you have to recuse yourself from every case that has to do with a group of people that you've already made a decision about, that you have an opinion about. My religion tells me not to go out and put a mom on the street. There are a lot of things I have to do that I wouldn't do by my faith.

> *Texas is changing. By the time I've retired, hopefully this whole gay marriage thing will have died down. Every generation seems to be improving on the last so far as bias and bigotry. This generation coming up is very non-judgmental.*—Hon. Jon W. Johnson, Smith County

I got the sense from my conversations that some of the judges who no longer perform weddings would actually still be doing them were it not for the possibility that the socially conservative voters who put them in office would use this fact against them in their next campaign. Thus, "to hitch or not to hitch" becomes, for them, a political calculation.

Then again, Tim Bryan (Gregg County) pointed out to me that he was elected "to do those things that JPs do." And though he didn't add this point to our discussion, my brain went there, nonetheless: how about those who cast their vote for a JP *wanting* them to officiate weddings, even same-sex weddings? Does their constituent voice also need to be heard within the precinct?

I do weddings. When the Supreme Court decision came down legalizing gay weddings, I stopped doing them because I wasn't sure if we were gonna have a run on the courthouse with all these people wanting to get married. But I saw very quickly that the justice court provides a service for people to get married, and I was not providing that service. So I waited a couple of months and let the newness wear off, and I started doing weddings again. I may have one person every other month who calls and asks if we do same-sex weddings.

In the wake of the Supreme Court decision, Theresa Farris (Freestone County) told me that she's still doing weddings. "I think everybody has the right to be married," she said. "I think everybody has the right be equally miserable." (Judge Farris has been married—and, one suspects, not miserably at all—since 1981.)

Travis Hill (Lavaca County) told me he's the only JP in his rural county still doing weddings. It's a no-brainer for him.

They come up with this deal about gay marriages and this stuff, and the rest of them are saying, "I'm not doin' that!" I don't give a damn. It doesn't affect me any!

> *I had a lesbian couple come all the way from Wichita Falls because nobody over there does that. I took an oath as a judge to follow the laws of the land and I feel like if I don't want to follow the laws of the land then I need to leave my job.*—Hon. Katy Marlow, Foard County

David Parker (Kent County), one of the most matter-of-fact philosopher JPs with whom I spoke, puts it this way:

I've done nearly as many gay weddings as I've done straight weddings. Life is hard enough without judging, so I don't. The thing about it is, it says in the Bible: "Judge not that you be not judged," and I can't take the judging.

Marc DeRouen performed the first same-sex wedding in Jefferson County. He expected to get blowback from disapproving constituents. He got none. In fact:

Once it hit the news, I received about six to eight letters from people thanking me and praising me. I received phone calls—people telling me things like, "I have a nephew who has a partner and I think he ought to be able to be married, and I'm glad there are people like you who will do it." My parents are Baptist and they also got compliments from people in their church who said, "We're proud of your son."

My thing is this: Uphold the laws and the Constitution; that's the oath I took and if that's what it requires me to do, I'm gonna do it.

That's not to say that some judges who sign the wedding licenses of same-sex couples *don't* get blowback—and even blowback from unusual quarters. A judge in central Texas said that when the SCOTUS ruling came down, he was asked by his clerk if he were going to marry gay people. When he said he was, she quit. She'd worked in that precinct for sixteen years.

Kelly Crow (Fort Bend County) takes a thoughtful Republican's view of things.

I personally believe that part of a JP's function is to perform weddings. People ought to be able to go to a JP to get married. It's not my job to determine whether I like a law or to care what my party thinks or doesn't think. The law is the law. There are a lot of Republican judges who are like me: mainstream judges. The American people are probably more mainstream, right down the middle. I don't care about gay weddings and I don't care about bathrooms. My values as a conservative are about my property taxes. If gay people want to get married, they have the right to get married. My job as a judge is to uphold the law as it is written, and if it gets changed, to uphold that new law.

I spoke with a conservative Republican JP in a fairly populated county who did not want her name attached to the following admission. She'd always wanted to do weddings, and so, two months after she came into office, she started doing weddings.

I don't just perform the ceremony. I ask them: How'd you meet? I want to get to know them because I want to be part of their happiness. I also started doing weddings because there was only one judge in the entire courthouse who married people. She's the only Democrat JP. She was raking in so much money it was unbelievable!

This judge does remind us that a good many JPs who don't perform weddings because they would be legally obligated to marry same-sex couples do not come by this decision lightly. In large counties where you find lots of people wishing to get married, a justice of the peace's religious convictions impose a sacrifice: the loss of comparable revenue enjoyed by judges who do not stand on similar principle. One small county judge told me that one of the things he really liked about being a JP was that "jingle" in his pocket. Big city JPs who marry have turned that jingle into a lucrative cottage industry. A judge in one of the state's most populated counties admitted that the extra income he receives isn't the only reason he's happy to continue to perform weddings; the joyful couples he marries are sure to hear from him during campaign season ("Remember how happy I made you that day I joined the two of you together in holy matrimony?"). There are those who don't see how a judge's decision not to marry gay people can be based on anything but religious intolerance or, at its most generous, a misinterpretation of scripture. But there are others who consider the stance itself as representative of a deeply rooted spirituality that cannot be extirpated even by the trowel of financial gain.

Same-sex weddings—they're usually a lot of fun. It's about love. We need more of that in the world.—Hon. Tom Rumfield, Callahan County

When Sylvia Holmes took office in Travis County, she wanted to make sure that gay couples knew she was an inclusive judge, so she put a gay pride flag and a picture of a same-sex couple on her website. She says that she's had couples who drive over an hour and a half for her to marry them. She's happy that she's been able to make her case for the importance of marital commitment for both straight and gay couples.

At the last training seminar, I was chatting with some of the JPs. A gentleman who was from a smaller county said, "I don't want to do those."

"I appreciate that, but you know, I have a completely different view. I don't care about religion and the sanctity of tradition. I just think people who want to be married should be able to get married. My generation, they all just want to live together. It's an anomaly now to get married. So when you've got two people who truly want to make that commitment, I'm all for it."

We sat around and chatted about property rights, about the right to see each other in the hospital when you die. He got my argument about the "sanctity" of marriage: A heterosexual couple can get divorced and remarried six times—this is "good" marriage? He was old-fashioned, but I could see him working out how he could explain this to those who might not like him marrying two men.

> *Being in a small town, I feel it's not fair for me not to be doing weddings when there's not anybody else around here. They'll have to go eighty miles to find a JP that does marriages.*
> —Hon. Evelyn Kerbow, Crockett County

Now, to be fair, there are other reasons besides same-sex marriage for why a JP may not perform weddings. Some judges have simply gotten burned out. Others have grown tired of driving to venues far from their courtroom.

With Harris Hughey (Denton County), there's a principle at stake here. It's actually a principle that, at the very least, deserves discussion among his colleagues.

Many times, as an attorney, I'd be representing somebody and we'd have a hearing in JP court. My client has paid me $300 an hour to go with him to the court. I walk in for a one o'clock hearing and three weddings walk in. And that JP does the three weddings before he gets to our case. The point being that I have a problem with me having a one o'clock hearing, and now there are three weddings ahead of us and my client is paying me

$300 to sit through three weddings. I'm not doing weddings during court hours; it just leaves a bad taste for me.

There are also JPs who don't do weddings because for one thing, there are plenty of people already performing weddings in their county. Judge Russell Johnson explained that "we have so many churches and pastors in Coke County. I feel like there are enough pastors to do the weddings."

> *We were in Sunday school, and an elderly lady who's in her eighties asked me about doing the weddings. I said, "Well, I'm not doing them."*
>
> *She said, "Well, what do you do, then?"*—Hon. *Kelvin Miles, Parker County*

Jackie Miller Jr. (Ellis County) gave me another reason that a lot of us can identify with. Most off-site weddings are performed on the weekends. Judge Miller values his weekends. And his family.

Life is short, and there are only a limited number of ballgames your kid's going to play.

NOTE

*LGBTQ: The most inclusive reading of this abbreviation is "lesbian, gay, bisexual, transgender and queer or questioning."

12

Four-Footed Constituents

I've tried cases where someone gave their dog away
and then wanted visitation rights.

—HON. RONNIE DAVIS, LIBERTY COUNTY

ONE OF THE LARGEST animal seizure operations ever undertaken in
the state of Texas took place on February 9, 2018, in Hill County. It
was ordered by one of the county's four JPs, Shane Brassell. He told me
that it was a two-day ordeal to get the more than 350 Texas longhorns
and crossbred cattle loaded onto trucks and removed from the eight-
hundred-acre ranch where they were starving from neglect. Brassell
said the emaciated cattle were literally dropping dead in front of the
Hill County deputies and the dozen cowboys hired to move them. The
operation, which involved the Humane Society of North Texas, was
deemed a success. The livestock's owner was ordered by Judge Brassell
to pay over $62,000 to reimburse the Humane Society for the cost of
the seizure and for the months of care that it would take to nurse the
survivors back to health.

The owner in turn filed a lawsuit against Brassell and numerous
others involved in the seizure for violating her constitutional and civil
rights. She accused the judge, the county attorney, the sheriff, and others of "fraud" and "racketeering" for robbing her of "cattle, property,
assets, and rights" and for committing "sabotage," "treason," and the
"overthrow of the United States government."

No good deed goes unsullied.[1]

With the exception of service animals, most visitors to Texas JP courts have two legs and opposable thumbs. This is not to say that non-human species don't frequently become the subject of matters that come before the court, as illustrated above. "All creatures, great and small"—especially the ones that bark—do find their way into quite a few small claims cases. Debbie Bindseil (Burnet County) told me about a case she heard in her court in which a man was suing his landlord because he'd been bitten by a dog.

In the course of the case, I was reading over the petition, and he had basically stated that he barked at the dog. I looked at the guy and I said, "It says you barked *at the dog." My clerk and the bailiff are sitting there and I thought they were gonna come unglued trying to keep from laughing. I later told them I could have made it worse: "You're fortunate I didn't ask him to please demonstrate, so I'd know if it was a* provocative *bark or a friendly* bark."

When Travis Hill (Lavaca County) was working as a deputy constable in Harris County, he served as bailiff for a particularly intriguing dog-bites-man small claims case.

You and I are out here walking our dogs down the street, and they go at each other. My dog bites you, so you sue me. However, you don't sue me because of injuries caused to you by my dog biting you. You sue me because your dog is traumatized by what happened, and the dog is suffering and has to go to canine counseling. So you're suing for damages to send your dog to canine trauma counseling. I want that job. I want to take up the job of canine counseling, buddy.

> *There are two things you don't mess with: a man's dog and a man's other dog. —Hon. Jerry Parker, Wood County*

Brenda Dominy (Cherokee County) heard a small claims case that concerned a stolen dog.

The owner saw the dog at a neighbor's house, but they wouldn't return it. The owner said he could prove it was theirs because he could make it do tricks. Picture this: a dog in the courtroom performing tricks on command!

Justin M. Joyce (Fort Bend County) shared his most interesting canine case. It involved a dog-owning plaintiff who was suing a dog-owning defendant for medical bills related to the defendant's dog attacking the plaintiff's dog. The defendant contested the case; he didn't think he should pay the bills because the aggression in question couldn't possibly have occurred. He presented evidence: a certificate that showed his dog had successfully graduated behavioral school.

> *What I see when I have to do a dog case is that people are more defensive about their dogs than they are about their own kids, especially when a complaint has been made against them. Cases like those are the ones where I want a bailiff in the courtroom.*
> —Hon. Marc Traweek, Yoakum County

Canine Texas isn't just pit bulls and Chihuahuas. But don't ask Nancy J. Pomykal (Calhoun County) if this statement is true.

I bring my little puppy to work once in a while—a three-year-old rescue Chihuahua. She's my bailiff. Don't make her mad, though. She can be hard on the ankles.

Randy Daniel (Henderson County) was set to hear a small claims suit in which the plaintiff alleged that he bought a dog from the defendant for breeding purposes, only to discover that the animal was genetically unfit to breed. The judge couldn't tell me how the case turned out because Judge Judy nabbed it for her TV show, and Daniel never got to see that particular episode.

In olden days, when local entertainment options were fairly limited, the citizenry of many a small Texas town used to tromp over to their county courthouse to watch that special form of theatre known as "puttin' on a trial." (Think: Atticus Finch in his summer seersucker or William Jennings Bryan fanning his perspiring face with a church fan.) Nowadays, Texas small-town folk don't generally gather in courthouse courtrooms to be entertained. But Judge Mike Towers can tell of a few times when an audience has shown up in Bandera County.

Interestingly enough, the cases that get the most attendance in the gallery in the courthouse are the ones having to do with animals. In my six years on the bench, the one that really packed the courthouse was a dog custody case. What happened was a woman of a certain age who was not doing so well and kind of in a fragile circumstance sold her dog to her elderly mother for twenty bucks so she could buy some beer. Her mother lived with her brother. The woman drove by one day and saw the dog out playing with the brother, so she stole the dog. We had this great dog custody case in the main courthouse with probably one hundred people showing up every day for this.

It came down to who actually had the right to possession of this dog. The woman was suing to get custody of her dog back because it was the brother who was taking care of it, and the woman hated her brother. Justices of the peace cannot, with a few exceptions, order injunctive relief*; however, someone can sue someone for something else, and we can do what we call a turnover order where we order them to turn over a certain item—a bicycle or a motorcycle or a cow or something like that.

Judge Towers ended up awarding the dog to the mother and the brother.

Speaking of cows . . .

Texas JPs will find a share of their civil suits devoted to bovine mischief, even in urban counties like Travis. It's just part of being a Lone Star justice of the peace. Judge Raúl Arturo González heard a case in which a cow was trespassing on a neighboring farmer's land and eating his pomegranates. Well, it was worse than that: "Once you have a rogue cow who gets a taste for pomegranate," said González, "she's going to come back and bring her friends." The case had to be dismissed because the total cost of the damage to the plaintiff's irrigation system and fences exceeded the court's legal jurisdiction at the time.

Then there are times when cows are just minding their own business when suddenly they get themselves cownapped. This from Jarrell Hedrick (Martin County):

We had this guy who went over to Midland, and he was trying to fill up his pickup with gas. But he'd been drinking a lot and couldn't get the hose lined up. He needs to go home, so he walks across the parking lot and gets into a semi and drives it twenty miles from Midland to Stanton and parks it in the street in front of his house. But little did he know when he'd stolen this truck that there were eight or ten head of cows in the back. They kicked and mooed and banged around in that truck all night along.

The judge who ended up magistrating him lived next door.

So after all the mooing and kicking and stuff, she got to see him next morning. I don't know what she set the bond for, but if I was her, I would have set it at a million dollars because she had to put up with that all night long.

Canine, bovine . . . cervine? Because Karin Knolle's precinct in Jim Wells County includes a number of deer breeding operations, her court receives quite a few game warden filings related to unpermitted breeding and records violations in this growing South Texas industry.

When Evelyn Kerbow thinks of deer in Crockett County, it usually involves all those who come to her neck of the West Texas woods to hunt them.

We have a lot of deer hunters out here. They'll come in and say, "Hey, can you do a wedding in my deer blind?" It'll be like twenty, thirty degrees.

"Oh, sure!"

(Judge Kerbow loves doing weddings.)

Since Texas is a dog state, it was the rare judge who told me a cat story. I got a twofer with Ronnie Davis (Liberty County): both cats *and* chickens, with a wink at ol' King Solomon!

I had a case where two women came to court together in the same car, fighting over a stray cat. I tell them, "What y'all do is this: you get that cat and bring it back here. On the way, y'all decide how you want to divide it. You want me to cut it longways?" I never saw them again.

Then there was this one lady that was working at the café. She called me one day, and she said, "Judge, my next-door neighbor's chickens are tearing up my flowerbeds, crapping in the yard, crapping on my front porch, and I can't get her to do anything about it. What do you think?"

I kind of say what I think: "I like dumplings," and hung up.

Three days later, she brought me the biggest damned pot of dumplings you ever had.

I suspected it was *chicken* and dumplings, but I didn't want to push it.

As Marc Traweek (Yoakum County) reminds us, animal cases aren't always just about the animals. They're also about the humans who have brought the critters into their lives. Judge Traweek talked to me about how a lot of citizens in his county will go to their local JPs to get help with problems that can sometimes fall outside the purview of a JP.

Years ago, I had a guy come into my office, and he was just crying his eyes out, and could hardly talk. I finally got him calmed down and set him down in a chair to find out what was wrong. He finally told me that somebody had tried to kill his dog.

"What do you mean, tried to?*"*

He said, "They sewed my dog's mouth shut."

"Really? Somebody sewed your dog's mouth shut?" I asked him, "So where's the dog?"

"Out in front of the courthouse."

So, we went outside and this little dog was sitting there shivering and distraught. He had a mouth full of porcupine quills. So I got the guy to understand what had happened, and I loaded up him and the dog and took them to the vet to have all those quills taken out.

Animal cruelty cases that wind up in Texas justice court don't just involve large herds of maltreated cattle or horses. Any animal, according to the Texas Health and Safety Code, that has been tortured; seriously overworked; unreasonably abandoned or deprived of necessary food, care, or shelter; cruelly confined; or caused to fight with another animal can be taken away from its owner. And it's the JP who signs the warrant for its seizure.

When animals are seized in animal cruelty situations, they become the temporary property of the county. Judge Jesse Speer, who deals with such cases in Eastland County, says that it's usually an animal advocacy organization that steps in to feed them and help the animals get their strength back so they can be adopted. In a sense, a special partnership is created between public and private entities to look after the welfare of creatures that can't look after themselves, and the justice of the peace plays an important role.

Sadly, Judge Speer said, the best you can do with some animals is to put them down when the vet has determined that the abuse has been too severe for the possibility of recovery. Some of it really breaks your heart, he added.

Tom Rumfield (Callahan County) isn't happy with how often the mistreatment of animals winds up in his court. Among the worst offenders are the "rescuers" who really aren't rescuers at all.

Animal cruelty cases are depressing, disgusting in some cases, but it's something that has to be done. We have these puppy mills out here. And people who have taken in horses under the guise of rescuing them. I guess they get some money from the state or the feds or somebody and they just use those horses as a way to make money. I went out on one where there were at least a dozen carcasses lying around. We're out here in a rural area and people think they can get away with that kind of thing, and sometimes they do—turning cows loose in pastures and not tending to them. Over time they become emaciated and diseased and are just left to die.

The one that got me the most was the girl who had a puppy mill and she was taking them in under the guise of rescuing them. I think we took some-thing like one hundred animals off that place in conjunction with Rescue the Animals. I actually had some folks come down from the Metroplex and take possession because there were just so many of them.

Judge Rumfield talked to me about the importance of non-profit groups like the ASPCA, the American Society for the Prevention of Cruelty to Animals, which pays to transport the seized animals and get them in good enough shape to be adoptable. He said that without them, he isn't sure what the county would do since it doesn't have the financial resources to bear this expense on its own.

The actual charge of animal cruelty isn't prosecuted at the justice court level, but the seizure warrant signed by a JP is the first step toward addressing the problem. Rumfield once dealt with a woman who was especially egregious in her treatment of the animals on her property. In his order he prohibited her from keeping any more animals for two years except for a household pet. He said she left the county and "started up all over again." Once that county contacted him, he sent them a copy of his order and they followed through with her arrest and yet another seizure operation.

Judge Rumfield works closely with both the district attorney, who files the cruelty charges, and his local sheriff, whose office submits the complaint and affidavit for probable cause to the DA.

I asked him if seeing what he sees gets him down, or does it help that he's making a difference.

I do get satisfaction out of those cases I'm able to do something about. What's frustrating and depressing is sometimes the length of time it takes with the process and knowing those animals are out there. Quite honestly,

I was a deputy for a number of years and it's just something you learn to deal with. You just have to leave it at the office. Anything having to do with law enforcement can be very depressing.

Texas being Texas, its JPs can also be called upon to step in and authorize confiscation of animals of the two-legged variety—those with feathers and beaks, "gaffs" and "slashers." Cockfighting remains a problem in the state, and it's a JP's job to remove the roosters (sometimes in mid-bout via planned raids) to the custody of animal rescue groups. Texas JPs also have the fun of dealing with cockfight aficionados when they run "afowl" of the law; in Texas you can be arrested and charged with a Class C misdemeanor for attending a cockfight.

Texas is filled with a whole lot of non-human residents, but also with a whole lot of folks who advocate for them and look out for them. It also has its cranks. Take, for example, the woman who, when it came to animals, didn't mind giving Kenny Elliott (Brazos County) her minority opinion. "I had a lady," he said, "who tried to file eviction papers on a dog."

Arf.

NOTE

*An injunction is a court order that either restrains a party from doing a particular thing or requires them to act in a certain way.

13

Forward and in Sensible Shoes (Sometimes Boots)

THERE'S AN OFT-REPEATED QUOTE about Ginger Rogers: She did everything Fred Astaire did, but backwards and in high heels. American women have often been forced by the cultural perceptions of the day to prove they can do the jobs of men by working harder, longer, and smarter. Female justices of the peace in Texas, especially in the state's smaller counties, do come up against wild west machismo-driven conceptions of what the role of women should be in their communities.

And yet, there has also existed in the state a countervailing attitude that Texas women are tough as nails and just as smart as the men they work alongside.

The first female governor voted into office in a general election in America was a Texan. The colorful Miriam A. "Ma" Ferguson served two non-consecutive terms: 1925–1927 and 1933–1935.*

Generally speaking, female JPs in Texas demand and command the same level of respect that their male counterparts do. Their communities have grown to accept them in these roles, and, as a rule, voters—both male and female—are comfortable returning them to office every four years.

Now retired, Sarah Miller was the first female judge elected in Erath County. She began her inaugural term in 1975. When she went in for her new judges' training, her class of freshman JPs was eighty-strong, but of those eighty justices of the peace, only four were women. Even today, "lady JPs" still haven't reached parity with male JPs in Texas when it comes to the numbers. They aren't so very far behind, however, and there are several counties, some with as many as four precincts, in which all the JPs are female.

I had the chance to talk to several justices of the peace who serve in these all-female JP counties. Debbie Bindseil (Burnet County) viewed working in a county with all distaff justices of the peace as a definite positive, though she said she wouldn't have a problem if at some point a worthy gentleman decided to join their judicial sorority. One of Bindseil's sister judges, Lisa Whitehead, addressed the advantages of black-robed sisterhood; she said they definitely have each other's backs.

Freestone County's four JPs are also all women. But two of them—Theresa Farris and Cinnamon Archibald—are more than judicial sisters. They're *actual* sisters. Judge Farris came into office in 2007, Judge Archibald in 2015. Judge Farris tells me that it's "great to have a sister who's a JP."

Because I trained Cinnamon, if she has a question and isn't sure about something, she'll call me. Or we might have something we need to talk about. Sometimes the law isn't very clear; you've got a real gray area on some things, so you have to discuss it. Once you discuss it for a while you come up with a solution. She brings up a lot of things that I don't catch.

That's not to say that female judges haven't had their share of struggles and frustrations along the way, especially those judges from the Baby Boomer generation. In those days the job required special skills at negotiation and quite a bit of finesse.

When the judge I worked for, Debra Ravel, assumed the bench in the 1980s, two other female Travis County judges took her under their wings: the Honorable Mary Pearl Williams, who, in the course of assembling a lengthy public service resume, had the distinction of being the first woman judge in the county,** and Travis County justice of the peace Leslie Taylor. Judge Ravel's two mentors imparted three pearls of wisdom, which she jotted onto an index card and taped to the top of her bench. Perhaps these kernels of advice were more relevant before the "Me Too" era, when female agency and empowerment were just coming to the forefront and female judges were still trying to be taken seriously by that sizeable fraction of male Texans who couldn't be depended on to take *any* professional woman seriously:

1. Less is more: In other words, do more listening than talking.
2. Use common sense: Judge Ravel was that rare commodity in Texas, especially in those days: a justice of the peace with a law degree. But she didn't run for office on the basis of that degree (in spite of the fact that she said it often came in handy); she took a pragmatic approach to rendering justice and she applied this same doctrine to the juries she sent off to deliberate, advising them to apply simple common sense and their own life experiences to the task of arriving at a just result.
3. Keep your sense of humor: You get more honey with the funny. Then Ravel added one thing more: Never let them see you sweat.

> *The female JPs I've gotten to know through the years, they are some smart women. They're sincere. They're turning their counties around on things.* —Hon. Tisha Sanchez, Palo Pinto County

In November 2018, a magical thing happened in Harris County. A group of nineteen African American women broke all records by getting themselves elected judges in one of the most ethnically diverse metro areas in the country. The group, which calls itself "Black Girl Magic," included two new justices of the peace, Lucia Bates and Sharon M. Burney. In fact, an astounding seventeen of these women were new to their benches.

Judge Burney had big shoes to fill: her own mother's. Zinetta A. Burney served as JP in the same precinct as her daughter from 2005 to 2018. A single mother who had Sharon when she was seventeen, Ms. Burney got her GED, then her undergraduate degree, and then a law degree, later practicing law in the county before being elected to succeed Judge Al Green, who had served as JP in the precinct for twenty-six years. (Green went on to become a high-profile member of the US House of Representatives.)

Sharon Burney wasn't the only JP I interviewed who has a strong family tie to another JP (past or present). Is there any bond stronger than that of family? Probably not. (Though Jon Glenn in Eastland County might point, with a wink, to the fact that the JP in Coleman County, Robert Nash, used to be one of his commanding officers in the national guard.)

Mothers, yes, but also aunts . . . Not only was Leslie Ford's aunt Faye Blanks a JP in Hutchinson County; she went on to become Hutchinson's first female county court judge.

The mother of Rodney Baker (Bailey County), Nadene Baker, was, for a dozen years, justice of the peace in adjoining Cochran County. She encouraged her son to run because she knew how much he liked people. "My whole family's that way," Judge Baker told me.

I don't care if they're black, brown, white, yellow, gray. I just like to meet people. I like to talk and visit. My mom always told us: you boys have a lot of common sense. You've got good heads on your shoulders. She said me running for JP would be the grandest thing. She really encouraged me.

There were, by the way, several male JPs I interviewed who were following in their father's footsteps, like Don Milburn (Lee County) and Wayne Money (Hunt County). Chris Acord (Grimes County) is also the son of a JP. His dad held that office for sixteen years. Acord remembers that when his father first started out, he worked out of his home—or, to be more specific, out of a converted garage. For sentimental reasons, Acord still uses his father's desk. Continuing the family tradition, Acord's son is thinking about following in *his* footsteps and running for JP someday.

Randall County Judge Tracy Byrd's grandfather was a JP in Potter County. "I was like ten or twelve when he started," Byrd said. "I remember electioneering for him as a young boy, standing in front of a school, passing out emery boards that said, 'Vote for my granddad.'"

But Randy Ellisor of San Jacinto County has them all beat. He is the son, grandson, *and* great-grandson of a Texas JP. His great-grandfather John Clayton Ellisor took office in 1892, and there has been an Ellisor serving as justice of the peace in San Jacinto County ever since.

Female JPs who bring their maternal instincts (otherwise known as "bringing mom") to the bench represent the rule more than the exception. Donna Wessels (Wharton County) told me this happens all the time:

Being in a small town, when I go to the jail, I know some of the people I see there. So I talk to them. I'm supposed to just be reading their rights and setting their bond, but if I know them, I'll say, "Why are you here?" and, "I don't want to see you here again." It's kind of like my mother instinct pops in. And I'll tell them, "You need to find some new friends because you're not hanging out with the right people!"

Kim Redman (Wise County) had to hear a case involving a teenager charged with disorderly conduct and language.

Just yesterday I had a kid come in with his mother. He was fifteen and there was another kid involved; he was seventeen. There was a lot of vulgar language being used down at the lake.

Judge Redman talked to the boy about the importance of choosing his friends wisely. Then it was time to talk to Mom. She asked his mother to step into her office.

I said, "This is mom talking to mom. It's very important that you keep him away from that other boy. I'm not saying this to scare you, but your son is very influenceable. He just wants someone to like him. The report I read was that the language was very disturbing. It's a situation where the older boy could take advantage of him. You need to be aware. There is nothing I can do about this as a judge, but I'm telling you this as a mom."

Judge Whitehead laughs when she thinks of the times men have indicated that because she's a woman, she isn't up to the job of JP.

When I was running for this office, there was a deputy who was running against me. He had thirty years' experience and blah blah blah, and I wasn't going to do any slinging, but he said to several people, hoping that it would get back to me, "She's never going to get up at all hours of the day and night," and I was thinking, are you kidding? I've been doing that since I was eighteen! Getting up to climb in my car and go do something is way easier than cleaning up vomit, or sitting up all night next to someone when they've got a fever and giving them a cold bath to bring their fever down. This job is a piece of cake. I get to go home and go back to sleep!

I can't imagine a job that better prepared me for being a judge than being a mom. When you're settling something between your kids, they're putting their own spin on it, and everybody's kind of lying a little bit, but they wouldn't really say they're lying. They're just omitting this or omitting that. So when they gave justices of the peace the discretion to ask questions and develop a case, it became really easy to go ahead and ask that question they don't want to answer, but which is going to change the whole direction of the trial. Like:"Mom! You're not supposed to ask me that!"

Olivia Neu (Cooke County) finds that success as a female judge depends on how you feel about yourself, and the degree to which the judge is able to instill among those who come into her courtroom respect, not just for her, but for the court itself.

I don't think I'm treated any differently because I'm a female judge. I find that if I carry myself with the kind of dignity and respect I expect people to treat me with, and I treat them that way, then I don't have to worry about it.

Good moms make good teachers. They also make good JPs who *used* to be teachers. Judge Ford used to teach third- and fourth-grade language arts. The three jobs overlap nicely for her.

The law has always been something I've been interested in. When you're a teacher, you're a judge, you're the jury, you're a lawyer—you're everything.

I asked her if a student she'd taught ever wound up in her court.

Yes. I've had several that I've either set a bond on in the jail or that I've seen in my courtroom for some Class C misdemeanor that they were charged with. I actually had one student turn himself in for me to set his bond. I went over and gave him a hug. I said, "You know, you kind of messed up, didn't you?"

"Yes ma'am."

I said, "You're doing the right thing by admitting it and taking your hit."

What I used to tell my students all the time is, "Once you're in my class, you're my baby—you'll always be my baby. I will watch you. I will know what you're up to."

Female JPs do have one problem that male JPs don't: When they aren't actually sitting on the bench or in chambers, they can be mistaken for clerks. Irma Dunn (Titus County) is one of the many judges this has happened to.

My clerks helped this boy who had a ticket. Then the mama came in. She just hit the counter with her hand and said, "I want to speak to someone in authority, not with you!"

I just look at her and say, "Ma'am, I'm the authority in this office. I'm the judge." She backed out of the office.

Most men have a way of pushing people's buttons just to show they're superior to others. A woman doesn't have to do that. A woman can just sit there and look at you and scare the bejesus out of you.
—Hon. Jeff Monk, Johnson County

Donna Schmidt (Cochran County) had worked as a clerk for her predecessor, Nadene Baker (mother of Rodney Baker above), for five years. When Judge Baker decided to resign before the end of her term, Schmidt, who wanted to replace her, found herself in competition with a gentleman who worked for the county in cemetery maintenance. She said he was good friends with a couple of the county commissioners who would, along with three of their colleagues, be picking the best person to fill out the retiring judge's remaining months in office. The gentleman garnered the two votes he was expected to get. Two other commissioners voted for Schmidt. It was left to the county judge to break the tie. Schmidt recalled that Judge Baker laid it out to the county judge in very clear terms: If he didn't vote for Schmidt, she'd be resigning immediately from her job as clerk. The new, erstwhile cemetery yardman would have no clerk to get him up to speed. Schmidt had no interest in working for a man who knew nothing about justice court, but who got the job simply because he had friends on the commissioners' court.

Judge Schmidt told me that Cochran is a "good ol' boys" county. In this particular instance, it was the "good ol' girls" who won the day. She's served as Cochran County's only JP since 2011.

Texas has a long tradition stretching back to the infamous Judge Roy Bean, who was appointed JP in Pecos County in 1882, of putting cowboys on the bench. Yet there has been no shortage of cowgirl JPs in Texas. Several of the female JPs I interviewed had ranching backgrounds. Some still owned and ran ranches even while they served as JPs, finding themselves just as often in the saddle as on the bench.

Take Judge Jane Jones in Borden County; she lives on a ranch and runs a herd. Jones told me she used to ride cutting horses for a living. One of her jobs as JP is unique to the state's rural ranching counties.

We put cattle in for people. If I see them, I'll put them in. The sheriff will call me: "Hey, we got cattle out on Toombs Road."

"I'm on it, Benny." Because that's like fifteen miles for him.

I used to have a big Australian shepherd—she died about two years ago—but I'd open the door and she'd get 'em. She was my ace in the hole. Nobody was gonna hit a black Angus cow at midnight, because we got that cow off the road!

But living in a wild west county has its downside for Judge Jones. She said that the judge who preceded her didn't take DPS traffic tickets; this resulted in a loss of revenue for the county. Eventually the highway patrolmen who worked in this region stopped bothering to file in Borden. Some of the ranchers liked the freedom this gave them to trundle all around the county without worrying, for example, that they might be cited for a broken taillight or a missing license plate. And yet, their offenses *did* get ticketed in neighboring counties. It was only Borden County that wasn't receiving the fine revenue. Jones explained that her county had a long history of keeping law enforcement at arm's length and attempting to resolve problems on their own. It didn't always work. And picking and choosing which laws to follow and which to ignore didn't make a lot of sense to her.

Take rattlesnakes, for example. The law doesn't allow you to shoot animals from a roadway, even snakes. "There were a huge number of rattlers on one side of town," Jones told me. "But you can't just go up and down the road hunting them. You're supposed to get ticketed for this. I caught a lot of grief over the rattlesnake deal. They were ready to lynch me for it."

One of the most famous Texas cowgirl JPs was Hallie Stillwell, whose life is chronicled in the Hallie Stillwell Hall of Fame Museum in Brewster County. Judge Stillwell was inducted into the National Cowgirl Hall of Fame in 1992. As JP, she had no problem upholding the law; she fined her best friend Inda, a habitual speeder; threw her grandson and his friends into jail for drinking underage; and even gave the local mayor a speeding ticket. A writer and public speaker, Stillwell lectured on life as a Texas woman rancher. Most importantly, perhaps, her adjudicating skills led to an invitation to serve as judge for the first Terlingua Chili Cookoff, held in 1967. (She continued in that capacity annually.)[1]

Amy Tapia (Matagorda County) once told her young daughters, who were around four or five at the time, that she was "going off to marry a couple of people." When she came home, her mother, who'd kept the girls, reported that her little granddaughters were very upset: *"We don't want Mommy to marry somebody else!"*

(Former Crockett County JP James Hearne had himself a little fun with the double meaning of that verb: "I'd have these girls come bouncing into my office, all bright-eyed and ask, 'Will you *marry* me?'

And I'd say, 'Well certainly, but my wife might not like it!'")

Notwithstanding that hiccup, Judge Tapia has loved being on the bench and has found a fairly good balance between serving as a justice of the peace and being mother to four growing kids. She admits that being a JP isn't an easy job, but she says it gives her great satisfaction knowing that she's making a difference in people's lives.

We have a lot of jerks, not the greatest people, but I don't mind those situations either. I'm a Hispanic female, I'm thirty-seven, I'm five-foot and I have dealt with my share of people who think they can run over me.

But I'm not someone you can run over.

About three weeks ago I had this one guy. I said, "If you don't want to let me finish what I need to say, then I'm going to have you escorted out."

In that moment, I think they see me as this little girl. That's one of the difficult things I've had to deal with: I don't look like a judge. When I'm out front in my plain clothes, male court visitors will ask, "When is the JP gonna be in, because I really want to talk to him." They assume that the judge is a man, that he's old, and, honestly, that he's white.

Tapia is the only female justice of the peace in a five-JP county. She says she works pretty well with her male colleagues.

They're really good about respecting the fact that I'm a female and that I'm a mom. I try not to pull that mom card, though, unless my kids are, like, throwing up. I don't want them to feel like "because she has kids, we've got to pull her weight."

And what is it like for the husbands of Texas JPs? I spoke with a female Justice of the Peace, who, when she first took office, had problems with her traditional husband accepting her new role as a professional authority figure. The couple had to work things out through marriage counseling. Most of the female judges with whom I've spoken haven't raised similar issues. In most cases, the men are proud of what their wives do for a living, though they do worry.

Then again, wives of male JPs do their own worrying. It goes with the territory.

James Hearne (Crockett County), a former border patrol agent, offered two examples of female judges that he personally encountered—one successful, one not so much. Judge Hearne succeeded a female judge, and then was himself succeeded by a different female JP. In the case of the former, the judge had been appointed to her job following the death of her JP husband.

She really tried to do the job, but she just didn't have a handle on it. An example would be when we'd have a death in the county, she wanted a deputy to drive her out there, and they were agreeable to doing that, but she didn't just go get in the car and go out there; she had to put her makeup on, and she might be a half-hour to forty-five minutes. Meanwhile, everybody's waiting for the JP to get there. It became a problem, and because of who I was, a group of citizens asked me if I would run. So I went down and filed for election. Would you believe that nobody had filed because of the political thing of running against a widow woman?

Hearne said that once he took the plunge, nine others did as well. The widow woman didn't make the runoff.

When it came time for Judge Hearne to retire, he was proud to pass the reins to his chief clerk, Evelyn Kerbow. Hearne told me that he didn't know what he would have done without her. When he came into the job, he "didn't know how to be a judge." He didn't just lean on his clerk.

"She taught me everything I know."

NOTES

*Wyoming's Governor Nellie Tayloe Ross was elected in 1925, the same as "Ma," but hers was a special election to succeed the place-holding governor who stepped into the job when her governor husband passed away while in office.

**Judge Williams served as the relief judge for Austin's municipal court in 1964, and, later, as Travis County Court-at-Law judge. She took the lead in establishing the first court administration program in Travis County, which began in January 1977. That program won national recognition as the Best Court Administration Program of a Misdemeanor Docket in 1980 from the National Association of Counties.

14

In God Some of Us Trust

My motto for this job is: I don't judge people. I judge choices.
God is the only judge.

—HON. SCOTT SHINN, VAN ZANDT COUNTY

IT'S OFTEN DIFFICULT FOR a justice of the peace whose religious faith plays a big part in her life to simply leave that faith at the courthouse door, although most do a very good job of respecting the wall between church and state called for by their office. But for those of strong Christian faith, mention of God is rarely limited to that familiar intensive for swearing in witnesses, "So help me God."

There continues to be some disagreement over whether a justice of the peace—as a holder of elective public office—should be conducting ostensibly religious wedding ceremonies while in the secular saddle. Judges with whom I discussed this issue contend that there shouldn't be a problem if the choice is left to the bride and groom. It's their wedding; they should be the ones to make the decision. And there are creative work-arounds for this problem. Debra Ravel (Travis County) reminded me of those times when she officiated interfaith ceremonies in which she brought in a friend of hers who was a rabbi to formally bless the union. I talked to several judges who marry people, but not as JP. Tommy Ramirez (Medina County) performs weddings in his capacity as Baptist minister.

Wayne L. Mack (Montgomery County) asks all the couples he weds to choose what kind of ceremony they'd like to have.

Since I became a judge on May 1, 2015, I've had a traditional ceremony with vows, scripture and a prayer, and I've had a civil ceremony. I don't force people to have a religious ceremony. I give them the option. Probably ninety-five percent of my couples opt for the religious ceremony.

There are other JPs, however, who believe that if a couple wants a religious wedding ceremony, they should instead go to a preacher, priest, rabbi, Imam, or other holy celebrant.

Stan Warfield (Colorado County) is an ordained Methodist minister. After a forty-year ministry in Oklahoma, he retired, but his wife laughs that he keeps *"flunking* retirement," and now he's back to being a pastor again—this time for a small Methodist congregation in a different county. When Judge Warfield marries people as a JP rather than as a minister (he's also a municipal court judge), he does what Judge Mack does, and he offers the couple an option: religious ceremony or strictly civil?

Only a couple of times have they said they'd like to keep it civil. It's usually: "We'd like you to marry us as a JP, but can you put some spirituality into it?"

Judge Warfield is careful about respecting the line between church and state.

I'm very clear about keeping my ministry and my work as JP separate. I have signs on my truck that say, "State of Texas Justice of the Peace," and whenever I do anything ministerial, I make sure those signs are off the truck. Very seldom do I even mention—unless there is a good example that comes up that fits the sermon—my justice court or municipal court. It's really not a part of my conversation when I'm talking to church people.

He says that inquests don't bother him.

I do my job with compassion, understanding, and mercy. I treat the family with the utmost respect. That's one of the reasons I ran for this job. With your attitudes, your actions, and your compassion, you can show people you care without dragging out the Bible. It's fairly well known in this area that I'm also a minister. A couple of times I've done an inquest and the family has come back and asked me to do the funeral.

Inquest JPs frequently find themselves in delicate situations in which they are interfacing with a grieving family at a moment of wrenching emotional pain. Comfort and solace are called for, and for many a Texas justice of the peace, religious faith is a deep well from which that comfort and solace can be drawn. Some families will ask a judge at a death scene to pray with them. When Judge Warfield is asked, he will pray with the bereaved. Other JPs told me that they will as well. The late Jimmy Miller (Jasper County) had no problem doing so. He was glad to be able to offer support in this way.

In that terrible moment of loss, questions are posed to judges—existential questions that fall far outside a JP's professional ken. Tim Bryan (Gregg County) told me:

I don't try to apply my faith to anybody, because that's not my job. But I have had multiple times where people are so lost and they say, "Do you think my sister went to hell because she killed herself?" We all want some kind of comfort that our loved one is in a better place. That's a hard part of life to deal with. I take it personal that I have that ability to be with people in that challenging time.

Carl Davis (Anderson County) is also asked those big, unavoidable questions.

When I go out on a suicide, I feel sorry for the family that's left behind. They're going to have to deal with this for the rest of their lives. I sometimes tell the family this: A person is like a house. In that house you have people. In your body you have a spirit. The house might get blown away like in a storm or maybe lightning destroys it. But the people got out. And everything's okay.

Sheron Collins (Hale County) talked similarly about the importance of being able to minister to families at such a terrible juncture in their lives.

Just a couple of weeks ago a young lady who was working the local high school football game came out of the booth and gave me a hug. She said, "I just want to thank you for taking such good care of us." Her brother had committed suicide some months ago. She said, "When I saw your face [when you came to do the inquest] I was able to handle it."

I thought, Oh my. We'd known each other thirty years. As horrible a situation as it was, being known here—that part of my job I look at as a ministry. I make no bones about my faith, and my being a Christian.

Before she came into office, Judge Collins didn't realize how emotionally difficult inquests would be for her, but she says her religious faith has gotten her through.

I never walk onto a scene, I never walk into the presence of death without prayer. Even before I leave home, I lift up prayer. My husband prays for me. I'll text him and whatever he's doing, he'll get up and walk out a minute and get that prayer lifted up. And then I go on.

I stay in prayer a lot. You have to. I pray before I go into that courtroom. I pray before I go on call-outs or to do an emergency detention. —Hon. *Tisha Sanchez, Palo Pinto County*

I asked Judge Scott Shinn (Van Zandt County) if he's comfortable praying with the family at an inquest, and he said he was. But the admission was followed by a caveat: while addressing the family's grief through the tools and sensibilities provided by his faith, he also has to consider the possibility that the family member presenting shock and grief may have had something to do with the death.

Which we wouldn't know at the time. So I'm very careful about not crossing that line. On the scene I'm the judge. I had to learn that over time.

Within the context of her own faith, Lisa Whitehead (Burnet County) was forced to re-examine her feelings about suicide.

I've always had just the worst opinion of a person who would kill himself. It's like, who does *that? How can you do that and leave your family? Then I was called to a horrific scene one night. A man goes into the bathroom and puts a shotgun under his chin and does the deal. It was a doublewide mobile home—his whole family was there, and you know how thin those walls are. There's a little four-year-old granddaughter there, and she runs off into the woods. This was February and it was really frigid, so agencies from two different counties had to respond, and they finally found the girl. She was okay.*

As I pull up to the scene, I hear wailing, just wailing and wailing and wailing, and that's unusual, so I get out and I go in, and the officers explain to me that this is the second brother who's taken his life in however many years. They kept saying, "How could he do this? How could he do this?"

It came to Judge Whitehead in that moment.

All of a sudden it was like God made it so clear to me that this person who killed himself, he wasn't even thinking about whether it was going to hurt someone else. People in this situation—they can't see past their own pain to get to where they can think of someone else's pain. I told the family: "He didn't do this to y'all. His pain was more than he could bear."

Those hadn't been my thoughts. They absolutely hadn't been my thoughts.

> **I don't force my religion on anybody and I don't think in this position I should, but I am a Christian and I believe that God calls us to positions and he gives us gifts to complete those positions.**
> —Hon. Scott Shinn, Van Zandt County

What about demonstrations of religious faith within the courtroom itself?

Jeff Monk (Johnson County) told me:

You don't give up your faith when you walk into the courtroom if you believe you walk as a Christian—and I'm not a perfect Christian—but what you do is you take what you learn in life and you share that with others. Each day that you're able to touch someone's life is reminiscent of your upbringing.

Gordon Terry (Garza County) likes to quote scripture when he's trying to get folks to work things out before he becomes involved. The applicable verses are Luke 12:57–59.

Yes, and why, even of yourselves, do you not judge what is right? When you go with your adversary to the magistrate, make every effort along the way to settle with him, lest he drag you to the judge, the judge deliver you to the officer, and the officer throw you into prison. I tell you, you shall not depart from there till you have paid the very last mite.

Perfect scripture for discouraging frivolous lawsuits!

> **Faith in God is important. I keep a Bible on my desk.**
> —Hon. Edward Marks, Floyd County

Faith played a big part in Judge Jimmy Miller's job as justice of the peace in Jasper County. He was often troubled when he had to make a ruling that comported with the law but not necessarily with what his faith was telling him. Yet he knew he had to rule by the law. Deciding to run for JP was something he had struggled with, and which he said he took to the Lord in prayer. The campaign involved knocking on a lot of doors, but it also gave him the chance to share his religious faith with others. He told me that he got to pray with a lot of folks along the campaign trail. Miller and his clerk bowed their heads each morning and asked the Lord to put them in a place where they could best be able to help people. He was also a founding member of the Jasper County Cowboy Church.

Christians don't have a monopoly on acts of charity and selflessness. Yet whereas a judge who isn't religious will credit their own independent conscience and instinctive moral compass for acts of benevolence toward others, Christian judges believe the inclination to be compassionate has been put in their hearts by a loving God. Douglas Zwiener (Washington County) sees people struggling every day, and acts accordingly, albeit with some judicial unorthodoxy.

I had an eviction case one day—a little Hispanic lady with about five kids with her. She was in one of the Housing Authority projects we've got here and she was at the basic $50 a month rent. She's working, like, two jobs; her husband has left her and gone back to Mexico. Her youngest child has just been diagnosed with leukemia, so she was having to drive down to Houston. Anyway, long story short, the amount of the judgment was, like, $350.

I leaned over and talked to the Housing Authority representative and said, "Is she a good tenant?"

"She is, but she's really had some bad strokes in life and she's going through a hard time."

I said, "Is there anything y'all can do to help her?"

"Not really. If we do a formal agreement to get her caught up on her debt, she's got to put money down and she doesn't have any money at all."

I told the defendant, "I'm gonna write you a check for $350 and let you stay, and we're gonna give it another month for things to change." She was very appreciative. I'd done my Christian duty.

She came back and she said, "I'm back on my feet and my daughter's gonna be okay."

Sometimes there is some good that comes out of doing something in an unexpected way. I do this all the time; I just wait until the evidence is such that the Christian side of you kicks in and you go, "Well, let's see if there's anything I can do about this."

Judge Wayne Mack (Montgomery County) had always wanted to be a minister, and in a way, he is. He told me that he'd given talks at a Catholic church, a mosque, a Baptist church, an Assemblies of God church, and a Methodist church. He says his wife refers to him as the community pastor.

Soon after becoming JP, Mack created a court chaplaincy program that invites courtroom invocations from local pastors. Mack says that "every mosque, temple, and synagogue" are represented among the chaplains who appear in his courtroom. Those in the courtroom who do not wish to be present for the public prayer are permitted to step out. That being said, the Freedom from Religion Foundation (FFRF) takes issue with Mack's program and have filed suit to stop him. They see problems with public prayer in a JP courtroom, including a potential violation of the Constitutional establishment clause. The foundation also fears the possibility that Mack might rule unfavorably and retaliatorily against lawyers and other parties who opt out of being present for the prayer but then must return to the courtroom and appear before him in his capacity as JP.

Those who defend Mack do so based on his established reputation for fairness and impartiality as a JP, regardless of whether the person in his court shares his faith or not, whereas those like the FFRF argue that the historic partition between church and state in the US should be inviolable and protected from even the smallest assaults, including within the Texas justice court system. The argument can be made that not every Texas JP who chooses to follow this precedent will be a Judge Mack.

Ultimately, it will be a court that will decide what happens in this particular court.

—⁂—

Sara Canady (Wilson County) wasn't the judge on call on the day of the 2017 mass shooting at First Baptist Church in Sutherland Springs, but she did help to process the scene and knew many of the people who died or who lost loved ones. The fact that this tragedy took place in a house of worship has made the journey out of this particular valley a difficult one, but one that Judge Canady says is buoyed by strong religious faith within the community.

God's just so awesome, the way he works through things and brings people together. Romans 8:28: "And we know that all things work together for good for those who love the Lord and are called according to his purposes." And Proverbs 3, verses 5 and 6 says, "Trust your Lord with all your heart. Do not lean on your own understanding, but in all your ways acknowledge Him and He will direct your path." I really rely on those two verses tremendously when things get rough and bad, because you just have to know that you're in the right place at the right time for the right reasons, and all the rest will just take care of itself.

> **When people ask the question, "Why are you a JP?" I say I really don't know, but I think this is a call from God.**—*Hon. Larry Flores, Frio County*

Keeping religion out of the JP courtroom while still recognizing the important role it plays in the lives of so many Texans, several hundred of whom don the robe of a justice of the peace, can be a challenge, and sometimes, as we've seen, even a legal challenge. While JP courts will always remain secular in theory and *mostly* in practice ("So help me God!") one cannot discount the fact that a lot of Texas JPs got elected because their constituents wanted someone of faith on the bench, wanted the decisions this judge would render to be informed by a spiritual conscience. While religion—and more specific to the state of Texas—Christianity—isn't the only motivator for conscientious behavior, there are many Texans who believe that faith puts folks on the right path, and this includes those who occupy justice court benches around the state. This is just a basic fact about the largest state in the southern Bible Belt: Great numbers of Texans who vote in accordance with their religious belief systems have decided that they'd like to have their local justice of the peace reflect their own faith and values.

Then all the people said, "Amen."

15

Brain, Heart, and Nerve

DOROTHY GALE WOULD BE comfortable in a Texas justice court. And this has nothing to do with annual Halloween visits by those who transact with the court while dressed in whimsical Ozian costume. It's because Dorothy would find in the lion's share of JP courts throughout the state judges who exemplify—as a credit to the profession and to the benefit of those they serve—the proper measure of each of the three desiderata of Dorothy's three Yellow Brick Road companions: brain, heart, and nerve.

BRAIN

You can sit across my desk and within three minutes
I can find out if you're lying to me or not.

—HON. ED FOLLIS, LYNN COUNTY

Justin M. Joyce (Fort Bend County) told me that over the course of his more than thirty years in law enforcement, he's learned how to read a situation and its participants and to know when someone isn't telling the truth. There are certain kinds of questions you can ask and certain ways that people will answer them that are revelatory. Judge Joyce studies eye movements for signs of deception.

Perhaps most important, he's raised kids.

All JPs are required to use their brains. But they don't all use them in the same way.

Susan Rowley (Lubbock County) is comfortable climbing around inside other people's heads. As a psych grad, a licensed mediator, and a defense attorney who offered psychological counseling to her clients, Rowley found that the skills she acquired through learning how to probe the human psyche have helped her glean why people do certain things and how the court can encourage them to stop doing the bad stuff and start doing more of the good stuff. As a judge, she's good at explaining the law in layman's terms and keeping it from going over the heads of those who come to court as self-representing litigants.

Wayne Money (Hunt County) is a "work the moment" sort of guy.

What I like about being a JP is that anything can happen at any time and you've got to be ready for it. I'm one of these guys that when something happens, it happens. It's history. We've got to go on to bigger and better things.

When Mike Nelson first came into office as JP in Galveston County, he was a textbook "second-guesser."

I'd come home, I'd be standing in front of the kitchen sink washing dishes, and I'd be going over what I did that day, to satisfy myself that I'd made the right decision. Or not. When I first took over, I was apprehensive and criticized myself if I thought I'd done the wrong thing.

I'd usually go to the house of the person I'd ruled against and knock on their door. I'd say, "I know you're upset, but let me at least explain to you how I got from point A to point B."

Most of the folks would say, "Now I understand how you ruled. I don't like it, but I understand how you got there."

I do know how to let go of it now.

You've got to be a listener and not a talker. You've got to listen to them and then you need to dig in to get to the rule of law that applies in the particular case before you.—Hon. Harris Hughey, Denton County

When it comes to interactions with those who come to court, Mark Russo (Rockwall County) has a pretty well-developed doctrine. It defines his courtroom demeanor.

Think before you speak. Be genuine. Be you. Be transparent. Do the

right thing for the right reason. Be humble. Be friendly. Don't come in with an ego. Don't be Judge Judy. When people come in to my court, they expect me to scream at them and not listen to them. But I'm not here to give a show. I say, "I'm only here for the facts."

Quite a few JPs with whom I spoke told me how helpful the classes offered by the Texas Justice Court Training Center have been to them. JPs are required to attend eighty hours of new judges' training arranged by the TJCTC within one year of being sworn in. Non-attorney judges then get twenty hours of additional judicial education every year, delivered by the center. (After the first year, attorney JPs may apply bar-approved continuing legal education courses to their ten-hour annual requirement.) The education a judge receives isn't just limited to classroom and on-the-job learning. Veteran judges advise and mentor newer judges. JPs exchange notes on their own experiences and research. Marc DeRouen (Jefferson County) spoke to me of the ancillary benefits derived from his annual TJCTC judicial training.

When I attend the schools, there are guys there who have been in office for thirty, thirty-five years. Everybody gravitates to them because we know they've seen and heard it all. That's where you gather your most valuable information. School is always a learning experience and I've never walked away from a training session where I haven't learned something, but sitting around during the breaks or after the class is over and talking to these more experienced judges, that's where I've got my notepad out.

Former Williamson County JP Patricia Ott thinks that smart judges could get even smarter if they were allowed to take law classes and get credit for them.

Let judges who, say, have been on the bench for eight years get into law school without the LSAT, because they're already sitting there judging the law. Let them get into law school and take classes and become better judges!

Irma Dunn, one of Titus County's two justices of the peace, is the first Hispanic elected JP in her county. Roughly 40 percent of the county's residents are also Hispanic. It comes in handy that she can conduct court in two different languages.

In the past, the kids would be the ones translating back and forth with the judge, but the kids would say to their parents whatever was convenient to them, not what the judge was actually saying! I always ask if they want

to do it in Spanish. I usually have the cases with the English-speaking
people first so that way I won't have them sitting there wondering what
I'm talking about.

She adds that she first makes sure that the Spanish-speaking court
visitors are comfortable with this arrangement.

HEART

I've set a bond on a guy and by the time I left the jail
he was bonded out, and I gave him a ride home.
    —HON. SCOTT SHINN, VAN ZANDT COUNTY

Nora Salinas (Brooks County) became a justice of the peace in part
to continue her advocacy for crime victims.

I've worked in county government for twelve years. Prior to that I
worked for the district attorney. I was a legal aid there. The one that stood
out: A young girl showed up at our office, a victim of domestic violence.
She stood there crying and told me the baby daddy had pulled out a gun
and shot at her and their children. The girl was telling me that she was
trying to do a protective order on him while he was in jail and none of the
JPs in her county would help her. That kind of chapped my hide. I was like,
how can this be? Because I worked for the district attorney's office, I knew
the history of this guy. I knew it was true. How do you not help somebody
who is telling you this kind of horror story?

That opened my eyes. Victims were being left out and not being taken
care of. It inspired me to run and be their advocate. There are programs
we have in the community, and I reach out constantly and refer victims
of domestic violence, of abuse. Victims matter, victims have rights. As a
JP, I have the ability to make a change.

Lisa Whitehead (Burnet County) agrees.

I've always been a volunteer and I've always felt like I was put on this
earth to help where I can. The Lord increased my territory, basically. I just
feel that as human beings, if we can help, we need to help. In a JP court we
have the best opportunity, because we're the people's court. And, of course,
I spent fourteen years in the county attorney's office; I saw so many people
who came in and they didn't know where to go because the criminal justice
system is not an easy path to navigate if you don't know how.

> *These people in the rural areas, they don't have a voice,*
> *especially minorities. They've taken* me *in and I protect* them.
> *They appreciate that. But that's just part of the job.*
> —Hon. Edward Marks, Floyd County

Judge Mark Russo likes to remind people who see a Texas JP for the very worst reasons that the worst doesn't *have* to be the worst. He's here to say, "You can get through this."

When you get arrested, you think your life is over. You're panicked. You're there because something bad has happened. Even an accusation can change someone's life. I'm the person who says, "Listen, life happens. Don't let this change the rest of your life. Learn from it and move forward."

> *The people who come in, they're so burdened, so beaten down*
> *by the system. To help them find that ray of sunlight, to help*
> *them climb their way back to the place where everybody else*
> *is—I think that's the most satisfying part of my job.*
> —Hon. Rodney Cheshire, Angelina County

One of the things that gives Christopher Lopez (Denton County) the most satisfaction is granting occupational driver's licenses.*

They walk in. They're thinking, "I'm just gonna fill out the forms and they're gonna give me an appointment for a later day, and then I'll have to kill another half-day missing work." But at the end of the hearing they actually leave with a license. I see the instant relief, I see their disposition completely change as they drive away with a license for the first time in months, even years. They don't expect someone who looks like me—a thirty-two-year-old Hispanic—to be asking them the very questions that will get them the license they need.

A lot of people have legitimate reasons for their mishaps.
Why make their lives worse by throwing the book at them?
—Hon. Fred Buck, Tom Green County

Jerry Shaffer (Collin County) talked to me about the insidious disease of poverty, which so adversely impacts those who come to his court. We first discussed his own background. He knows these people. He's lived his life among them.

A significant portion—probably three-fourths of the cases we hear—involve poverty, and in a lot of cases, extreme poverty. I grew up in Fannin County. Even today it's really poor. I came from very impoverished circumstances myself. We were in a three-room house five miles out from Leonard. My dad was a day laborer. We didn't have running water or electricity when I was young.

What I see happening a lot of times is that circumstances get out of control because of bad choices that people make. I'll give you a scenario that's quite typical. A fellow and his wife—neither one has very much education—have two or three kids. They're just living from paycheck to paycheck. The old boy, the husband, he gets in an accident and he's out of work for three months. During this time, he's got to decide whether he buys medicine or food or rent or pays the speeding ticket he got. So he signs this ticket that says he promises to appear in a certain amount of time in the JP court. Well, of course he doesn't show up because he doesn't have the money to pay it, and now he ends up with a violation of a "promise to appear." A warrant's gonna be issued on him.

But not just that: when he got the speeding ticket, they ask to see his insurance, but his insurance has lapsed because he couldn't afford it. When you do that, you lose your driver's license. Now he's got a no-insurance ticket, he's got a speeding ticket, and he's got a "violate promise to appear" ticket. It's ends up there are now three warrants out on him. The next thing you know, he gets a headlight out and he doesn't have the money to go fix the headlight. So he gets pulled over because of that, and when they run him through the system they discover he's got all these warrants and they take him to jail.

Now I can have some impact. I explain to him that he can get an occu-

pational driver's license. I can give him community service for whatever I feel like is warranted. I can adjust his fines to fit his economic situation. We might even give him brochures on the local food pantry. We might put him in touch with the various social agencies that he can avail himself of. We can rescue him from that spiral.

> **I try to do what I can for people. Everybody's going through such a hard time right now.**—Hon. *Margie Anderson, Shelby County*

There are great things that JPs do for their constituents that fall outside the usual job description. Sometimes they do them anonymously or without drawing too much attention to themselves; but the press does like to sniff them out, especially if it helps in getting people to take advantage of that good thing. For several years, Judge B. H. Jameson has been giving away free gun locks for anyone who needs them—his way of helping to reduce accidents involving unsecured firearms and kids in Gregg County. Who pays for the gunlocks? Judge Jameson does.[1]

Stan Warfield (Colorado County) doesn't give away things. Rather, he gives the gift of time.

I had a gentleman I was magistrating one day; can't remember what he was charged with—a misdemeanor that he just wanted to sit out. Five days. He didn't want to do community service. But he said, "Can I start tomorrow?"

"Why? I can already give you two days credit because you were arrested yesterday."

"Judge, let me tell you. I have a niece graduating from high school tonight. No member of my family has ever graduated from high school before. I'd like to be there to see her."

"I tell you what: I'll cut you loose this afternoon, but I'll be back here at the jail at nine o'clock in the morning. You better beat me back here. If not, you'll be in deep doo-doo."

When I hit the jail the next morning to magistrate, one of the jailers says, "Judge, he's back. He checked in at 8:30. We asked him why he came back. He said, 'The judge did right by me. I want to do right by the judge, so I'm keeping my word."'

> *Sometimes just a little help along the way can make a big difference and go a long way.*—Hon. Stephen Y. Taylor Jr., Castro County

As a member of Dallas County's African American community, Michael Jones Jr. says he was motivated to run for justice of the peace to make sure that people in his county got the fair shake that he's seen denied them in the past. In fact, long before the Black Lives Matter movement took itself to the streets of nearly every city in America, judges like Jones and his fellow JPs of color in Texas were striving to provide justice, regardless of the law enforcement culture of their communities, that was equitable and colorblind. Jones respects the challenges faced by the low-income constituents he serves. He works with defendants, making adjustments to their fines when he's able and setting up payment plans that fit their income situations. Education has always been important to him, and now he's in a position to educate the people who come to his court about their options when they get in trouble.

> *We're a small town. A lot of these people know me. They look on me as kind of their counselor. "What do I need to do, judge?" "Where do I need to go?"*—Hon. Evelyn Kerbow, Crockett County

Jeff Monk (Johnson County) believes that one of the most important jobs for a Texas JP is knowing not only when a decision you make should be detached from emotion, but also knowing when you must listen to your heart to understand why a person did what they did. He's well acquainted with the emotional state that a lot of people find themselves in when they visit his court:

When you have people coming in with the burdens of life on their shoulders, and you can sit there and crack a funny with them and give them some relief, it makes a difference. When people walk into my courtroom and they see this judge with long hair and a beard, they think: this ain't some fat, old, bald-headed guy.

There was this young man who'd been in my court multiple times and he was just messing up left and right, and his mom said, "Why don't you go and talk to Judge Monk? He'll listen."

The son looked at his mother and said, "Mom, he scares me. He reminds me of a pissed-off Jesus."

Incidentally, when Monk first ran for office, he was told by one of the doyennes of his local Republican party that he'd have to cut his ponytail if he wanted her vote. So he cut his ponytail. He laughs, "Back in 2002, beards and ponytails were *not* in the Republican party!"

There are times, though, when nothing in the judge's toolbox can do the trick. Or, even worse: The JP is pulled in too late, and, in the worst-case scenario, only when it's time to perform a death inquest. "All you can do then," says Jarrell Hedrick (Martin County), is "just shake your head and go on. You wish you could have fixed it, but you can't." Hedrick mentioned a couple of young men in his county who had shot themselves over losing their girlfriends. "They thought it was the only way out. *No, it wasn't.*"

Sergio L. De Leon (Tarrant County) related to me one of the saddest cases he'd had. Here is an instance in which a judge's hands are tied, regardless of what his heart is saying. It involved a driver's license revocation hearing.

An elderly gentleman had failed his test. The family, siding with the state, had produced two letters, one from the family physician and the other from the optometrist. The optometrist was saying the man's eyesight wasn't what it used to be and was only going to get worse. The other doctor said the gentleman was in an early stage of Alzheimer's.

When it was the defendant's time to speak, he gave me the greatest speech I'd ever heard. "Your Honor, I'm pleading with you not to take away my driving privileges. I want you to know that I've been driving since before I was even the legal age to drive. I did so because I was on the family farm, and I was helping my father pick the produce from the farm and drive it into market to sell so we could sustain our family. I drove myself to high school, didn't finish college—I was drafted and I was in World War II. Then I found myself driving munitions to and from the front line to General Patton's platoon. I did that in Italy to defeat fascism.

I got married and took a job selling insurance and I drove all over the country. And that's how I put my kids through college. Then I was driving my grandkids around, and then my wife got sick and I was driving her to her doctor. She passed on, and all I do now is just drive to and from the grocery store and the coffee shop; that's my social life. I'm asking you: Please don't take the very last thing I have in my life."

I was floored by such an impassioned speech, I was moved to emotion, taken away by what he said. I don't think I'd ever shed a tear until I had to do that difficult thing and revoke his license based on the fact that two physicians were recommending it.

And it gave me no great pleasure to do it.

Incidentally, not all driver's license hearings leave a JP regretting his decision. I had an interesting conversation with Sylvia Holmes (Travis County) over the complete absence of any qualms whatsoever regarding her assessment of a female applicant's suitability for an occupational driver's license:

Judge Holmes: *We had a woman who was blind and couldn't hear very well who was trying to get an occupational driver's license. We actually had to take the keys from her and call Uber.*

Author: *To be clear: "Ms. Magoo" was blind, but she wanted you to let her keep driving? Was it hard for you to keep a straight face?*

Judge Holmes: *I don't know that I did, but she couldn't have seen me anyway, so it wouldn't have made much difference. She was only ten feet away from me and couldn't hear me either.*

I said, "Ma'am, do you have an essential need to drive? Ma'am? Ma'am? MA'AM!"

"I do, Your Honor."

"I see that you just wrote something on that piece of paper. Can you read me what you just wrote?"

"Well, I can't really see it."

"Bailiff, would you please take her keys? Ma'am, MA'AM! How'd you get here?"

"I drove."

There are, as Judge Holmes has demonstrated, times when a JP has to put her heart in temporary layaway, not even letting love for a family member get in the way of doing your lawful job. Like Dallam County's

JP Carol Smith's love for *her* kids. They think Mom's going to get them "out of stuff."

"No, honey, you're on your own. So just deal with it." I do have a daughter who's gotten a couple of tickets in this court. I'm like: You know what? You did it. Take care of it, suck it up, move on, and don't do it again!

NERVE

I have to sleep at night. I'm not going to rule for someone because they have power in the town. Sometimes doing right is hard.

—HON. DEBBIE HORN, POTTER COUNTY

Being a justice of the peace isn't for the faint of heart. Magistration puts judges face-to-face with some pretty tough customers. Police officers will tell you that their riskiest interactions with the public come in the form of domestic disputes. Yet justices of the peace are quite often required to step right into just that type of dispute in their courtrooms. Some are family squabbles that end up as heated small claims cases, and other times, court proceedings wind up involving the justice court remedial tool known as the peace bond.

Debra Ravel (Travis County) told me an unsettling cautionary tale about what happens when a JP's best intentions produce something very different from the desired result:

I put a couple under peace bond, as I often did, so it looked like I was trying to be fair, even though it was the young woman who was bleeding when they came in. Under the terms of the order, each side was to have no contact with the other. They were living together, but we made arrangements for one of the deputy constables to go to her place and get his belongings and take them back to his place. Which is what occurred.

What happened during the hearing was that he kept interrupting. Finally—I was kind of fearful to do it—I held him in contempt and put him in jail. A week later he came by and told me I'd been fair, admitted he'd lost his temper and wanted to apologize to me. I was impressed by that. I said, "John, if you can stay clean and don't have any more problems in my court for a year, I'll try to help you get a job at the end of that time."

Six months later he came in again. I thought he was going to be a great success. Instead, he said, "I'm in trouble and I need your help."

I said, "What's the problem, John?"

He said, "Well, the feds are looking for me, judge. I've got some guns at my apartment and I'm on parole."

"What?"

"I have guns in my apartment and they're gonna pick me up. What should I do?"

I said, "Did you have an attorney who represented you when you went to jail?" He said yes. I said, "I think you need to surrender yourself to him."

So he called his lawyer and went in and surrendered himself. He ended up going back to prison for several years. The attorney told me the whole story, which was that he'd been in prison for killing two women and he'd been in jail for most of his life. I'd had no idea of his past but was pretty horrified to find out that I'd been helping this man and was naïve enough to think that my involvement was changing his approach to women.

Signing an emergency detention order (EDO) for a citizen with mental health issues can also be a disquieting experience. Judge Irma Dunn is familiar with the risk.

Sometimes the family comes and talks to me, and then I send the constable to go and talk to the person, because I would hate to put somebody in the hospital who doesn't need to be there.

But there are times when it is the judge herself who has to get personally involved.

I had one that kind of scared me a little bit. I had to keep backing out and when I get close to the door, I'm like, "I need to let you know that I just issued an emergency detention warrant and you're gonna be detained here for at least three days." He looked at me like, "I'm gonna kill you!" People can get aggressive.

Tisha Sanchez (Palo Pinto County) used to get personally involved with EDOs, but not anymore. Which isn't a bad thing; she told me that there's definitely something in the water in Mineral Wells, Texas. For a county of only around thirty thousand people, she signs an awful lot of these orders.

I'm not exaggerating this: Our county has one of the highest numbers of mental health patients for a county our size. The judge I worked for as a clerk swore to this: These are the offspring of the people who came to Mineral Wells for the water. Pecan Valley** had to build a new building and had to hire more case workers and staff. They said that two years ago *their numbers were in the two-hundreds. Now they're over five hundred.*

I'm not usually face-to-face with the patient. For my safety, I just don't go to the homes anymore. The last one I went to, the gentleman had taken a butcher knife to the furniture.

> **I spent a lot of time in the beginning of the pandemic calming people's fears, including my clerk. As you know, there are only two of us. I think, overall, this would be what I did the most of—being the voice of reason.**—Hon. *Karin Knolle, Jim Wells County*

Circumstances sometimes require a judge to step outside both her job description and her comfort zone. Barbara McMillon (Cass County) found herself in just such a situation one Saturday morning. A man had barricaded himself in his home and wouldn't come out. He'd destroyed his apartment and slashed up the interior of his pickup truck. Now he was holding off the police with a long-blade knife and threatening harm both to the officers and to himself. After relaying the situation to Judge McMillon on the phone, the police chief told her he wanted her to come and talk the man out.

I asked the chief if he had a dead body at the scene. He replied, "No, but I need you to get your backside over here and talk to this guy." I continued to take a stance that I did not have any business being at a police scene if he didn't need me for an inquest. I finally agreed that I would go and try to talk to the man. I knew the man, and in the back of my mind I was thinking that he must be suffering from a chemical imbalance of some kind, as the incident that was described was out of character.

As I got out of my car, I noticed the destroyed pickup and the exterior damage to the apartment that the chief had described to me. He said they had been dealing with the situation for over two hours.

As I approached the apartment door, I heard other officers caution me to not get very close, as the windows were knocked out and he could injure me with the knife. The officers were also concerned that it was possible that he had some other weapons, possibly a gun. I stood back from the door and called the subject by name and identified myself.

He immediately said, "Yes, ma'am!"

I asked him to put his weapon down and come out and talk to the police chief. He shouted very plainly that he was not coming out. Again, I called him by name and said, "If you do not put the weapon down and come outside, the police officers have guns and they are going to kill you!"

This did the trick. The door opened and the man emerged without a weapon. Judge McMillon could hear several of the officers snickering. Since she had effectively neutralized the situation in two minutes, they began calling her their new hostage negotiator.

All in a day's work.

Courage is important to the job. But so is staying vigilant. The whole time Judge Patricia Ott (Williamson County) was JP, she worried about her colleagues not exercising enough caution when they went about their jobs. Even in retirement, she still worries. Some courthouses have metal detectors, but most JP offices aren't located in their county's courthouse. Texas justices of the peace are supposed to have bailiffs, but the job is usually filled by the constable or one of his deputies, whose presence is officially required only for formal courtroom proceedings.

Ott has worked to raise the consciousness among judges about the physical risks that go along with the job. JPs are uniquely vulnerable to the public because accessibility to their workplace is a chief feature of the people's court. At some point in their lives, a majority of Texans will need to visit a justice court. Many of these folks will be angry and aggrieved. Most will display their umbrage via tongue and brow, but there will be those who'll choose to ratchet things up. "You protect yourself best when you don't treat courtroom security lightly," Judge Ott told me. "The odds of the worst happening are small," she said, "but when it happens, you don't want to be the judge it happens to. Be vigilant."

Being armed helps. I talked to a West Texas judge who confided that he'd been accosted four times by dangerous people he'd dealt with—though in one instance, it was a case of mistaken identity, as it was actually the *district* judge the person had the grudge against.

One of the four came to my house after I magistrated him. He got out, and the bondsman told him where I lived because "he wanted to talk to me." He's right there knocking on my front door. The other times were on the courthouse steps, once in a restaurant, and then once at a convenience store. Because of that, I am constantly armed. All four times, even though

I didn't have to resort to pulling a handgun, just the presence of it kept things from escalating.

There are JPs who think that asserting a little authority and maintaining firm control of the courtroom is the best way to keep the judicial train on track. Other judges prefer the carrot approach to the stick, or, at the very least, they set the stick aside. To Amy Tapia (Matagorda County), that stick is her gavel.

I don't like to use my gavel. I knew a judge who used the gavel along with this very stern voice. Part of it just seemed very egotistical, in my opinion. The only time I saw it used was when he was yelling or frustrated, instead of trying to defuse a situation by taking his tone down while looking them straight in the eye. You shouldn't take your position and authority to a level at which you're telling the people who come to your court that you're better than them. I did use the gavel in the very beginning, to dismiss my court. I kind of snickered to myself because it felt so inauthentic. It wasn't me.

Steven T. Kennedy (Uvalde County) was called upon to hear a politically charged Class C assault case against a county commissioner. The case involved physical contact on the stairs of the courthouse between the male commissioner and the female district clerk. The trial was set to be heard by a jury, but was switched to a bench trial at the last minute, with the change putting Kennedy in the political hot seat. He ended up fining and rebuking the commissioner. Judge Kennedy has a transcript of the case; the district clerk's husband happened to be a court reporter and he'd asked permission to record the emotionally charged proceeding. Kennedy, who can now look back on the trial with the kind of composure and humor that comes with time, said that he learned something about himself from this case (in addition to, I assume, what he was made of in terms of judicial grit): "I sure used the phrase *mighty fine* a lot."

He decided he'd work on that.

There are those rare occasions when courage requires that you deal with disturbed court petitioners who put homemade bombs on your counter. This happened to Debbie Horn (Potter County).

We had a man come in and file for a peace bond. He said his mother and his sister were trying to kill him. He feared for his life. So there was a hearing. There were no grounds. It was all "he said, she said." The case was dismissed.

He came back with his girlfriend and his children. He had one of those old oil cans wrapped in paper towels. He set it on the counter and said, "I told you they were trying to kill me. I just found this behind the tire of my car."

The APD [Amarillo Police Department] bomb squad came. It really was a bomb. It turns out that he made it himself at home and there was gunpowder in the ridges on the screwed-on lid. APD said just the friction of moving it and bringing it to the court could have exploded it.

He went to prison for this. He's out now. He still comes to our court.

Constituents sometimes make unusual requests of their local JPs. Some are outlandish and completely untenable. Others are legally problematic. Henry Alvarado (Sabine County) was once offered a foot rub in lieu of payment of a fine. Clyde Black (Houston County) hadn't been in office any time at all when he found his mettle tested by a similarly nervy constituent.

I was a brand-new judge, and the clerks tell me that a lady's come in with a speeding ticket. They said she'd pled guilty but wanted to talk to me about getting some help with the costs. They brought her into my office and I didn't notice that they'd closed the door when she came in. She sat down on the couch, looked me in the eye, and kind of pulled her skirt up and said, "Judge, I'll do anything."

I said, "I'm brand new. Let's talk to my clerk!"

In the words of Dorothy Gale, "We're definitely not in Kansas anymore."

NOTES

*An occupational driver's license is a special type of restricted license. It can be issued to one whose driver's license has been suspended, revoked, or denied for certain offenses (other than a medical reason or delinquent child support). It authorizes the driver to operate a non-commercial motor vehicle only for the purpose of getting to and from work, getting to and from school-related activities, and performing essential household duties.

**Pecan Valley Centers for Behavioral and Developmental Healthcare.

16

In the Opinion of the Court

TEXAS JUSTICES OF THE peace are paid to render opinions from the bench. That doesn't stop them from rendering opinions *off* the bench that often put them in disagreement with each other. For example:

Should Texas JPs Be Required to Have Law Degrees?

The question isn't new. Since Texas justices of the peace started acquiring Juris Doctor degrees, there has a been a debate within the fraternity over whether, like every other judge in Texas except for constitutional county court judges,* justices of the peace ought to have law degrees. Granted, there are few JPs who can make a strong case that *every one* of Texas's 804 JPs should have that diploma. There are some counties in Texas where you'd be hard-pressed to even *find* a lawyer, let alone one willing to accept the very small salary that goes along with being a rural justice of the peace in a county with a beggarly tax base. (Although there are a few lawyers who, because their practices involve areas of the law outside justice court jurisdiction, are allowed to continue their private law practice while serving their community as JP. Judge Kathleen McCumber, below, is one.) The real argument plays out somewhere in the middle: Should counties of a certain size be required by law to have attorney-JPs? There are interesting arguments to be made by each camp.

Pro

Jeff Wentworth (Bexar County): Judge Wentworth practiced law and served in the state legislature for twenty-five years. He chaired the senate jurisprudence committee that has jurisdiction over the entire judicial branch of Texas state government. Wentworth uses that experience to say that he "can't imagine that it isn't significantly easier and invaluable to have a law degree if you're a justice of the peace."

Kathleen McCumber (Galveston County): Judge McCumber uses her skills as an attorney every day. Though she still practices family law, it rarely conflicts with her duties as JP. She finds frequent opportunities to apply her training as a lawyer to matters that come before her in justice court.

Duncan Neblett Jr. (Nueces County): One of the good things about being justice of the peace with a strong legal background is the opportunity to mentor other judges. Sometimes the State Commission on Judicial Conduct will direct a JP to sit in on Judge Neblett's court proceedings to see how he does things (correctly). The downside to being a lawyer-JP is always having to fight the inclination *as* a lawyer to give legal advice to one (or both) of the parties that come before him. As a judge, he must remain neutral and impartial through each and every wince and cringe.

Harris Hughey (Denton County): Hughey points out that even if one sets aside an attorney-JP's familiarity with the law, those justices of the peace with law degrees still have a distinct advantage over lay judges: the experience they've gained from the time they've spent as lawyers who've actually practiced in justice court.

I've been in enough courtrooms to know what questions to ask to get to where we need to be in order to frame the issues and apply the law. That's the big difference. I've got a lot of practice doing that through the years and that's where I think a licensed attorney is more than worth his salt.

Sharon M. Burney (Harris County): Judge Burney told me that in a county as large as Harris, it's important to have some JPs with solid backgrounds in the law. She is proud to be the third lawyer-JP of color in her precinct.

Kelly Crow (Fort Bend County): *The JP lobby—the JPCA [the Justices of the Peace and Constables Association of Texas]—they say they represent the interests of JPs and constables, but they're very much against requiring JPs to be lawyers. Some of us attorneys would like to see that happen in larger counties, like Fort Bend, because the case load is so much greater, because of the availability of lawyers in the area, and because of the complex legal issues we have to deal with from a civil standpoint. We have a lot of pretty complex statutes we have to address in the property code, in the civil practice and remedy code, deceptive trade practices, things of that nature.*

Judge Crow thinks both sides should be looking for some middle ground that makes sense. She admits there are plenty of non-attorney JPs with backgrounds that are helpful to being a justice of the peace, such as those who work in real estate. But she believes there should be requirements for being a JP that go a little farther than "just being eighteen and having a pulse. Right now, you don't even need a high school diploma to be elected JP."

Crow has noticed a troubling lack of understanding by some non-lawyer judges of some of the fundamentals of criminal law: that one is presumed innocent until proven guilty, that the state has the burden of proving guilt. She told me that she's worked with JPs who still don't understand what probable cause is. A good many of them, she added, want to learn more and want to be proficient, but some of them don't.

Olivia Neu (Cooke County): *I think a JD is actually necessary to be a JP. Yes, you have to use common sense and not be so rigid that you let the law override equity, but we do so many different things, the number and types of cases we hear are so vast, and some of the things we do have strict laws governing them. There's no way you can know all that. A legal background helps you to go and research and make sure you're complying with the things you are required to comply with, and to use your judgment on the things you can use your judgment on.*

I can look at it the other way and say this is even more of a reason you ought to have a law degree. When I was an attorney in private practice and practiced in district court, I'd go to the judge and argue my case. I'm going to hand her the law and I'm going to lay out my legal arguments and the other side is going to do the same thing. In justice court, I'll have two parties completely unrepresented. As the judge, I'm the one who has to know where to look for the appropriate law; I have to analyze it and then I have to apply it to the case. I don't have the advantage of two attorneys doing that for me. In some ways it's more incumbent on the JPs to know and be able to apply the law than in a court where you have attorneys.

Susan Rowley (Lubbock County): *It's funny because I looked back on my election, and the guy who was the most competitive running against me, he kept using this argument that, "It's the people's court, so we need a regular person on the bench who isn't an attorney." I'm thinking and thinking about it and, yes, it's a people's court in the sense that the "people" come in, but I really think the* people *would rather have someone who has a knowledge of the law on the bench, just from a standpoint of efficiency.*

Travis Hill (Lavaca County): *I'll probably weigh in on the side that JPs should be lawyers. I've dealt with JP courts as an attorney; there are a bunch of them that are run by laypeople, and they just run them as little fiefdoms. "We're not about* the *law, we're about* my *law, and I'll just make it up as I go along."*

You say, "Here's some case law, judge; read this."

"I don't care what that says. I'm the JP. I'm the law around here. This is what I say."

"Well, you're totally wrong and now my client is gonna have to spend money to appeal to county court and we have to start all over again!"

Con

Travis Hill (Lavaca County): . . . then again, Judge Hill is willing to admit that there are attorney-judges whose bench practices can *also* raise an eyebrow:

*There's one of those fiefdom counties over here; the judge is an attorney.
He hates credit card companies, so he always rules against them. No matter what the law is, no matter what the facts are, he's gonna rule against
the credit card companies.*

Nicholas Chu (Travis County): Sometimes, ironically, it's lawyers
themselves who are best at pointing up the advantages of having non-
lawyers in justice courts. Judge Chu, who served in both the county
and district attorney offices before taking the JP bench, found himself
doing a little reassessing after he became a justice of the peace himself.

*When I went to my classes, I was thinking, There are lot of these new
JPs who aren't lawyers. And I was thinking that, for lack of a better term,
they'll be out there shooting from the hip. But I found out that the vast
majority of people there care about doing right and getting justice. Even if
they don't have a law degree, they're working very hard, sometimes harder
than the lawyers. I think the lawyers are thinking, I have a law degree. I
don't have to worry about this stuff.*

Judge Chu told me that lawyer-JPs have a tendency to glance over
nuances to the law that non-lawyer JPs have to really drill down on. I've
heard this from non-attorney JPs as well. And perception plays a part;
most lay JPs have a sincere desire not to disappoint their constituents
by appearing insufficiently grounded in what they're expected to know
and do.

Judge Chu has friends in high places—or, rather, higher courts—and
he tells them that he really likes the faster pace of justice court. It's lib-
erating when a judge doesn't have to carefully develop a record that will
be consulted on appeal.** Because the rules are geared toward self-representing litigants, "a JP can kind of help out; they can ask questions
and get to the important parts of a case. You get to drive the ship more
than in other courts."

On the One Hand, on the Other Hand

Bill Price (Coryell County): *I'm gonna tell you about the lay judges.
Nine out of ten of the non-lawyer JPs I know are really good judges. They
study harder than the lawyer judges. They understand that they've got
that deficiency. But what gets them in trouble is violating ethics rules.
Lawyer judges are familiar with these rules and don't get in trouble.*

How Do You Feel about Lawyers Practicing in the "People's Court"?

Charlie Hodgkins Jr. sees very few lawyers in his courtroom in Palo Pinto County. "Lawyers," he says, "don't have time to come to a little old court in the middle of nowhere." But this is becoming more and more the exception nowadays.

There are those JPs who welcome lawyers into their courtrooms and others who would rather they just keep their distance. Lay JPs don't relish face-offs with attorneys, who, in some instances, will have a better command of the law than the non-lawyer judge. On such occasions, the judge may take the matter under advisement and do a little boning up on the law at play, even taking a recess right then and there to get up to speed. It's especially satisfying when the lay judge discovers that the attorney's argument is actually incorrect.

As a judge who is also a lawyer, Judge Price has a thing or two to say about those among his counselor-brethren who practice in justice court, specifically the ones who engage in intellectual bullying.

I gave a piece of advice to another justice of the peace—a young judge— one time. He was a non-lawyer. He complained that some of the lawyers in town would bring cases in and just harass him. Here's how you stop that: You look them in the eye and you scratch your chin and you say, "Counselor, that's an approach I'd never thought of before, and I don't know the law on that. Would you please write me a brief and have it on my desk Monday morning?" And when you do that, that's the last time they'll pull that stuff on you!

We have some lawyers who think that because I hear cases in justice court, I'm somehow inferior to the district and county courts. The law doesn't say I'm inferior. It says I have a different jurisdiction. What happens is that they'll come and say, "I can't come to court tomorrow. I've been set in district court on such-and-such case." I may give them one bite of that apple but after that, they're gonna have to bring me a setting sheet that shows me that district judge set them before I set them, because if I gave them their setting first, they belong to me.

Not that there aren't attorneys in justice court who can be just as entertaining as individuals who choose to represent themselves. There was the time Nancy J. Pomykal (Calhoun County) was hearing a traffic case in the Port Lavaca courthouse:

The defendant was represented by an attorney out of Houston. He was a couple of minutes late and came flying into the courtroom. He had on a seersucker suit and one of those funny Panama hats. He whisked his hat off and the first words out of his mouth were, "Your Honor, I object!"

> ***I've had trials with attorneys on both sides. When you have attorneys, what should last an hour or two ends up lasting most of the day.***—Hon. Kenny Elliott, Brazos County

Mike Smith (Harrison County) said that one of the big things he learned when he became a JP was how little the state's law schools teach about justice court. There are obvious reasons for this: Some Lone Star attorneys will never set foot in a JP court for the entire length of their careers, especially if the kind of law they practice falls outside the jurisdiction of this court. But with the increase in the monetary jurisdiction of the court to $20,000, and the ever-expanding judicatory portfolio of a justice of the peace, they could very well find themselves one day in the land of "different rules" without a roadmap.

Jim Cavanaugh (Brown County), a lay judge, has some strong opinions about a certain kind of lawyer who shows up in his courtroom: One who buys up credit card debt at a substantial discount for the chance to roll the dice in JP court.

The attorneys we see in our courts, most of them are the credit card attorneys; we call them the "bottom feeders." People get behind in their credit card payments and these clowns will buy, like, $2,000 of debt for five bucks. They add in their fees and their overhead and now, instead of $2,000, you owe $5,000. We get the hospital debt cases in here, too. It's sold on the internet. Every night these attorneys will go online and say, "Look! There's one for Brown County. Let me get that one!" They'll buy it and the next thing you know, you're being sued because you went to the hospital last year. You owed $500 but you get a letter saying, "You owe us $1,800 now."

How Do You Feel about Your Fellow JPs?

There are JPs who get along swimmingly with the other justices of the peace in their county (and in neighboring counties, with whom they sign cooperative bench exchanges). Then there are those other JPs who would prefer to have nothing to do with their colleagues.

Mark Laughlin (Grimes County) is a member of that first group. He told me that when he took office, the other two judges in his county "pretty much took me under their wing and helped me get off on the right foot. Also, when we run into something that needs to be addressed and where we need consistency between the three of us, they've been very receptive to that."

Harris County's sixteen JPs meet once a month, usually by phone. (I suspect by the time this book comes out, they'll be holding virtual meetings online.) They schedule three-day work sessions once a year, which Judge Louie Ditta says are helpful in addressing matters unique to their county.

One of the big things when I came into this office, it was like everyone was on his own—everybody had different forms, different ways of doing things from one court to the next. Now we've become much more standardized, which is a good thing. We have discretion when we need it, but standardization too. The judges who've been around for a while mentor the new judges. That happens at our work sessions, too. The new judges raise their hands and ask, "What do I do in this particular scenario?" We've got a wealth of history and judicial wisdom there.

Judges in other counties are equally supportive of the new kids on the block. And there is always a new crop. Some Texas justice courts have high turnover rates. Ambitious JPs move on, move up. Others can't handle the workload or the stress of the death inquests, and turn in their robes within weeks of taking office.

But when Texas justices of the peace gather each year for judge school, they discover that—while a lot of big city JPs and small-town JPs can find things to relate to and agree on, which facilitates comity and judicial fellowship—there is a great deal they *don't* have in common. This promotes feelings that run in entirely the opposite direction. The differences that get highlighted in these city vs. country encounters can translate into suspicion, and even, in extreme cases, contempt. There are large-county JPs who think small-county JPs don't have nearly enough to do; they're hayseed lollygaggers who, should they ever find themselves sitting on a big city justice court bench, they wouldn't know what hit them. Then again, the more populous the county, the more likely a judge is to specialize in one or two functions: "She's the truancy judge." "He handles most of the occupational driver's license hearings." Big city JPs will hand over to their municipal court counterparts the job of jail magistration. Big metropolitan JPs also don't have to look at dead bodies . . . *lots* of dead bodies. These differences can fester into deep animosities between JPs.

> *I'm not really a slick-talking politician. I'm just kind of an ol' country boy. When you go to the JP conferences, you can tell the big city people: slick dressers, some of them obviously attorney JPs. They're pretty easy to spot, even if they're dressed in their shorts.*
> —Hon. Russell Johnson, Coke County

Judge Margaret O'Brien estimates that there are half a million people living in her precinct in Dallas County. As large urban counties like Dallas and Harris and Travis mushroom in population, other counties, all of them in rural parts of the state, are, conversely, losing residents, a phenomenon that is not unique to Texas. The ratio of cow-to-human in some Texas Panhandle counties like Hartley, Castro, and Deaf Smith (its county seat, Hereford, is heralded as the "Beef Capital of the World") can be as high as eighty-to-one.

The ways in which a judge like O'Brien and her JP counterparts in the sparsely populated counties in the Panhandle and on the high, arid plains of the Llano Estacado interact with members of their communities can be radically different from one other. For example, JPs in urban precincts with limited free parking frequently hold tow hearings, which might sound completely alien to rural county JPs. Judge Kelly Crow points out that in very urban/suburban Fort Bend County, she has to deal with a lot of health and safety code violations. Smaller counties either don't have the officers to file these cases, or, if they do, they simply don't file them. In a rural county, a septic tank improperly installed by someone who isn't licensed might prompt a JP to haul the guilty party into court and demand that he get out there and repair the septic tank he had no business putting in. Whereas in a large county like Fort Bend, the law is the law, and violations carry penalties and have prescribed legal remedies.

Being a small-county JP presents its own challenges. Trisher Ford (Tyler County) once had to recuse herself from hearing a small claims case because she'd had a bad personal experience with one of the witnesses. When magistrating at the jail, a small-county JP like Ford will frequently find herself reading rights and setting bond for people she knows, and, just as important: people who know *her*.

Several of the classmates I went to school with have had to come before me. A couple of them have said, "You know me, Trish!"

I'm like, "I'm Judge Ford and I'm here to magistrate you. I don't know you. I'm the judge, and we're gonna go about this the way we're supposed to."

It's hard. Especially when you go to Walmart to buy ice cream, and there they are.

Yet there are sometimes advantages to knowing a defendant and the family when you're trying to decide how much bail to set or whether they pose a flight risk. Judge Ford cites this hypothetical:

Here's a guy from Louisiana who got caught with marijuana. He's got a criminal history a page long. I don't know if he's gonna show up for court. But ol' Suzy Q over here, caught with the same amount, she's been here all her life and she's always showed up for court. On a conviction for marijuana, she's gonna show up. I'm not gonna set her a high bond.

Bobby McIntosh (Uvalde County) doesn't think large-county JPs understand the difficulties that their small-county counterparts face when they're called to deal with things that come up on the civil side of the court, things they might see only once in a blue moon. Maybe they learned how to do something in the past, but now they're having to learn it all over again.

I have to go back and start from scratch on things we don't do very often. Recently, within a ten-day span, I had two individuals come in and file for a writ of restoration. That restores the power to the tenant after the landlord goes in and turns it off to try to make the tenant move instead of going through the legal eviction process. Before those two, in all the thirteen years I've been on the bench, I'd never had even one.

And JPs in small counties are sometimes, at least initially, left to their own devices to work through problems and issues for which there are adequate tools, mechanisms, and protocols already in place in large counties. Judge Russell Johnson in rural Coke County had to face hours and hours of run-around and buck-passing with regional and state officials when, early in the pandemic, a suspected virus-related death left him holding the bag when it came to responsibility for testing and sending the body along for autopsy.

Geographically myopic big city JPs can be appalled by the kind of informal judging that goes on in tumbleweed Texas. Likewise, small town JPs don't see assembly-line justice as anything they'd care to sign up for. Yet the simple fact is this: a small-county JP, like retired judge Sarah Miller (Erath County), might have slapped a $200 fine on her neighbor for burning his trash during a county burn-ban, because she just happens to *know* all her neighbors, and recusing yourself from all the cases in which you know folks just isn't an option. But by the same token, Judge O'Brien in Dallas County can't help it that she has to employ a rigorously systematic approach to getting through all the time-sensitive evictions filed in her court. It's just a fact that there are going to be a lot of forcible entry and detainer (eviction) suits filed in that precinct. O'Brien told me that on her very first day in office she had to hear over eighty.

The disparity between the two courts is reflected in the complex challenges that an advocacy group like the JPCA faces. Former Williamson County JP Patricia Ott spent a lot of time looking out for her judicial sisters and brothers before the Texas state legislature in her day; she points out how important it is to educate those who write the laws about the many different *kinds* of justice courts there are. "Every law doesn't work for every court," she says, "and, in fact, many of them can make things much more difficult for certain JPs." When it comes to educating the judges themselves, Ott says that one-size-fits-all classes don't make any sense. Continuing education for JPs should take into consideration the size of the county, and it should be noted that rural counties (especially in suburban areas) can become mid-sized counties; and that mid-sized counties like her own can become large counties. Round Rock had 26,000 people when Ott took office. Its current estimated population is over 130,000. (Incidentally, Judge Ott hasn't just been an advocate for JPs. She's worked hard at improving training for clerks, and even authored a clerk manual focused on justice court process.)

Beth Smith has watched her precinct in Hays County go from around four or five thousand people when she came into office in 1999 to between 50,000 and 55,000 today. Her caseload has grown with her population.

> *Our county is really growing. It used to be nothing but*
> *cedar posts and moonshine liquor around here.*
> —Hon. Ronnie Webb, Somervell County

Would It Be Better for JPs in Texas to Run as Non-Partisan Candidates?

Another point of disagreement that crops up between judges is whether justices of the peace should run without any mention of political party affiliation. Such a move would, no doubt, incite blowback in a state in which political parties wield significant power and influence, especially at the state level. Yet down at the county level, except in the area of campaign assistance and certain perceptual benefits that redound from being a member of a particular party in a particular county, perhaps party identity has been oversold, and losing partisan labels might be a blessing. With the demise of the Yellow Dog Democrat and the "rouging" of rural Texas, and the expansion of urban and suburban Democratic strongholds, JPs throughout the state are scrambling to brand themselves in the way that best serves their efforts to stay in office. Emblematic of this period of seismic political party realignment among Texas JPs is the fact that no fewer than nine elected county office holders in Lamar County decided to all hold hands in January 2011 and take the Republican plunge together. This group migration from blue to red included four of the county's six JPs.[1]

Judge Crow sides with those who'd like to see party affiliation for JPs go away.

I would love to see a movement for judges not to have to run along party lines, because I don't think it matters. What matters are your qual-

ifications, your knowledge of the law, your ability to evaluate certain situations.

Jon W. Johnson (Smith County) sides with Judge Crow.

As a judge, I'm non-political. One of the comments I made in my debate when I ran that raised eyebrows was my wish that judges would have to run without affiliating with a party. If you run as a conservative Republican, the first time you have a liberal person come in, the appearance is that you're not going to give them the same weight. You need to be unbiased.

> **I'm a UT grad but I grew up in Midland, so my politics are somewhere between John Wayne and Kinky Friedman. I believe in that Constitution. The system works. Just let it work.**
> —Hon. Mike Towers, Bandera County

Even more telling, only once in all of my two hundred phone conversations was the name of President Obama invoked—in this particular case, as an example in the judge's view of someone whose upbringing in a foreign country "just might have had an impact on his Americanism." Likewise, only once did a JP slip into our conversation that he was "a Trump guy." Conversely, there were only a couple of times in which the name of Donald Trump was negatively injected into our conversation, this by liberal judges who felt comfortable extending the parameters of our chat a bit. My interviews weren't about politics—or, more specifically, about political *parties*—except for a few fun campaign stories: One JP lost in his first race for the job by one vote. There was a recount, which resulted in a loss by *two* votes!

Doing away with expensive JP primaries and having everyone run in the general on the basis of their experience and their promises and their proposals, could, in fact, save their counties millions of dollars and put a smile on the face of the judge who told me that she always dreaded having to run for re-election. "*First* I have to campaign for the primary. *Then* I have to campaign for the primary run-off. And *then* I have to campaign for the general. I'm *so* tired!"

Should a Texas Justice of the Peace Wear the Robe? If So, How Often?

There are JPs in the state of Texas who *always* wear their robe. Yadi Rodriguez (Hutchinson County) believes it sets the right tone for the court, so anything she's doing as a judge, she does while donned in her black robe. Stephanie Frietze (El Paso County) says she wears the robe about 95 percent of the time; her last name is on it. It's a point of family pride. Other justices of the peace will only put on the robe to perform weddings. Others eschew the black vestment altogether. To them, it's sort of like an English judge's periwig—a silly anachronism.

Tim Walker (Lamb County) recalled that when he was in judge training, JPs were advised not to discourage people from calling them "judge," *and* to wear their robe whenever they're on the bench.

It establishes a decorum. Even though sometimes there will be lawyers in there who are so well-versed in the law, and they're gonna want to bluster and try to bum-rush, never be afraid to establish whose court this is.

Mary Hankins (Bowie County) wouldn't agree. She's one of those judges who forego the robe. "Out here where I am," she says, "if these people saw me in a robe, they'd laugh."

—⚬—

Some of the differences in opinion between judges end up being less about differences of opinion and more about differences in personality. Angie Pippin (Fisher County) and I talked about what I'm now calling "grumpy old man-judge syndrome": There are colorful curmudgeons whose cantankerous temperaments belie their true warm natures, but there are also—let's just cut to the chase—bona fide "you kids get off my lawn" judicial old coots. Judge Pippin understands the difference; she's gotten to know both varieties.

There have been men JPs I've known—oh my gosh, what a grumpy, old, rough attitude! They're like old roosters or something. Either they've been in office too long, or they're really not happy with their life, or—Just go fishing, dude! We'll sit around at our annual training, talking about cases and stuff, and they'll say, "What'd you do?" And I'll say whatever it was I did on a particular case, and they're like, "Well, I wouldn't have done that. *I would have thrown them in jail." Oh my God! We try not to do that except as a last resort!*

(I was fortunate. I got to talk to the judges who actually *wanted* me on their lawns.)

How Beneficial Is Sending JPs to School Each Year?

The mandated training sessions arranged by the Texas Justice Court Training Center are designed to help JPs in the state stay on top of the periodic changes in legislation that affect their courts, and keep them fresh and sharp on the many duties required of them. JPs are given helpful tools and practical strategies. Frieda Pressler (Kendall County) also likes the opportunities that the classes afford to mingle with other JPs and find out about how they're working through challenges within their own precincts.

Other JPs question the wisdom of a comprehensive approach to educating Texas justices of the peace. Not only was Debbie Horn (Potter County) a clerk for her predecessor JP for sixteen years before becoming a judge herself, she has been a teacher of both JP court clerks and those JPs who don't even have clerks (and have to do all their own paperwork). Her commitment to judicial education stands in marked contrast to the philosophy and day-to-day practices, she said, of the judge for whom she once clerked, "who didn't believe in continuing education for justices of the peace." Her former boss once confessed to her that he'd take out his hearing aid during class. This judge's dismissive attitude toward "judge school" was shared by other JPs Horn knew. She told me about the night before she was supposed to teach a class when one of her judge students walked up to her and asked if she minded if he slept through her presentation the next day, "because there's nothin' you're gonna teach me." There were other JPs, she said, who spent the class time "playing on their tablets and reading the newspaper."

Then there are JPs like Cyndi Poulton (Jackson County) who recognize the importance of paying attention in class. This is where they learn about changes in the laws and become familiar with those fine points of legal procedure they might someday have to deal with.

In the classes, I'm left saying, "What are you talking about? I've never heard of that. I might have heard about it, but I don't know what it is because we don't handle it in my court."

But I can tell you, when I get back from training, somewhere down the road somebody will walk through the door and say, "I need to do this thing," and then I'm like, crap! I should have listened better!

Texas JPs will always disagree, especially given the fact that justice courts are set up to give judges a wide berth for independent thought—a way of looking at matters that come before them, which, while respecting and applying the law when required, does afford them avenues for applying common sense and some creative problem-solving.

Disagreement among judges isn't necessarily a bad thing when it exposes JPs to other ways of thinking about all the things that go into being a Texas justice of the peace. But respect for one's colleagues remains paramount. The phrase, "Let us agree to disagree," as hackneyed as it has become, still has merit. And where better to understand that very human proclivity for disagreement than in one of the places expressly set up to air and resolve it?

NOTES

*Every county in Texas has a *constitutional* county court; in less populous counties this court has two functions. Its county judge and commissioners serve as the administrative arm of county government, while the county judge (who, like a JP, does not have to be a lawyer) also exercises judicial functions, such as hearing cases appealed from justice court and cases related to Class A and Class B misdemeanor charges. In the more populous counties of Texas, *statutory* county courts have been created (known as County Courts at Law) to aid the single constitutional court in its judicial functions. The presiding judge in these state legislature-created courts is required to have a law degree.

**A case that is appealed from justice court to county court is given a trial *de novo*—a "new" trial, which takes the case back to square one, as if the previous trial before the JP or justice court jury never happened.

17

Disrespecting the Robe

THE LATE COMEDIAN RODNEY Dangerfield famously "got no respect." Yet there were a lot of folks who respected him for his success in the profession. Texas justices of the peace are the Rodney Dangerfields of the state's judiciary, largely appreciated for all they do, but still finding themselves on occasion the brunt of discourtesy, incivility, and governmental disregard.

DISRESPECT FROM CONSTITUENTS

The most direct form of disrespect is boorish and impudent behavior from those who appear before the judges in courtroom and jailhouse, something with which Mark Holt (Walker County) is well acquainted.

I maintain a professionalism just because of my prior experience in law enforcement, and you have citizens you're dealing with. So you kind of have to temper it down a little bit. I had a little old lady come into the court over a roofing incident, where she didn't pay the roofer, and it turns out she was really eccentric, probably on the verge of losing her mind. I ruled against her because she flat-out didn't pay the guy who put a roof on her house. She said, "I hope you die and rot in hell."

And what do you say? She's like eighty-something years old. "I'm sorry"?

Former JP Debra Ravel (Travis County) was once pushed to the limit.

I remember one situation where this woman came in. She was bleeding. We got the fellow to come to court. He called his attorney. Apparently, there were criminal cases pending against him involving this same woman. The attorney ordered him to keep quiet and not to say anything during the hearing. So the woman took the stand and this man just wouldn't shut up. He kept raising his hand and saying, "Judge! Judge! I need to tell you something." I warned him and warned him. Finally, it was either let him speak or hold him in contempt and put him in jail. He said, "Judge, I just need to tell you a couple of things. I want you to know I never used a stick on her. The other thing is I may have pulled her hair out but I never beat her face." The deputy constable told me later that he'd never seen me with that expression before. Somebody should have nailed down my robe because it was all I could do to keep my cool in that room after what he'd admitted doing.

> *I've probably held people in contempt about five times. Knowing you can do it means you don't have to. I'm not big on the gavel. I'm more of a yeller. You can ask my daughters. I can make your ears bleed.* —Hon. Jackie Miller Jr., Ellis County

It isn't widely known that JPs have contempt authority just like other Texas judges. In my conversations, I enjoyed finding out which JPs ever had reason to exercise this authority to maintain order in their courtroom, and who came dangerously close. Sparky Dean (Taylor County) sought the counsel of the assistant district attorney who prosecuted in his court when there was no doubt that one of the defendants in a trial was lying under oath.

We had traffic court this month and the guy kept lying over and over again. Took a recess and called the assistant DA into my office. "I kept giving the guy an out. I'm fixing to hold him in contempt of court."

She said, "Judge you can do that, or you can file perjury, which is a third-degree felony."

I'm thinking, Oh crap, we're just talking traffic court here. I did hit him for contempt of court and fined him $100. I said, "Dude, you can't do that under oath. Everybody in here knows you're lying."

In JP court you've got direct contempt and indirect contempt. Direct is where they're actually right there, saying things like, "Judge, you're a blankety blank." You can fine them $100 and/or give them three days in jail.

I asked one of the district judges, "How do you keep decorum in your court?"

He said, "What do you mean?"

"Well, I have people go off and they won't listen to me."

The judge laughed. He said, "I don't have that problem in my court. I hold them in contempt."

"But I do too: $100, three days in jail."

"Well, that's your problem. My contempt is six months."

Stuart Posey (Victoria County) shared the story of a woman who literally lost control of herself in his courtroom. She was in her mid-fifties, described by Posey as a "cougar"—in this case, though, a cougar with some very sharp claws.

She was married but she and her husband were going through a divorce. She was living in the house, he was not. She brought in her seventeen-year-old boyfriend, who had a drug problem. The husband, who still owned part of the house, wanted him evicted. I listened to the case and I listened to the family members and I made my decision to evict him. The mother went off on me—total lack of respect in the courtroom and my constable not really taking charge of things the way he should have. I finally had to order him to get the woman out of the courtroom. Otherwise, there was going to be a riot. I went ballistic. I've never yelled like that before because I'd never seen that kind of disrespect in a courtroom. I was astounded that they would be yelling at a judge.

Judge Posey said the incident gave him a headache that lasted for four days and got him so scared that he went in for an MRI.

Jeff Monk (Johnson County) isn't averse to holding people in contempt for misbehaving in court, but this doesn't happen until after he's issued multiple warnings. He told me that he'll look at the offender and say, "This is your last warning." At that point it's all about that button—pushing that last button.

I have a phrase: "If you push my button, I will light you like a rocket at NASA on launch day." Once they do, my gavel is used only for contempt. That's to let my constable in the courtroom know that it's time to step up here and put this person in handcuffs.

The line between fining someone for contempt and putting them behind bars is the demeanor of the individual. I've held someone in contempt for $20. I've held someone in contempt for $100 and three days in jail. I understand the emotions and I will allow a certain broadness, but as a judge, you have to keep people on track. You have to be the cut horse. You pull one cow out of the herd and you're not gonna let it get back in. You're gonna separate it.

Judges are often tested when they magistrate, and are required to read rights to some pretty angry and refractory customers. Rick Hill (Brazos County) has dealt with a few.

I had a lady one time who called me an f'in' idiot. I knew that if I got judgy with this woman and tried to have a conversation with her, then that would prove I'm an idiot. I said, "Ma'am, would you like to request a court appointed attorney?"

She said, "I would like to request that you burn in hell, MF."

I said, "I'll take that as a yes," and moved on. If I had said, "How dare you disrespect me like that!" she wouldn't care. It's a bad day for these people. I'm not going to engage in that. They call it black robe-itis or judge-itis or whatever, but when you get to the point where you feel like you're more important than other people, that's a problem.

Temper is a dangerous thing, but mostly for the person losing it. J. Treg Hudson works in a small court in a small county, Mason, and often has to answer the phone himself. If it's about a ticket the person has received, he informs the caller that he can't discuss it because he's the judge. It often starts with the caller being cussing-mad, but then, hearing that he's actually talking to the JP, he'll suddenly become docile and respectful. On one occasion, Judge Hudson got an early earful, but the caller—a female this time—was the bigger loser in the exchange.

I don't answer the phone as the judge. I answer the phone with "Justice Court, Mason County," or something like that. So I get a lot of people who just go off on who they think is the clerk. I had a lady go off on me. She was just livid she'd gotten a ticket between here and Fredericksburg—just irate about it. I'm trying to get a word in edgewise to tell her that I'm the judge and I can't talk to her about the details of her ticket, if you want to plead guilty—

All that stuff. And, kind of typical of a lot of people in our culture, it's always somebody else's fault, the deputy's fault or the trooper's fault. She was so mad at that trooper.

She said, "I. WAS. NOT. GOING. NINETY-ONE MILES AN HOUR! I WAS GOING EIGHTY-EIGHT!"

I said, "Well ma'am, first of all: I'm the judge. And now you've just kind of ruined me so far as my neutrality." I told her, "If you plead not-guilty at this point, I'm most likely going to recuse myself because of what you've told me. But I will tell you that I'll probably be the prosecutor's star witness, because you just admitted to me that you were going eighty-eight." It's just amazing that people get so indignant over something they think is a mistake. It's the old strain-at-a-gnat and swallow-a-camel mentality.

Donna Wessels (Wharton County) was sold on video magistration even before the pandemic put most Texas JPs into that same boat. Her preference has always been for not having to head over to the jail and get herself too up-close and personal with not the most well-behaved members of her community.

There was this one wild lady. She told me I was fat and gross and the whole bit. Because she had a new charge on her, I had to see her again face-to-face. When I got to the jail, she was attacking one of the guards. Oh my God, this same crazy lady again! She was a handful. The next time I saw her they had her in some kind of straitjacket thing and she looked like a mermaid. Eventually I think they sent her somewhere else.

Judge Wessels thinks it was probably some kind of mental health facility.

> *Once I was so frustrated with a defiant litigant who just would not stop arguing that I banged my gavel so hard to get his attention that I hit the base off-center, causing it to fly up into the air and across the room, barely missing my clerk's head!* —Hon. Jeff Williams, Harris County

During her thirty-six years on the bench, retired Justice of the Peace Suzan Thompson (Matagorda County) has had to hold several people in direct contempt. She didn't like to do it as a rule, but there have been times when she was inescapably compelled by circumstances. "Everybody's in a bad mood once in a while," she said, "but you still need to check your attitude." And if you're incapable of doing that . . .

This is a true story: I had these two brothers in for truancy. I'd say they were regulars. The mom was there, and, bless her heart, she was doing the best she could. She did have a drug problem, and these boys were doing the best they could. The boys approached the bench with the mom between them, and this young man—the one brother—he had a toothpick in his mouth and he was playing with it to the degree that I thought he was going to choke in my court. I said, "Please take the toothpick out of your mouth and place it on the bench. You can get it when you leave."

He didn't remove the toothpick. Instead, he cleared his throat, preparatory to spitting on the judge. "Don't even think about it!" Thompson admonished him. The boy responded with profanity. Judge Thompson held him in contempt and called the bailiff over.

When the bailiff went over to grab his arm and place him under arrest, the war was on. The boy resisted. His brother reacted. I had three police officers in the courtroom and there one of the officers was, right on top of the other brother. Mama jumped on the back of one of the other officers and got him down on the ground. It was a free-for-all.

One of the attorney tables got shoved off to the side, catching and bruising the finger of one of Judge Thompson's clerks. A visiting judge—a retired DPS trooper who'd come to observe—stopped observing and leapt into the fray. Judge Thompson discovered him "down on the ground with his knee in this kid's back." She could hear him saying, "You just need to move *one* time. That's all I'm wishing for!" Reinforcements arrived and "Mama and her two boys all went to jail for contempt and for disturbing the proceedings." The mother served three days, the boys were sent to juvenile detention.

Judge Thompson's story has an epilogue:

About three months ago I was here in my office in the municipal court when a young man walked in. I looked up and I said, "Well, look who's here."

He said, "Judge, how are you?"

I said, "Better yet, where have you been?"

He said, "I got my life together. I got a good job. I made right what was wrong. I learned my lesson." He's doing well. He didn't have any animosity, now that it had been several years. We talked for some time.

DISRESPECT FROM THE COMMISSIONERS COURT

Problematic constituents aren't the only source of headaches and jangled nerves for Texas JPs. Judicial headaches can also come from those who control the purse strings of the county: the county judge and his or her fellow commissioners. After "Your Honor, I was *not* going that fast!" the sentence most frequently heard by a Texas justice of the peace is, "The county can't afford it."

Granted, quite often it can't. As a result, county facilities remain in want of renovation. Some JPs are forced to work out of poorly retrofitted public buildings, clunkily converted doublewides, or, in some cases, their own homes. Texas county courthouses—among the most ornamentally interesting public buildings in America—can reek of mold and mildew, have roofs that leak, or Victorian garrets rife with avian trespassers. Computer systems and software need upgrading.

There isn't money for hiring additional clerks or for providing extra training for the ones a JP has. Some judges have to make do without any clerks at all. Wayne Denson (Lavaca County) told me that he's now into his second term, and every year his civil docket almost doubles. Still, he can't get the county to give him even a part-time clerk to help out. He wonders how long he'll stay in the job without clerical assistance.

Even though ours is a court of no record, we still have lots of records to keep. Most of my time is spent with paperwork. If I had a clerk, that would just be Heaven!—Hon. *Katy Marlow, Foard County*

The list of things that Texas justice courts in the state's more financially crunched counties are forced to go without is lengthy and demoralizing. Yet there are also times when you're given to wonder if the money is there, but the county commission simply isn't willing to share it with their justices of the peace. One judge told me that he's fairly certain his commissioners don't have a clue as to what their JPs actually do. Another very busy judge who has no clerk bristles over the times that constituents can't reach her, and then they whine to their commissioner, who makes the knee-jerk (and patently wrong-headed) assumption that the judge is sloughing off. Then there's Kendall County, which continues to grow, more people die, the jail gets more crowded, and yet, Judge Teri Nunley told me, the commissioners remain unmoved.

They still think that being a JP is a part-time job. In the old days a lot of JPs had other professions because the job really wasn't full time. But I'm up here all day every day, and what's really frustrating is that we're on call 24–7. Our magistration numbers have gone up substantially, so we can spend half our day at the jail, and we magistrate on the weekends. It's just not a good solution when they're not giving us help or hiring us a medical examiner. The commissioners in every county need to recognize the importance of what we do.

Judge Nunley said her county commissioners were thoughtful enough to hire one new clerk . . . to be shared among all four justices of the peace in the county.

You take what you can get.

And sometimes you pray you don't lose your job, or, rather, your very precinct. At one point, Galveston County had nine justices of the peace. Thanks to retrenchment, they now have only four. Kathleen McCumber is the luckiest of the four; she only has to travel to one court to perform her duties as JP. Billy A. Williams, however, is required to divide his time among offices in Galveston, La Marque, and Crystal Beach.

After Sharon Maxey (Falls County) and her constable husband, James, sold their family business, which doubled as their precinct's justice court and constable's office, their county commission was anything but helpful in getting them another building to do the people's business.

They said they weren't going to provide us with an office. "You're going to have to drive to the courthouse every day." We butted heads for many years, because that's not even where my constituents are! They were of a mindset that they weren't going to provide an office, even if I had to hold court on a street corner. Finally, God blessed me with enough money to ask the Mennonites, who lived in Lott, to build me a small office. This office belongs to me and the county doesn't pay for anything but my utilities. My husband's [constable's] office is here as well.

When we were broken into a few years back, we had to pay for repairs out of our own pockets. Every year the county commission gives us a form to fill out for budget requests. We might as well make paper airplanes out of it!

Texas JPs aren't afraid to complain. In 2014, the four justices of the peace in Johnson County filed an official grievance with their commissioners. They pointed out that not only were their salaries significantly lower than those of JPs in counties of comparable population, the Johnson County JPs made thousands of dollars less than the commissioners, whose job it is to decide how much their justices of the peace get to make.[1]

In the meantime, a lot of JPs—as we saw in the case of Judge Maxey—are forced to play with the cards they've been dealt. This often includes making do on salaries that hardly suffice, that require some Texas JPs to hold down second jobs to pay the bills. Every county commission uses its own criteria for deciding how much to compensate those county employees who wear the robes. Sometimes the decision-making process is a rational one; at other times it doesn't make any sense at all. And there are some counties, some would say, that pay their JPs *too* much.

Yes, you read that right.

According to the Texas Association of Counties 2020 salary survey, the JP for Loving County, Texas's least populated county (with around 190 people)[2] takes home over $98,000 a year. That same survey reveals that the lone JP in Motley County—with around six times the people of Loving County—makes only $17,000 a year.[3] Granted, Chuck Ream, the judge who nobly serves this county located just south of the Panhandle, indicated that the job really *is* just part time (although, like almost all the justices of the peace in one-JP counties, he's expected to be on call 24–7). Judge Ream says that his office hours at the courthouse in Matador are from 1:00 to 3:00 weekday afternoons, which is good, because his salary requires him to work another job as well; he serves as maintenance director for the Motley County Independent School District.

The differences in JP salaries get even more dramatic when you compare populous counties—where, arguably, justices of the peace *ought* to be making a lot more—with sparsely populated counties about which one could make a case for the total opposite. In the six Texas counties with populations over one million—Bexar, Collin, Dallas, Harris, Tarrant, and Travis—JPs are quite comfortably compensated; their annual salaries exceed, sometimes by quite a bit, $100,000. But in Williamson County, which, after experiencing a whopping 44 percent increase in population over the last ten years, is now home to nearly 615,000 Texans[4] (and continues to grow), its four overworked JPs each take home a comparatively underwhelming $91,468 a year.[5] At the other end of the population spectrum, Kenedy County has, at last count, 371 people.[6] In terms of population, it is number 252 out of 254 counties. Even so, it has four justices of the peace, each of whom makes $53,404 a year.[7] They are paid by their generous county commissioners a total of $213,616 a year to serve an average of 93 people each.

Lucky are those JPs who have a special, even consanguineous, relationship with their commissioners. But there are other justices of the peace who benefit from the simple fact that their county commission understands the importance of adequately funding their offices and fairly compensating them for their work.

Many of the county commissioners who actually treat their JPs respectfully do so simply because they're decent guys (and gals). For example, the two JPs in the sister Panhandle counties of Dallam and Hartley, whose county line bisects the aptly named city of Dalhart, share duties, such as jail magistration, with the two county judges. According to Dallam County JP Carol Smith, this was actually the county judges' idea! The result of this four-partner arrangement is that Judge Smith in Dallam and Judge Beth Bezner Moore in Hartley County get time off—a precious commodity for JPs who serve in single-JP counties.

DISRESPECT FROM ONE'S OWN STAFF

One of the saddest forms of disrespect for JPs is that displayed by a judge's own clerks. This is unfortunate, because a judge's clerical staff are usually regarded as the backbone of the court—indispensably smart, loyal, and scrupulously conscientious attendants to the judges they serve. But there are, alas, a few bad apples who use the job for illicit, personal enrichment. I spoke to a judge in Uvalde County who discovered that not one, but ultimately *two* of his clerks had been stealing from the court coffers—taking payment on tickets and writing out receipts from a dummy receipt book, then entering dismissal in the docket and pocketing the money.

DISRESPECT FROM THE TEXAS STATE LEGISLATURE

Texas JPs suffer the slings and arrows of their state legislature in two different ways. Mike Smith (Harrison County) decries poorly written laws that sow confusion for the judges whose job it is to interpret them. When we spoke in 2019, he cited a good example: the recent raise of the legal smoking age to twenty-one, which carves out an exemption for young men and women in the military. Where is the exemption in effect? Everywhere? Only on a military base? Why isn't the law clearer?

> *Every two years when the Texas legislature convenes, it's like a side-show. Get your popcorn and watch them go.*—Hon. Jim Cavanaugh, Brown County

The bigger problem inflicted by the legislature is the passage of laws that negatively impact the operation of the state's justice courts either through overburdening them with even more responsibility or by casting nets around the citizenry that JPs are left to untangle. Most insidious and consequential are those laws often cobbled for the purpose of patchwork revenue-raising in a state that tries assiduously to avoid the institution of a state income tax. One law, insipidly named the "Driver Responsibility Program" (whose ostensible purpose was to fund trauma centers around the state), involved slapping severe surcharges on repeat traffic offenders. The program pushed the poorest Texans into downward spirals that progressed from fines and suspended licenses to heavy fees and jail time. The program wreaked havoc on millions of low-income Texans by thrusting them into inescapable cycles of debt. After years of complaints from members of both parties from all corners of the state—with some of the loudest coming from the justices of the peace, who scrambled to find ways to help the most vulnerable of their constituents—it was finally repealed.

> *I knew one case where a guy had almost $30,000 in surcharges.*
> —Hon. Larry Cryer, Chambers County

Talyna Carlson (Gregg County) spoke for a number of her JP colleagues:

If you're working, let's say at Walmart, you don't have enough money to pay the $400 fine to the city or the county [on the ticket] and then have to pay the state of Texas $350 a year for three years in a row and pay for insurance. So I'm very grateful that those surcharges are going away. It was horrible for these people. You'd have a single mom, or a guy walking into your court in his work boots and the soles are worn out, and then he's got those surcharges to worry about.

The only thing good about the Texas state legislature, as some JPs will tell you, is their propensity to sometimes change their mind.

DISRESPECT FROM EVEN THE DANGED DISTRICT ATTORNEY

Texas justices of the peace can get dissed for traveling outside their lane, so to speak, since others in the criminal justice industry tend to have their own ideas about the kinds of things that JPs ought and ought not to be doing. Bob Shea Jr. (Taylor County) found this out after only six months on the job.

This sheriff's deputy from another county needed a search warrant for suspected child pornography. He came to me because I was only about five miles from where the house was. I said sure, I'll sign it. So they conducted their search and everything was good and then I get a call from the district attorney and he says, "Why did you sign that warrant?"

"Well, I could do that."

He said, "I don't like that, if you don't mind. Let's let a district judge do that."

And I said, well, okay. He was really ticked off. I think he was a turf person. I've never done another one. I tell them they have to go to the district judge.

Trisher Ford (Tyler County) told me that she had to conduct court for several years without any district attorney at all. "Our DA was missing in action for the last four-and-a-half years. The DA just didn't show up for court. The new DA is still trying to catch up."

DISRESPECTFUL PORTRAYALS OF JPS IN THE MEDIA

TV and the movies have played their part in perpetuating the kinds of stereotypes of JPs that contribute to a lack of respect for the profession in Texas. At their least offensive they depict justices of the peace as grizzled old dudes who marry you and your honey and pretty much do nothing else. Or they play less innocuously on the mythology of dime novels and pulp magazines, drawing straight from the Judge Roy Bean school of six-shooter adjudicating.

In a February 1960 episode of *The Danny Thomas Show* that served as the pilot for *The Andy Griffith Show*, Griffith plays an embryonic version of Sheriff Andy Taylor, a lawman who, lo and behold, is also the local justice of the peace. Andy's "court" could just as easily be located deep in the heart of Texas were it not for a throwaway reference to some strange beverage called "pop."* Ol' Andy hauls Thomas in for running a stop sign, and infers from the wad of cash Thomas flashes that a shakedown of this big city high roller might pay off nicely. As in other media portrayals of justices of the peace, Sheriff-cum-Judge Taylor is depicted as a countrified rube, though he does come off as slightly less clodhoppery than Archie Campbell's "Justus O'Peace" on the cornpone comedy show *Hee Haw*.

Not that this latter reputation doesn't have the occasional tablespoon of authenticity, as Larry Cryer (Chambers County) will tell you. And he'll also be the one to tell you how to fix it:

A lot of the criticism that justices of the peace have gotten, and get every day, are still old-hat, dust-on-the-shelf from TV shows like Hee Haw. *So many JPs have left such a poor record—the way they dress, the way they act, chewing tobacco, smoking cigars, using spittoons.*

Cryer tells judges who inadvertently remind folks of those negative media impressions that it would be helpful for them to wear a necktie every day, along with some decent clothes.

DISRESPECT FROM THOSE WHO DON'T EVEN KNOW THEY'RE SHOWING DISRESPECT

Most people don't *mean* to disrespect the judge. Or the court. Or to drop dead ticks all over your courtroom table. "We called him the 'Ticks Man,'" said Debbie Horn (Potter County).

We had an eviction suit on someone who lived in one of the family services homes for people who are mentally ill. He was filing all kinds of paper and wanting to countersue the landlord. He comes to court wearing this big, thick wool coat that looks like a horse blanket, and ticks were dropping off onto our table. He'd told his landlord that his apartment had ticks, and they kept sending the exterminator but he wouldn't let him in.

He couldn't *let them in because the ticks had surrounded him like circled covered wagons, and he couldn't step outside that circle.*

He also gave me papers that said he had committed suicide five years prior in Oregon and that he was no longer alive.

Respect *and* disrespect go both ways, and quite often, you give as you get. Katy Marlow (Foard County) told me this.

I just really believe that if I show respect, I get respect back. You, as the judge, might be upset at the moment because the person has done something bad, but you remember that we're all human. It's okay. We'll get through this.

Food for thought, throughout the state of Texas. Including Morris County.

Its county seat: Daingerfield.

NOTE

*Texans, when last I checked, don't drink "pop" or even "soda." They drink Coke and Dr. Pepper.

18

Goin' Rogue

If I know a guy has done something wrong, I'm going to jar his ass . . . I don't want this bond thing to be punitive, but dammit, if someone does something wrong, we don't owe him anything . . . I don't think there's a case in JP court worth a jury trial . . . People get all upset because I won't marry a black and a white . . . I'm not an angry man, just frustrated.

—ROBERT COLE, DALLAS COUNTY.[1]

DALLAS COUNTY HAS GIVEN us some of the state's most colorful and controversial judges, but Judge Robert Cole had a reputation for roguery on the bench that put him in a category all his own. His quick-draw temper and antiquated views would seem to place him in the earlier, wilder days of Texas, but in fact he missed that era by more than a century; he was on the bench in the 1970s and '80s. Cole felt it was his calling to solve all the ills of society, but in his own way. He had a special affinity for his fellow landlords and a special abhorrence for marijuana and "long-haired hippies." They made him "see red."

Another JP from the pantheon of memorable Dallas judges was the honorable Bill Richburg, otherwise known as "the law west of the Trinity." Richburg didn't appreciate being compared to Judge Bean. "Roy Bean was a tyrant," the judge pointed out. "*I* like to help people." Richburg, who served from 1944 to 1973, signed 125,000 peace bonds, held court seven days a week, chewed out welfare cheats, and exercised a form of bygone paternalism that skirted the rules but often got results. Some of those results came courtesy of a fake lie detector device he set up in his courtroom, which he said helped to get a whole bunch of folks to fess up in court.[2]

Bending rules, breaking rules, and even creating your own set of rules simply goes with the territory when you're a Texas JP. There are those judges who color scrupulously within the lines while others blithely color outside those lines, and then there are those who have been known to toss the whole judicial coloring book into the county dumpster.

> *When I give a speech before the local bar—even though some of those guys think that JP courts are different from district courts and county courts at law—we do have to abide by the rules.*
> —Hon. Fernando Villarreal, McLennan County

Goin' rogue, as we see with the mixed bag that is the biography of Judge Richburg, isn't always a bad thing. Sometimes, circumstances require a little creative problem-solving that generally won't get a judge into *too* much trouble. Billy S. Ball (Angelina County) told me about the time he simply couldn't help himself. There was a certain courtroom situation and a particular response he felt was warranted.

I had a fight in the courtroom. This was when I first took office and I had an elderly constable. I had this young male about twenty-five, twenty-six years old. I revoked his bond and we were going to put him back in jail. The constable probably hadn't put the cuffs on anybody in about twenty years, so he was kind of fumbling around there. The young guy was kind of pushing the constable, fixing to head out the door. I thought, Well, hell, I better get down there before the constable gets hurt.

I went to put the cuffs on the guy, and he grabbed me by the lapels of my new suit and the only thing I could think was: Don't you tear my new suit! *There was a big scuffle. We were wrassling around, all over the courtroom.* Man, don't you tear my new suit! *I thought I was going to mess around and get hurt fighting with this young guy, so I just took him out. (I was raised on policing in the sixties. I couldn't remember what they had or hadn't outlawed.)*

I look up and all of the sudden, the doors are flying open. The clerks had called over to the jail. Here come all the jailers, but by that time I already had the guy handcuffed.

It seems like back in the old days, JPs had a little more latitude when it came to devising unconventional solutions. Tracy Byrd (Randall County) told me about a judge back in the seventies:

[He] had a box on his bench, and kids would come in with their tickets and he'd ask them for their driver's license and they'd hand it to him and he'd throw it into that box and ask them to come back in a month, "and then maybe I'll give it back to you." Unofficially, I guess, that was "suspending somebody's license," but he wouldn't file anything on them. He'd just keep their license while they thought about what they'd done.

And going rogue with a wink and a swagger can apply to *aspiring* JPs, as well. Singer-songwriter and humorist Kinky Friedman launched an unsuccessful bid for justice of the peace in 1986 in Kerr County with the campaign slogan, "If you elect me the first Jewish justice of the peace, I'll reduce the speed limit to 54.95!"* He also promised over the course of what he called his "tragically misguided adventure" to keep Kerrville out of war with Fredericksburg.[3]

When judges get the impulse to misbehave, they can do so in a myriad of ways. Judicial misconduct can range from moments of relaxed propriety to temporary lapses of judgment to the premeditated perpetration of multiple homicide. In the case of the first, a JP was privately sanctioned by the State Commission on Judicial Conduct in September 2018 for having worn a Halloween costume "during the performance of her judicial duties."[4] One wonders what kind of costume would provoke such a scolding, since JPs have long been known to dress up on Halloween to perform the judicial duty of marrying folk. Sherri LeNoir (Limestone County) said that one Halloween she officiated the wedding of a costumed couple in the city park while dressed as the Queen of Sheba. Former JP John Payton (Collin County) performed a New Year's Eve wedding in which the couple, who were adherents of a naturist religion, had no qualms about asking the judge to strip down to fig leaves to marry them in their own fig-leafed but otherwise wholly Edenic state. They even brought him a set of fig leaves to wear. He politely declined, though one wonders if a more adventurous JP might have taken them up on the offer.

Some Texas JPs find that they have to resign from office following involvement with their brother in defrauding state lotteries. Such was the case with Fayette County JP Tommy Tipton who in 2017 pleaded guilty to felony crimes related to a rigging scheme that targeted the multi-state Hot Lotto game.[5]

In a category of villainy all its own, one finds perhaps the most notorious act of criminality ever committed by a Texas justice of the peace in modern times: the cold-blooded act of triple murder. Kaufman County's Eric Lyle Williams committed offenses against humankind, which have landed him smack-dab on death row, that involved plotting and carrying out the revenge killings of two prosecutors in his county in 2013. Kaufman County District Attorney Mike McLelland and Assistant DA Mark Hasse had together won a burglary conviction against the JP for stealing $600 worth of county computer monitors, a crime that was captured on courthouse surveillance cameras. Williams was forced to resign from office and surrender his law license. The death of Williams's third victim, McLelland's wife, Cynthia, was a real head-scratcher, even for Williams's accomplice, his wife, Kim.

Kim Williams said that her husband's plan was hatched right after the conviction. She told true crime writer Kathryn Casey that Eric likened himself to a character in the movie *Tombstone*. He carried out his assassination of Hasse on January 31 in broad daylight near the county courthouse. Williams was dressed in black "like the character in the movie." The killings of McLelland and his wife took place during a home invasion two months later.[6]

Ms. Williams testified that Eric intended to carry out additional killings, but his plans were thwarted when a friend of his, who'd been renting a storage unit on the murder-obsessed JP's behalf, went to the police. Something just didn't seem right to Eric's Texas national guardsman buddy. Maybe it was the size of the arsenal Williams had stockpiled inside: sixty-one firearms, a crossbow, jars full of homemade napalm, and thousands of rounds of ammo.[7]

The judge who had presided over Williams's burglary case, District Judge Glen Ashworth, was apparently next in line for extermination. Ms. Williams testified that her husband "was gonna shoot [the judge] with a crossbow, then bore his stomach out, and put napalm in it. He thought about kidnapping him and bringing him back to the house and putting him in the freezer . . . he was going to be buried in the backyard—in the flower bed."[8]

In Irving Berlin's musical *Annie Get Your Gun*, Annie Oakley sings, "You Can't Get a Man with a Gun." In 2007, Michelle Araujo, justice of the peace in Floyd County, did "get her man" with a gun: three shots into her husband's stomach. She pleaded guilty to aggravated assault and was sentenced to ten years of probation and a $5,000 fine. Needless to say, Araujo had to surrender her position as JP, a job she'd held since 1999.[9]

The State Commission on Judicial Conduct has privately sanctioned a number of justices of the peace over the last quarter of a century for a variety of rule infractions and intriguing acts of judicial impropriety. Of course, "privately sanctioned" means the JP's name is kept off the ten o'clock news. Here's a sampling:

- Releasing magistrated family members on personal recognizance bonds or without any bond at all. (It perhaps goes without saying that justices of the peace who perform magistrations have no business Mirandizing and setting bail for family members, including, in one case, a JP's own son.)

- Reducing fines on defendants who gave donations to non-profit organizations supported by the judge, including a scholarship program the judge himself had started.

- Ordering various individuals in his court into "time-out," and when two of them tried to leave during the time-out period, ordering his bailiff to handcuff them.

- While acting as magistrate, routinely opining to defendants that a local towing company was charging excessive fees.

- Ordering defendants in bad check cases to pay the face value of the checks to the court, rather than make restitution in this amount to the petitioning merchants.

- Conducting court proceedings while barefooted and wearing a T-shirt and shorts.

- Sending a fictitious notice to someone critical of the judge, leading him to believe he'd been charged with a criminal offense and was facing possible arrest. The threatened individual was a county commissioner.

- While traveling on a state highway at night, chasing, stopping, and arresting another motorist for committing a traffic offense. During the incident, the judge displayed a handgun for which he did not have a license.

- During a hearing, making sarcastic comments to a juvenile defendant charged with a traffic offense and then following the defendant and his parents out to the parking lot, where a verbal confrontation ensued.
- Accepting personal property from a criminal defendant in lieu of payment of court costs. (The imagination runs wild.)

Behavior that warrants public sanction usually involves judicial misconduct taken to an even more egregious level.

In June of 2018, the commission issued a public warning and order of additional education to one of Kleberg County's justices of the peace over a statement made by the judge from the bench during a small claims jury trial that "this is redneck court." The judge testified that he used this particular statement to open court every day. Since the case had to do with a tenant vacating a landlord's rental property before the expiration of the lease due to the property owner's purported "aggressive and intimidating conduct," and since that conduct involved the flying of a Confederate flag on the property, the question of the day became, "Redneck—good? Or redneck—bad?" The judge contended that the term *wasn't* derogatory.

Considering the circumstances of this particular case, the commission didn't agree.

A former judge in Trinity County in 2013 asked a favor of a colleague JP, who was preparing to magistrate a woman who'd been arrested for DWI. He said he'd like to magistrate her himself.

Which he did.

He set a personal recognizance bond for her, later explaining to the commission that he did this because he knew her and knew she "wouldn't run."

She was his girlfriend.

The commission received two different complaints on a former Harris County JP, which resulted in a double public admonition in March 2012. In the first case, a Vietnamese American attorney representing a client on a disorderly conduct charge found himself engaged in a verbal contretemps with the judge over the attorney's need to subpoena various school records that he believed benefited his client's case. According to the lawyer, the judge resorted to profanity, called the lawyer "boy," and told him that "those records are none of your goddamned business." The attorney also reported that the judge had called the defendant a "little brat-nosed, punk-ass kid with a foul mouth and a bad attitude." Things escalated from there.

A year later, this judge found himself in even more hot water with the commission. This time the complainant was the mother of a thirteen-year-old boy who was appearing in the judge's court after being charged with "disrupting school transportation." While waiting for her son's case to be called, the mother listened to the judge:

1. ask an African American parent "if she was on welfare and expected the government to pay her fine,"
2. wonder aloud if a Hispanic parent had "six or seven kids," and
3. tell a Pakistani American parent that her son should be "stoned to death."

Later, the woman said the judge "yelled at her son because his hair was long and fell over his eye."

A Brazos County judge was admonished by the commission for referring to a Texas Parks and Wildlife Department game warden as the "bird and turtle sheriff." The judge also objected to the fact that the warden was writing far more alcohol citations than "bird and turtle" tickets.

A judge in Montgomery County was publicly admonished in March of 2002 for "sleeping on the bench." Although he denied ever falling asleep during a trial, his clerks observed and discussed among themselves the judge's "propensity to fall asleep." In a sworn statement given to the commission, the JP wrote that "it is the judge's opinion that no one should say when the judge may rest during a twenty-four-hour period."

The commission saw things differently.

It was the determination of a review tribunal appointed by the Texas Supreme Court that a justice of the peace in Jefferson County be removed from office upon recommendation by the commission and be barred from holding future judicial office in the state of Texas. The opinion, effective immediately, came down in April of 2004. The judge was found to have used abusive and obscene language in the courtroom, failed to follow the law, exhibited incompetence in the law, attempted to interfere in the lawful arrest of an individual, and participated in or used corporal punishment in certain truancy matters before the court. Accusations of numerous incidents of roguish behavior from this judge abound: handcuffing children accused of not attending school, threatening to hit juveniles on the head with his gavel, punching a juvenile in the chest, hitting another on the head with his knuckles, administering corporal punishment to juvenile twin brothers in his chambers, threatening to jail children, actually jailing one alleged truant for seven days before she could finally make bond, tossing a local newspaper reporter out of his courtroom, and telling magistrated inmates at the county correctional facility that he intended to engage in sex with their wives while they were incarcerated.[10]

Though barred from ever being a judge again, this former JP, as of this writing, serves as mayor of a city in Jefferson County.[11]

One former Brazos County justice of the peace encountered trouble when he allowed pride in his alma mater to get the best of him. When magistrating a college student charged with taking a much-venerated school ring from another student who was matriculating at a fairly well-known university located in that county and "throwing it in the grass," the judge asked the accused if he knew what an "Aggie" ring was. Of course, the implication was: "Do you know how *important* this ring is?" When the defendant answered that he did not, the judge held up his right hand to bring the student in close proximity to the judge's own school ring. Later, he explained to the commission his reason for educating the young non-Aggie standing before him: "The Aggie ring is a manifestation of one of the highest traditions in the community. It is an outward, visible symbol of the wearer's commitment to the school."

The judge's Aggie pride was further confirmed when he set the young man's bond at $50,000, which is $45,000 over the bond threshold for such an offense.

One case that didn't make it to the commission, which a currently serving JP told me about, involved a judge in the South Plains region of the state who threw a woman in jail for contempt because she used profanity on the witness stand. There was actually a reason for the profanity: she was quoting verbatim the threat made by the individual who was, in fact, on trial for "assault by threat." But this judge had a reputation for banning all cursing in his courtroom, even, apparently, cursing that occurs between quotation marks.

—⁂—

In Lubbock County, two JPs formed the very definition of contrast. Susan Rowley, who worked in their courts as a prosecutor, outlined the stark differences between them:

There was one judge in particular—Judge [Jim] Hansen, a good guy who's fair. He really knew the law, really knew what he was doing, and we got along so well. It was like a well-oiled machine.

But the one I replaced couldn't care less what the law was, he was against drinking and he made sure that anyone who had a drinking offense would get a conviction. He'd throw the book at them without even reading their case. When I was a prosecutor, I'd come in and I'd say, "I want to give this kid a 'deferred.' It's his first offense." He'd say no. And I'd say, "Judge, you're just saying this because it's an alcohol case. You aren't considering the full range of punishment options."

There were other apparent issues with this judge. He left office with a 27,000-case backlog. A great many of the Class C misdemeanor charges that came into the court had gone far beyond the statute of limitations. There were complaints that had never been signed by the attending officers. According to Rowley, some of these complaints even had warrants issued on them, so there were people who were actually doing jail time on warrants for tickets that should have been dismissed ten years earlier. Judge Rowley mentioned a woman she personally saved from a similar fate:

When I was still a defense attorney and running for office, I remember going down to the jail—I think I was bonding one of my clients out of jail—and there was a woman, probably in her sixties, sitting there wanting to turn herself in, and I said, "What are you doing here?"

"I'm gonna have to spend two weeks in jail on warrants on all these old cases."

I couldn't use my cell phone because I was in the basement, so I said, "Give me your name, date of birth, and the kind of tickets you're talking about." I ran upstairs and I checked on the tickets, and there were no complaints on file, so they should have been dismissed. I put in an appearance on the tickets and called the DA, and they dismissed them. Apparently, she got out of jail that day. She didn't even know who I was, but she didn't have to sit in jail for two weeks.

When I spoke with Judge Rowley, she still had quite a lot of work ahead of her, cleaning up the disarray she'd inherited. She longed for the chance to stop cleaning up files, to stop having to get thousands of shucks (case jackets) put into their proper record boxes. She was wistful when imagining the light at the end of the tunnel:

It's going to be so nice. I get to be like all the other JPs. I walk into their office and they're just so relaxed! I'm so jealous because I'm just an extra clerk right now going through stuff, and those fleeting moments when I'm actually in the courtroom I'm like, this is so great. I love this part!

In the wake of *his* predecessor's departure, Mike Nelson (Galveston County) had his own prodigious clean-up to deal with.

He was in the office maybe thirty minutes a day. Consequently, I've had to dismiss 2,500 criminal cases due to the statute of limitations. He left me with, like, seventy-five civil suits he'd never given any attention to, and thirty-five jury trials. So it's been a big workload for me and my staffs.

(Judge Nelson holds justice court in two different cities.)

Wayne Denson (Lavaca County) speaks to what can go wrong when a JP finds himself out of his element. That JP in question *wasn't* Judge Denson:

Just after being sworn in, I was directed to the county clerk's office to "pick up" all the records belonging to my predecessor. I was told to "bring a truck." As it turned out, they had twenty-seven file boxes containing all the records they could find at the home of the deceased JP. Some of the boxes looked to be in pretty rough shape and I was informed that those had been found inside a barn. None of the boxes was labeled, and they contained records going back over twenty years. It was a jumbled mess with a mixture of criminal and civil records haphazardly thrown together in no particular order. A few of the boxes had live insects and at least one, a rat carcass.

It took me six months and quite a bit of fumigating with insecticide before I finally worked up the nerve to go through the contents of those twenty-seven boxes. I found several money orders and personal checks that had never been deposited from years before. Miscellaneous papers and documents appeared to have been dumped in boxes with no regard for any sense of order. The old docket books full of silverfish weren't much better. I couldn't tell from the handwritten entries what cases were still outstanding, and, ultimately, I ended up dismissing almost a thousand cases because the records were so awful.

Gina Cleveland (Jasper County) was one of several judges I interviewed who talked about the various problems she and her staff had to fix, which had been left to them by her predecessor. In Cleveland's situation, there were criminal cases in which money was taken in, but there was no record of the defendant having entered a plea. (A plea must be taken before the court is allowed to accept a fine.) She noted that the judge was never in his office, not that the office hadn't been otherwise occupied. Judge Cleveland found (I feel a theme developing) dead rodents there.

Lest these accounts give the impression that all JPs do is clean up the messes left to them by those who came before, I should note that quite a few of the justices of the peace with whom I spoke held their predecessors in such high esteem that they patiently waited to hear an announcement of retirement before deciding to run to replace them. Jimmy Miller (Jasper County) said he couldn't thank the previous JP in his precinct (the Honorable Freddie Miller, no relation) enough for all the help he gave him.

If I have a question and I don't know the answer and he doesn't know the answer, he starts studying right then. He's been a godsend to me. I'll gather up all my stuff and, just like I'm still in school, I'll go to his house and we'll sit down at the kitchen table on Saturday morning and get to studying until we get the answer.

Jeff Hightower was inspired to become a JP when, as a deputy sheriff in Bosque County, he often found himself working with the late Judge Bennett Morrow, whose twenty years on the bench exemplified the best that a JP can be. But Hightower is aware his experience isn't likely the norm. He does find that there is a certain breed of older judge "who gets set in his ways and refuses to adapt," even when laws come down from the legislature that require him to.

> *The JP world is so different—there are over 254 ways of doing things. Everybody does it differently.*—Hon. Angie Pippin, Fisher County

Debbie Horn (Potter County) has studied rogue judges. After all, she's been a justice court employee in one way or another for thirty years!

I've dealt with people who were normal when they got elected. First thing, oh my gosh, they were wonderful and they're really going to serve. By the second term, they start to change, and by the third term, they "know everything. There's nothing you can tell me."

I told my clerk when I took office: This is my job. This is not who I am. I'm still gonna go home and I'm gonna scoop poop out of my backyard that my dog left. I'm not going to be above that. But if at any time you feel like I've crawled up onto some high horse, you need to knock me down quickly.

As this chapter has demonstrated, there are rule-breaking, even law-breaking, JPs who deserve to be knocked down a few pegs, or perhaps kicked out of the profession entirely. But they are the exception.

What *isn't* exceptional is the very real possibility that every JP may have a bit of the rogue and scamp living within. Perhaps the JP who conducted court proceedings "barefoot and wearing a T-shirt and shorts" wasn't atypical at all!

NOTE

*The joke would have worked even better had there not already been a Jewish JP serving only 100 miles away in Travis County. I should know. I was one of the Hon. Debra Ravel's clerks.

19

Just a Member of the Community

Small town JPs are marriage counselors. We're grief counselors.
You stay in touch with the people in your precinct.

—HON. CHARLIE HODGKINS JR., PALO PINTO COUNTY

EVERY COUNTY IN THE state of Texas is unique, though there are similarities that bundle them in interesting ways. In terms of area, Texas's smaller counties in the east are dwarfed by the gargantuan "don't fence me in" counties of the far west. You could fit forty-one and a half Rockwall Counties into mammoth Brewster County, which is larger than the state of Connecticut. Still, Brewster County has only three JPs, who, one would assume, spend a lot of time in their cars. (I could never pin one down to ask!)

As I noted earlier, Harris, Dallas, Tarrant, Bexar, Travis and Collin Counties are each home to over one million people. Harris County is within striking distance of five million. Conversely, there are eight Texas counties with fewer than one thousand inhabitants. There are counties where most of the residents are fluent in Spanish. Other counties' denizens have deep roots in Poland, the Czech lands, and Germany. Another thing I've noticed about how different one Texan is from another comes through in their accents. In my many phone conversations with JPs throughout the state, I detected at least a dozen different Lone Star micro-accents. (It's interesting to note how many different ways Texans pronounce the word "interesting.")*

Every Texas justice of the peace must accommodate herself to her county's unique geographical and demographic profile. She must execute her job while both respecting the various dynamics and idiosyncrasies of her community and living among those she serves.

A JP's role is contextually shaped by his community. The smaller the county, the greater the likelihood that a judge's constituents will also be his neighbors, his friends, and the people who worship next to him at his church. In poorer counties there is more of a chance he'll see people in his courtroom he knows—people in straitened circumstances. Judges in more affluent counties interface far less frequently with those they know. Matt Beasley (Montgomery County) told me that he has a very good collections rate on traffic tickets. He happens to serve a precinct whose residents have deeper pockets than most Texans; they're much more willing to use their disposable income to simply pay a fine and be done with it, as opposed to soliciting the court for alternate resolutions to their troubles.

There are judges for whom serving the community to which they belong is an easy lift. They come into office and set people straight right off the bat: they aren't doing favors for someone just because they're an old friend or because of a blood or marital connection. There are judges who set out to be fair and impartial, and ultimately disappoint. Even worse, there are those JPs who never promised such a silly thing in the first place! In fact, one of the most frequent infractions brought before the State Commission on Judicial Conduct (as touched upon in the previous chapter) involves JPs who felt nary a compunction over giving a legal advantage to someone with whom they were personally connected, either through the exercise of their official duties or by using the cachet and influence that devolved from their judicial title.

Then there are those big-hearted judges who just like to bend over backwards, period. One JP told me that her predecessor had gotten himself in hot water with the county when the auditor discovered an envelope filled with checks—payment on fines and the like—that the judge had held back and not deposited simply because he felt sorry for the defendants and thought they should keep their money. The county eventually announced that the county wanted its revenue, and it was the former judge himself who had to make good on all those undeposited checks.

When you live in a small town, it's a lot like being in a family. We fight amongst ourselves and everybody knows your business, but nobody cares. People help each other out. They just want everybody to be decent and respectful, and mostly that's the way it is.
—Hon. Edward Marks, Floyd County

In small counties, the job description of a justice of the peace is far more fluid. Jane Jones told me that in Borden County (home to around 660 residents), people tend to pitch in wherever needed, even JPs. She offered a good example. "We're more hands-on with the inquests. I stay and help them load the body, I help them bag it up and get it into the ambulance. We don't have a lot of personnel, so you get in the full effect of it."

"It can be hard being a JP in a rural county, where everybody knows everybody," Glenn E. Klaus (Medina County) told me. "They'll stop you at the Shell station." And anyplace else, because JPs aren't good at blending in with the local scenery in small Texas towns. In his book *Inquests: Living with the Dead*, Mitch Shamburger (Smith County) writes about visiting his dad in the nursing home and recognizing the room's other occupant as both a customer of the family's Texaco station and a visitor to his court

"Leo—Leo Barber: do you know who I am?" Shamburger quizzed the man.

"I know *you*," the old man whispered. "You're the son of a bitch who took my driver's license."[1]

Donna Schmidt (Cochran County) has a soft spot for the people in her county. It even shows up when she magistrates the ones who step out of line and break the law.

People are always like, "Why are you so nice to me?"

"Why wouldn't I be nice to you?"

"Well, you're the judge and I'm in trouble all the time."

I'm like, "I'm going to be fair with you."

There are these guys I've magistrated over and over again, and I see them when I go down to arraign them and they're crying. "I know I disappointed you!"

I'll hand them a Kleenex, and I'll say, "You didn't disappoint me. You let yourself down. The last time you were in here, what did I tell you?"

"I don't remember."

"You've got to get up one more time than you fall down."

In small communities, it's impossible not to have personal connections with the people you have to Mirandize and set bond for. Mark Holt (Walker County) told me about a young man he magistrated whose face was familiar, but he just couldn't place him. "I was on the calf scramble, Mr. Holt." Now Judge Holt remembered.

"A super good kid," Holt told me. "He got caught with marijuana."

It isn't unusual for Donna Wessels to see a lot of the same people at the jail when she performs her duties as magistrate for Wharton County.

It's kind of like Otis in Mayberry. We have a few Otises that we see weekly. We may say, "How much money do you have in your pocket?" This way we know how much bond to set, since they have to come up with ten percent. If they say five dollars, we say okay, your bond is fifty dollars, so you can get out of jail. There are a lot of no-trespass warnings from different businesses around town. They just don't want people hanging around. But when the weather is bad or it's cold outside or they're just hungry, the people I magistrate will intentionally go to one of those places so they can get put in jail and get their three hots and a cot.

In Potter County, Thomas Jones finds many of these engineered return visits to the jail to be symptomatic of a severe national mental health crisis.

People arrested for criminal trespass, they go right back to the place that they'd originally trespassed. Those repeat offenders with mental health issues, they realize that the weather is changing and it's going to get brutally cold, and they will get picked up on criminal trespass so they'll have a place to go and get warm. Most of them are homeless. It's creating a lot of pressure on local government.

Texas JPs are more than just residents of their towns and counties. They are also spouses, parents, grandparents, aunts and uncles, sons and daughters, church members, church leaders, members of civic and social service organizations, soccer dads, Little League moms, coaches, den mothers, troop leaders, PTA members, school bus drivers, volunteer firefighters, EMS technicians, book club members, VFW members . . .

Ed Follis (Lynn County) does more in his community than just serve as JP. He does woodwork, making furniture repairs, putting in cabinets.

"I do what I can to help the community," he said. "I do a lot of work for my church. I'm active in my museum. I'm active in my cemetery association."

JPs even go to the gym. John Guinn (Coryell County) was one of the longest serving judges with whom I had the privilege to speak. He's been in office since 1981 and says that he intends to keep being a JP "until they carry me out or I lose my mind, one or the other." To keep himself in shape, he makes an effort to get to the gym three or four times a week. He tries, when he can, to put on a suit before donning the robe, although the day I talked to him, he didn't have time, and held a hearing in shorts and tennis shoes (under the robe).

Hey, it happens.

How do JPs balance family time and judge time? I asked this question of Talyna Carlson (Gregg County). For example, what happens when your inquest calls intrude on the time you need to spend with your family?

We don't look at it as an interruption. I just go and do my job and come back and we rock on. I don't like for law enforcement and families to wait on me at a death scene. I think that's disrespectful to everyone involved. I get there as quickly as I can, do my job, and get out of the way.

Judge Nicholas Chu is the first Asian American justice of the peace in Travis County, and possibly the first in the state.** He performs a lot of weddings for members of that community. Because the University of Texas is located in his precinct, international students from Asia may anticipate some form of favoritism from a Chinese American judge, but, Chu says, "they get disappointed."

When she first became a JP, Sharon Maxey (Falls County) hated to impose fines on people she went to church with.

But I just sat myself down and said, As long as you treat everyone that walks through the door the same, it doesn't matter if you know them or not. You give each of them the same opportunity, the same options. It should never be a hard decision. I want to go home at night and feel that I've done my job well and followed the law by the letter.

She did say that when it turns out that a defendant had been a customer of her family business, she'll give the person the option of requesting that another judge hear the case. Some take the offer; others don't worry at all that she isn't going to be fair.

For Larry Cryer, not only is being civic-minded part of being a JP, it is also part of being Larry Cryer. Back in the 1980s, he became deeply committed to getting ambulances for Chambers County. After an explosion that killed six local men and required him and others to transport the injured in the beds of pick-up trucks, he decided then and there to work to get an effective emergency management system put into place in the county. When he was younger, Judge Cryer did ride-alongs with local law enforcement officers and developed a good relationship with them. This has redounded positively in the area of community cooperation.

Stephanie Frietze comes from a strong public service-oriented family, that has been a part of El Paso since before it became a county in 1850. Her deep roots have given her a strong commitment to her community—a commitment that goes beyond just being a JP.

I've always wanted to make a difference here. As a JP, I get to do it every single day. I work with our local commissioner to clean up parks and streets, and with the mayor of Vinton to clean up the Rio Grande and the local highways.

She's also set up a payment plan to help people pay their fines. Others may opt for the community service opportunities she offers.

Like judges Cryer and Frietze, Michael York (Lee County) enjoys numerous community affiliations outside his job as JP; he's active in the local Masonic lodge and serves on several local boards and commissions, including the National Child Passenger Safety board for his town.

And some Texas JPs aren't just another member of the community; they're an indisputably *important* member of that community. When Judge Trisher Ford (Tyler County) sees people at the edge of emotional extremity, she knows that it's her job to address what is upsetting them.

People who come into the court—they're scared. Most of the time they're mad—not at you, but at their circumstances. But it comes off directed at you. You've got to know how to defuse that, to be firm, but understanding. Most of the time I could have someone come in stark raving mad about a ticket they received and by the time they leave, they're laughing.

Being "just a member of a community" has its drawbacks, especially if your tenure in office is dependent on navigating the shoals of local politics. A South Texas justice of the peace told me that a lot of people said she was "crazy to run" and characterized a potential race in David and Goliath terms. But this judge felt that her incumbent just wasn't "doing the job at hand" despite his many years on the bench. And in spite of the fact that she couldn't find enthusiastic support outside her family and in spite of the fact that she was reminded repeatedly of the political ugliness she would face if she ran . . . she ran.

And won.

By twenty-two votes.

Even after taking office, this judge told me that she was "smeared" and often felt that she was the only person standing for what she strongly believed was the right thing to do. The political turmoil she said she'd faced has been difficult, but she still enjoys being a public servant and serving the public the best she can.

It never hurts for a JP to set a good example for his community. Edward Marks told me about an exchange he had with one of the other office holders in Floyd County.

He was out driving around shooting rabbits off the road. He was hopping mad when he got his ticket. He said, "I didn't know this was against the law."

"Well, you do now."

"Well, you can fix that."

I said, "I could, but I ain't going to. People like you and me need to be held to a higher standard."

There are those who are intimidated by the justice court; others express awe that they are about to be part of something they've seen on TV. Yadi Rodriguez (Hutchinson County) told me that people ask her clerk things like, "Am I really going in front of the judge?" "Is there really a courtroom?" Some of them ask if Judge Rodriguez has ever "met Judge Judy."

Not all JPs have their own courtrooms. For large trials, they might borrow the district or county courtroom in the county courthouse. There are judges like Brenda Smith (Newton County), who holds court in front of her desk, or, in the case of Angie Pippin (Fisher County) and Travis Hill (Lavaca County), at a conference table. The conference table becomes, in effect, the courtroom.

Incidentally, when Judge Smith became JP in 1996, her JP office was located behind her general store. Louie Ditta (Harris County) told me about a judge he knew whose court was next door to his family business, a sausage company.

There was another judge I got to know many years ago. He had a restaurant, and his courtroom was in his restaurant—like in a little side room. The county paid him maybe two hundred a month for setting that room aside for his court. He would just leave his restaurant and go do a trial.

Brad Henley (Hill County) works out of a converted mobile home that was once used as a branch bank. He likes it there. It's right on the highway and only two miles from his house.

Julie Sanchez is one of four justices of the peace serving Hudspeth County; in size, it's the third largest in the state. The county has a lot of open land where people live off the grid. Sanchez said that she most often sees these maverick homesteaders when they have trouble getting along. They don't have the money to file lawsuits against each other, but they show up at her justice court office nonetheless. After all, she *is* part of "The Law West of the Pecos."

What we have is a lot of people who've bought property out here in the middle of the desert where there's no water and electricity. They move out here and they barter with one another. "I'll give you my water container for your horse." Then all of the sudden, they start fighting. The sheriff's department sends someone out to talk to them. You do this and you do that or you're gonna have to file on one another. But nobody has the money to file. And a lot of them think that because there's no water out there, well, they just aren't gonna bathe, so they subject all of us to the smell. There's a couple that come in here. I'm like, where's the Lysol?

Not every community in Texas has the advantage of a thoughtful and enlightened citizenry. And there are JP precincts you'd never confuse with Mr. Rogers' neighborhood or Mayberry R.F.D. I spoke with one Texas JP who confessed behind the cloak of anonymity:

I've had them come in here for writing hot checks and say, "Judge, I don't understand this. We put money in the bank to pay our bills with and now they tell us we don't have any more money. But we've still got half the checks they gave us still in the checkbook!"

Around here, we've got a lot of inbred people. You can take one finger and punch both eyes.

Ed Follis (Lynn County) has at least one bozo in his community. But it isn't him.

I've got an answering machine with caller ID. I have an announcement that goes out that says leave this information and I'll return your call. One morning I got in about five after nine and I had a message that said, "Hey, bozo, it's after nine o'clock." That's all it said.

I happened to see this man's name and telephone number. I called that number and I said, "This is Bozo." And he hung up. I haven't heard from him since. But I've got it marked over here on his unpaid shuck. One of these days, sooner or later, we're going to see each other.

> ***People come in here, they'll pay a ticket, and then we spend about thirty minutes talking. I punish them, but they won't go away!***
> —*Hon. Katy Marlow, Foard County*

Ronnie Davis (Liberty County) loves his community and loves his job. He was seventy-seven when we spoke, but told me, "As long as my health is good, I'm gonna stay here." He has a special relationship with the members of the community he serves.

If somebody dies, they call me first. If somebody needs an Avalanche [grain cart] they call me first. The other day when we had that forty inches of rain, I'll bet I got thirty-five calls. "What roads are closed?" "When is the school going to open back up?"

I have to walk about eighty feet to get to my office from my house. I'm here every morning at about ten minutes to six. I'm making coffee, I'm reading a little in the Bible, and my friends come in here. I'm liable to have twelve of them in here drinking coffee. I open my court at seven because we've got so many people that need to be at work at eight. They want to take care of their business before they go to work.

> ***I'm a JP in Coke County for a reason. I like the slow pace of life here. I'm happy being here.***—*Hon. Russell Johnson, Coke County*

Mike Smith (Harrison County) is another JP who has no problem engaging in a personal way with his constituents. He has an open-door policy where people can drop by and pick his brain. He sees a lot of older people who want his advice on matters for which a professional opinion might be helpful. Even if a particular matter seems inconsequential to most folks, he knows it's important to the person who's come to see him, and he's happy to help. Just so long as his friends abide by a set of rules he came up with to govern his interactions with the public:

- *If we're going to talk about something that's private to them, then it needs to be private to me, so I make them take their telephones out of their pockets and lay them up on my desk and show me that they're turned off.*

- *With the people I think might end up in my court at a later date, for instance in a civil case, I'll tell them that I'm glad to talk to them about the process, filling out the paperwork, help them decide if they should be talking to a lawyer, but I won't discuss the facts of their case.*

- *A lot of people want to talk about their neighbor and the problem they're having with this person or that person. I'll tell them that I don't discuss other people and their actions, because that keeps me out of a lot of he said-she said situations.*

- *If a female comes in and talks to me, for example about a citation, the door that connects to my clerk's office is always left open.*

Duncan Neblett Jr. (Nueces County) likes serving a small community. (Port Aransas, though a big tourist destination, only has a year-round population of about 4,200.)

In a small community like we have, I feel like the judge is in a position to help the people—especially young people who need a little guidance because they don't have a father figure or an authority figure in the house. We work closely with the school. We're blessed; in this community the people respect the judge. They may not like how he rules sometimes, but they feel like they got a fair shake.

Over the years, it seems that we have been able to keep a lot of things from escalating, from getting out of hand. I work hand-in-glove with my constable. I hear judges in other counties talk about, "that goddamned constable—he won't do anything. I won't even say hello to him." Here, we're blessed with a good relationship.

Susan Ruiz-Belding (Frio County) spent most of her pre-JP professional life in banking and working as a retirement consultant. Her parents, both of whom only had a third-grade education, encouraged her to pursue her schooling. After years of selling banking products, Ruiz-Belding likes the chance to shift gears; she now gets to be a community partner, working to improve the lives of those she serves with the tools the justice court gives her.

> **I've had people come to my house and want to pay a ticket.**
> —*Hon. Edward Marks, Floyd County*

Charlie Hodgkins Jr. (Palo Pinto County), who has no clerk, often gets calls outside of office hours from people who have business with the court.

I get calls on Christmas, Thanksgiving, New Year's Day—someone wanting to pay a fine or something, and I say, "Well, the court's not open, but this is what you need to do," and I give them the information. It's just the way I've always handled my court. I feel it's my obligation to help the people. They wouldn't be calling if they knew what to do.

When Janae Holland was thinking about running for JP in Wood County, she considered ways she could serve her community beyond what the job required. She kept both of her campaign promises, the first of which is: The judge gets to the county jail every morning between 3:30 and 4:00 a.m. to magistrate. She does this because it gives those who have been in overnight custody the chance to make their bond, get home, get themselves cleaned up, and make it to work later in the morning.

She told me another promise she made: She'd hold Saturday court every three months. I asked her if her clerks minded coming in on Saturday. It turns out they don't mind at all. Judge Holland cooks lunch for them two days a week; she actually has a well-earned reputation for her cooking. When I asked how her family feels having a judge in the family, she said it was fine just so long as it didn't keep her from fixing the fried chicken and the mashed potatoes they love so much.

Holland also enjoys having informal chats with kids who just want to come in and talk. She keeps a food and sundry pantry in her office for people in need.

The kids come in. I buy Gatorade for them and make it comfortable for them. I keep things people need, personal items, female items. I was at church and this guy said, "Hey, I have something for you. I know you see a lot of people because you're right there on the highway and so people may come by and they're hungry so I'm just going to give you these Vienna sausages and you can just give it to them." A lady brought me two bags of baby clothes. I may not be able to use them in my office but there's juvenile probation, there's child welfare. I was on the child welfare board for ten years. I adopted my son through that child welfare board.

Holland keeps a lawn chair in her car so that when she's driving around and sees someone she knows, she can stop, take out the chair, and they can "sit and chitchat."

Back in the olden days when I worked as a clerk for a justice of the peace, social media meant one of two things: sending someone a letter or a telegram (remember telegrams?) or calling them up on the phone. Today's JPs and their staffs are faced with a profusion of electronic communication opportunities and must manage social media access in such a way that there isn't a negative impact on the court. Mike Smith (Harrison County) told me about the restrictions he's put on his clerks when it comes to their use of social media. His reasoning is sound: people often use the personal accounts of clerks to make private appeals for leniency and special consideration in their dealings with the court. Smith wonders if other judges shouldn't be more attentive to the kinds of digital conversations that are going on via the public access features of social media, which can undermine the primary objective of the JP court to be fair and impartial.

There are those who have no idea what their local justice of the peace does or doesn't do. Judge Michael York received a call from a county resident complaining about graffiti on an abandoned car. He wanted York to issue an order to have this taken care of. (Writ of Spic and Span?) Judge Edward Marks said that most of his precinct's "solid citizens" want their JP to "stop crime completely."

"There's people over here dealing drugs! Why don't you go do something about that?"

Living in a small town, whether a JP likes it or not, places him right in the middle of pretty much everything that goes on there. Judge York thinks about this all the time.

I've had people come up to my house wanting to settle disputes. I'm sitting at home trying to eat some dinner and hear a knock on the door. When they see me at the Walmart or the grocery store, they're like, "Hey, my aunt got a ticket. What do I need to do?" Life in the fishbowl!

One thing I've done is I have a mobile office, so even if I'm at home and have to issue warrants, I don't have to run into town anymore. I tell them I don't look good at three o'clock in the afternoon. And I certainly don't look good at three in the morning!

> *These Republic of Texas folks—they file all these motions, but they're all null and void because they've created their own special notary. They don't believe you have to have a driver's license. They're amusing in some ways and frustrating in others.*
> —Hon. Jackie Miller Jr., Ellis County

"Republic of Texas" is a general term for a bundle of organizations that subscribe to the belief that Texas justices of the peace are illegitimate because the state of Texas is, itself, illegitimate. Members of these fringe groups claim that Texas is its own country. They consider their justice court a convenient local forum for waging protest, wherein they can make their valiant stands—in microcosm—much to the exasperation of the JPs who find themselves bearing the brunt of their mischief.

> *They keep quacking about how the constable and the JPs don't have any jurisdiction. I give them a little history lesson.*
> —Hon. Mike Towers, Bandera County

Douglas Zwiener (Washington County) had an eviction case in which the defendant wasn't making his mortgage payments, so a foreclosure was in the works. It ended up being a Republic of Texas remonstration. Zwiener ultimately ruled against the man, but not before the defendant took a stand against the legitimacy of state-of-Texas justice courts, which, he argued, have no jurisdiction in the sovereign *nation* of Texas.

On the day of court he comes in and literally tries to file a banker's box of the most superfluous crap you've even seen on paper. I was like, "What do you expect to do with this stuff?"

"This is my case! I'm gonna go through this box, sheet by sheet."

"No, you're not. Do you have anything in that box that is remotely related to Texas law?"

"But you don't have jurisdiction!"

"Honey, I have jurisdiction going back to the sovereignty of the soil. And I was a history major in college. Don't come and tell me about the history of Texas."

He had said he was going to bring in all his Republic of Texas friends. I brought in extra security. Nobody showed up.

Judge Zwiener also had the pleasure of magistrating a woman on a warrant who also contended that a justice of the peace didn't have jurisdiction over her. She was an "incorporeal being."

How do Texas JPs lighten the stress of dealing with problem folk in their communities? Humor helps. There is the potential for levity in quite a bit of what a Texas justice of the peace is required to do. Inevitably, this involves either someone within their community or a visitor from points beyond unknowingly "making a judge's day" . . . through laughter. And what's funny can sometimes come from a pretty dark place.

Wayne Money (Hunt County) magistrated a man who was arrested while trying to break into a truck. There was something off about him—*really* off. "Have you seen the cartoon where the guy stuck his finger in the light socket?" Money asked me. "His hair is standing on end, smoke coming out of his ears, his eyes spinning?"

I could picture it.

Well, I didn't arraign him on the first day, because he couldn't even understand me if I read him his rights. The second day he could understand, but he just wasn't complying. We appointed him a lawyer to make sure his rights weren't violated. But he was feeling no pain. He had been on, like, a six- or seven-day high with drugs. He was just completely and totally out of it.

As for the defendant's electrically charged hair and spinning eyes, Judge Money explained that this is what happens when you've been tased six times.

—Ⱳ—

Thomas Jones (Potter County) escapes through music, sports, and fishing.

I can have an eviction hearing, where I have to let people know that they have to vacate the premises; two hours later I'm at an inquest and have to deal with a family that's lost a loved one; then an hour later I'm setting someone's bond. You go from one thing to the next in such a short amount of time. With this job you definitely have to have some sort of stress reliever. You have to have a way to get some time for yourself and kind of decompress. I go fishing.

Oralia Morales (Brooks County) has her own ways of peeling away the stress from her job. She prays. She sends up a prayer before she heads out to do an inquest and then afterwards, and then she says she lets it go. She takes care of her plants at home, throws herself into her housework. This helps. Her boys, whom she raised by herself while serving as a JP (since 2002), are now all spread out, so she travels a lot to spend time with them and help out with the grandchildren. It helped a lot, she said, that when her sons were growing up, they were understanding of their mom's special job, and that she was able to keep her family life separate from her JP duties.

Sara Canady's county—Wilson—was tragically tested by the Sutherland Springs church shooting in 2017, but she reminds us that Texas communities are strong and resilient. They inspire the justices of the peace who serve them to be equally strong and resilient.

My mom had hernia surgery a couple of weeks ago. The doctor said after the surgery that he'd decided not to replace the old mesh with new mesh because it had, for the most part, done what it was supposed to do. It had become part of her skin. That's just like how we are in our communities.

You think about a grain of sand in an oyster, and that grain of sand is an irritation. But because an oyster can't expel that grain of sand, it exudes a chemical that, in the end, becomes a beautiful pearl.

They're a part of you, and you're a part of them.

NOTES

* Not every Texas JP was born in Texas; I spoke with justices of the peace who had Illinois, Arkansas, Ohio, and Louisiana accents; one of my interviewees, Margaret O'Brien (Dallas County), hails from the same place as the Blue Northers: Canada.

**To the best of my knowledge there exists no comprehensive historical record or database containing the names of all the men and women who have served as justices of the peace in Texas going back to the days of the Republic, let alone biographical data on each one. The herculean task of reaching out to county clerks and historians in all 254 counties for the purpose of compiling an exhaustive biographical and historical listing of every Texas JP awaits that Texana researcher of special mettle indeed.

20

And In Conclusion, Your Honor

WHAT DOES THE FUTURE hold for the Texas justice court? Although the job of justice of the peace is being significantly reconstituted, subsumed, or abolished altogether in other states, Texas won't be following suit any time soon. Indeed, the trend has been going in the opposite direction, with the court being invested with even broader jurisdiction, and its purview and the range of duties for which JPs are responsible continuing to expand. Stuart Posey (Victoria County) has noticed that every time the state legislature raises the monetary jurisdiction in civil cases, "more goes rolling downhill from the higher courts to the justice court."

Though Texas justices of the peace now play a less consequential role in truancy prevention and reduction than they used to, the granting of essential-need driver's licenses has been tucked into their portfolio. The state legislature is inching closer to making possession of small amounts of marijuana a Class C misdemeanor. That C misdemeanor means JP court—which means a lot of tokin' Texans getting into the hair of a lot of Texas JPs and their clerks. Doubling the monetary jurisdiction for civil suits heard by JPs means a lot more lawyers crowding the corridors of Texas's justice courts, but it also means the presence of more *non*-lawyers willing to represent themselves in disputes over even higher debt and damage claims than ever before.

> *When we first started [in 1986], it was pen and paper and big docket books. You handwrote your warrants out. Maybe writing in the docket books accounts for the callus that I have on my right hand. The best thing that ever happened to the JP courts is the computer age!*—Hon. Frieda Pressler, Kendall County

Some Texas JP courts are now virtually paperless, with all operations completely electronic. Others are moving into the twenty-first century with the speed of cold molasses. JPs in Dallas County have been pushing their commissioners to upgrade their operations for years, and only recently have things started going in the right direction. It's been a real headache for Judge Margaret O'Brien.

I have a staff of nine people. We have no electronic filing. Everything is paper here. Dallas County is a snail. It's been a $30 million fight between the commissioners to get us a $2 million system. This has been going on for almost a decade. We have a 1980s Forbes system that's awful. When you go into court, it's all paper files that get all out of order.

Several months after my chat with Judge O'Brien, her words rang true in quite a dramatic fashion, the result being a tremendous loss of revenue to the county. When fellow Dallas County JP Katina Whitfield came into office in early 2019, she discovered an enormous backlog of criminal cases in her court—over 100,000. Other Dallas County JPs were faced with a similar challenge. Judge Thomas G. Jones was dealing with nearly 275,000 cases that had been in the system longer than ten years. Dallas County District Attorney John Creuzot ended up having to dismiss hundreds of thousands of these cases throughout the county's justice courts, clearing the books of unsettled tickets and hot checks never made good.

This meant clearing the books to make room for a future in which there will be no more books, or, at least, no more cases that are only as good as the paper they're printed on—paper that hasn't been mislaid or inefficiently filed. Dallas County's travails are a worst-case scenario for what happens to justice courts when a county drags its feet on computerization and digitalization.

Then again, there are still some very small counties like Borden, where Jane Jones serves as at-large justice of the peace, that receive so few civil filings that she can easily continue to record case-related information by hand in the large, old-fashioned docket books.

The justice court of the future will inevitably cater to a more educated species of Texan. Connie Hickman (Navarro County) has already noticed this trend. She came into office in 1991 and was a JP court clerk for several years before that. Over the years, she's seen justice courts working with more and more efficiency. Computerization helps a lot. Some JP courts are now completely computerized, digitized, and futurized, and that bandwagon continues to grow even more crowded with the need, which expanded greatly beginning in 2020 during the pandemic, to take more court operations online.

I feel like there will be permanent changes coming out of our response to the COVID-19 virus. We're discovering ways to make our courts more efficient. —Hon. Mark Russo, Rockwall County

Judge Hickman might also agree that those who appear in her court aren't nearly the lost lambs they used to be, in fear of being juristically sheered or slaughtered.

I think people are more aware of their ability now to file things on their own, pro se. They're a lot more educated about doing things now than they were in the early '90s. People are more exposed to information now, through TV and the internet, court shows, people going to court in the news, people exercising their legal rights. They're not nearly as afraid of going to court as they once were.

No JP in Texas is more focused on the future than Randall Slagle in Travis County, whose court, at the time of the implementation of his paper-free program, was the most electronic justice court in the state.

We don't print any paper unless there is some legal requirement or if someone asks us to do it. Like if they don't have an email address. If, say, a defendant in an eviction doesn't show up and we don't have their email address, we'll mail them the judgment. But anyone who we have an email

address for, we'll send it that way. We've given demonstrations to almost every county in Texas.

Slagle told me that they've been visited by members of the Georgia state legislature and even shared their system with a judge who flew over from the United Kingdom. Judge Slagle has some thoughts about those JPs who are resistant to change.

In Houston, some of the courts don't want to go paperless. They're fearful that the server could be corrupted and they'd lose things. My argument to them is: "Look at the last hurricane you guys dealt with." They spent millions of dollars having paper repaired so they could preserve these records. They had to bring in these remediation companies to come in and save their paperwork.

Slagle teaches classes on the intersection between rapidly innovating technologies and the Texas justice court system. He predicts big changes in what JPs will be dealing with ten years from now.

Such as in the area of DNA testing and the "internet of things": Rather than talking about how the internet affects us, we should be looking at the different forms of electronics that we interact with, like Ring doorbell, like Alexa. In my keynote address to trainee judges this year I talked about drones. Maybe ten years ago people didn't know a thing about drones. Now they're getting them for Christmas.

Slagle foresees the use of unmanned aerial vehicles as an aid in doing inquests and in the area of traffic enforcement, where they can be equipped with radar to go after speeders.

—⁂—

Throughout this book, I've tried to strike a balance. I wanted to educate the reader on what a Texas JP does (and doesn't do, for that matter) while also sharing how it actually feels to have this unique and fascinating job. But I couldn't do this without partnering with the judges themselves to tell their story.

So let's posit some conclusions, the judges and I. Have a seat. Court is now in session.

Hon. Jackie Miller Jr. (Ellis County): *I will tell you, this is the way I see JP court: most people never appear in a county or district court. They don't get in trouble. For the majority of people, the only visual they get* *of the court system is a JP or municipal court. You try to treat them with dignity and respect. You're dealing with a lot of pro se litigants. You can't give them legal advice, but you try to be as helpful as legally possible. And you let the chips fall where they may.*

I'm your best friend or your worst enemy. Choose wisely!

Hon. Nancy J. Pomykal (Calhoun County): *I told someone one day who asked, "What's it like to be a JP?" I said, "It's easy. First of all, you have to be a Philadelphia lawyer. You have to have the patience of Job, and you have to have the wisdom of Solomon. Also, compassion. It's extremely important to have good people skills because of all the upset people you have to deal with."*

Hon. Billy Hefner (Colorado County): *My job is to make people better citizens, and that's the way I look at it. I work with kids. I work with adults.*

My takeaways from all my talks with judges are three-fold.

The first: how often I found JPs agreeing with one another. I'd ask what was the best part of the job, and only rarely would I not hear: "the chance to help people." Over and over again, their care for their communities and their desire to be a source of assistance came through, not only via their statements of commitment, but also through the active example of their outreach to their constituents. I don't think these judges woke up one morning and decided to pursue a life of civic succor. I believe it's something ingrained in them, a part of who they are, perhaps even dating back to childhood. Darrell Longino (Polk County) recalled sitting on the porch with his grandfather, who owned the local general store.

He became kind of an elder to the working-class people. We had a bunch of cotton farmers and truck farmers down in the river bottom, and a lot of them couldn't read and write. So they'd go to my grandfather to help them decipher letters and things like that. Those folks would come up and say, "Mr. Craig, how are you?"

"Mighty fine. What's your trouble?"

I've thought so many times how proud he would be to know that I'd grown up to become a justice of the peace by following in his footsteps.

> *Everybody has problems, everybody has things that go wrong in their*
> *lives. If they want to straighten their lives out, I want to help them.*
> —Hon. Stacy Spurlock, Jack County

Another area of agreement involves death investigations. Seldom did I speak to a JP who was comfortable doing inquests, though some would say they'd reached the point of at least being able to sequester that close association with the stark and repeated reality of death in their backyards, emotionally partitioning it in such a way that it didn't end up short-circuiting the other areas of their lives.

Others continue to struggle with how to process and compartmentalize the kinds of visceral reactions to situations that tug and assault—and not just those that arise from dealing with the dead and the grieving. There are many other heart challenges that go along with the job of being Texas JP: having to evict people from their homes; working with at-risk, troubled kids, who often seem beyond help; having to formulate action plans to assist people beaten down by financial struggles; mediating conflict between families torn apart by baked-in animus and calcified resentments; and having to extend judicial lifelines to those who are at the end of their tethers without easy recourse to making themselves whole again. Yet as difficult as all this sounds, these are the very things that give them the most gratification in their jobs: being there for people and extending a helping hand, not only to the most helpless and vulnerable of their constituents, but also to those who just need to be shown how to help themselves.

My second takeaway contrasts sharply with the first, as exemplified in chapter sixteen, "In the Opinion of the Court." There are a lot of different ways of doing all the things that JPs are required to do. Likewise, there are divergent perspectives on their job. There are judges who perform weddings and those who do not, judges who act as county coroners and those who don't, judges who hear one or two eviction cases a year and those who hear hundreds a month. There are JPs with neighborly, open-door policies and those who do everything by the book to obviate even the whiff of favoritism.

> *The law is black and white, but life is gray.*—Hon. Steven T. Kennedy,
> *Uvalde County*

The third takeaway for me is the degree to which the job, even for those judges who have been in it for decades, continues to inform them, to educate them, to surprise and amaze them. Douglas Zwiener (Washington County) is frequently stumped:

You think you know about this job, but I guarandamntee you that every day some oddball, weird thing comes along and it's all inside the gray area of the law and that's why you have judges. How gray is this? Is there a law that's going to be applicable to this? How far on the legal chopping block do I go to make this work?

> *The job really throws curve balls at you.*—Hon. Marc DeRouen,
> *Jefferson County*

Not that there aren't some JPs who have seen so much over the years that it's a little hard to admit to ever being surprised by anything perpetrated by a member of the human race. "I've worked for the public since I was about fifteen or sixteen years old in one capacity or another," says Bobby McIntosh (Uvalde County).

I've been in their homes, I've seen things that just make you want to run backwards. I've seen human nature at a lot of different levels. I tell people that there's not one thing a human can do that surprises me. It will really tick me off, but I'm not surprised.

Texas JPs are positioned at the locus of oddball human behavior and at the nexus of those various strains of contradictory human interaction. They learn early on that there is no such thing as a control group for human beings.

Many Texas JPs are guided by a matrix of logic and common sense that they have acquired through a lifetime of experience in a variety of outside professions, exposure to contrasting sets of family dynamics, and the kaleidoscope of social constructs they have witnessed along the course of their lives. Others are guided by religious faith. Still others find within themselves the light of evolved conscience and discernment that illuminates their way.

Not every judge, as we've seen, is a paragon of civic responsibility and virtue, but I still remain astonished at how often the profession of justice of the peace in the state of Texas seems to attract the helpers, the cockeyed optimists, the genuinely engaged, the thoughtful, the conscientious, the honest, the fair, the funny, the joyous, the winkers, and the all-around stinkers that make Lone Star justice so gosh-darned colorful.

In the course of gathering material for this book there was something else I learned about Texas JPs—how representative they are of every Texas stereotype *and* every *anti*-stereotype. Like America itself, the state lends itself to entertaining generalization and mythology made manifest. But Texas is also a study in contrasts as wide as the Palo Duro Canyon. I don't know what part of this process I enjoyed the most: discovering that those rowdy, rustic western archetypes that frequently define (and sometimes caricaturize) the culture of the state are alive and well in justice courts throughout Texas, or getting the chance to squint through that chromatic prism of unpredictability that is Texas in its twenty-first-century incarnation—a state that embraces both the Harris County sorority of judicial sisters of color *and* the good ol' boy junior varsity Judge Roy Beans.

My chat with Randall Slagle in Precinct 2 in Travis County was one of my favorites. I was pleased to have the chance to visit over the phone with the current JP occupant of the court where I worked as a clerk over thirty-five years ago. Not only did we discuss what it was like to be a Texas JP at the end of the second decade of the third millennium of the Common Era, we talked about what it's like to be Texan. Then, since I was informally cataloging from my phone conversations all those *different* Texas accents, we spoke about what it means to "*talk* Texan." For a time, Judge Slagle served as a criminal prosecutor on the island of Maui, then returned to his Texas roots:

Sometimes just to relate to some folks when I'm training, not when I'm actually doing the presentation but afterwards at happy hour or something, I'll start talking in my Texas twang and turn it up a little bit. I can do it because I've got a dad from Odessa, Texas, and a mom from far East Texas, but I was born in Austin, the big city. In Hawaii, everyone wondered why I didn't have a very thick accent. It's because I didn't want people to just assume I was some horse-riding hillbilly from the middle of nowhere, not that I have anything against that. But I know that people outside of Texas sometimes assume that we're all these country cowboy people.

Which would be quite wrong.

And which would also be a little bit right.

Viva country cowboy judges *and* urban cowboy judges!

Viva, Texas!

—ᴍ—

I had intended to give the last word in this book to one of the JPs with whom I'd been in touch and whose insights into the profession of judgin'—granular-wise—go far deeper and are far better articulated than my own. The competition for that honor was stronger than I expected, so valedictory comments actually go to *five different* judges, each of whom gave me their heartfelt takes on what it's like to have one of America's most interesting jobs.

First, the Honorable Keri Jones, from the "wild, wild West Texas county of Winkler." Before becoming a judge, Jones was a nurse. She says she went from "fixing boo boos" to "taking money for people's boo boos." In her court she sees many of the people she'd cared for at the hospital (both inpatient and outpatient), including a good many of their family members. She sent me a list of some of the things she's learned since becoming a JP:

I have learned that an eviction is not a quick process, and I can't understand why some people expect to live somewhere for free!

I have learned that people will look me in the eye and give me the biggest line of crap just to get out of paying a traffic fine, but still complain about the status of our decaying roads and the lack of safety on our highways.

I have learned that everyone deserves a second chance, and some people don't realize when they have been given one.

I have learned that issuing an occupational driver's license can made a grown man cry because he won't have to cringe each time he sees a police officer.

I have learned that I will encounter many situations that were not taught to me in a class.

As far as sitting behind the bench in a hot black robe, I sometimes have to pinch myself and take in the depth of my power, influence, and respect for this position. Not all of the people I sit in front of know that I'm not an attorney, so winging it is an understatement! It scares me, and I try very hard to perform this job with due diligence and treat everyone like I would want to be treated. I figure that after each court hearing, if both parties walk out—both a little piffed—then I did my job, fair and square!

The Honorable Rick Hill (Brazos County) leaves us with the following four rules by which he lives his judicial life:

One: Know my job. So I'm always studying and reading and trying to get better at this.

Two: Do my job.

Three: Do only my job. Judges get in trouble when they step over the line.

Four: Remember the Golden Rule and treat people with respect.

The Honorable Wayne L. Mack (Montgomery County) puts a very real and very human face on all that we talked about.

I'm in charge of justice and peace in our community, and at my level in Texas, justice courts are the highest volume courts in Texas. We interact with millions of our citizens. Ninety percent of Texans that have any interaction with the judicial branch of government happen into a justice or municipal court, so I want them to have a positive experience. But also, in that role, I want to draw a bright line about what responsibility and accountability look like.

The Honorable Kim Redman (Wise County) *really* likes her job.

I was told by the judge I worked for as clerk that if "you win the election, this will be the best job you've ever had in your life."

I said, "Really?" When I got the job, I called him and I said, "You're right. It's just interesting every day."

It's just the whole variety of it, I think. You wear so many hats as a judge. You're in here and you talk to juveniles and then you talk to an older person. Then you go to jail and you see someone who's totally whacked out and then you go to a death and you have to talk to the family. A lot of the time you pray with the family, and a lot of the time you just hold their hand and walk them through it. It's just the most interesting thing I could ever do. I love the job, I really do. I hope that I can do a good enough job to get re-elected!

Getting a great deal of satisfaction out of your job as Texas JP gives Judge Redman a lot of company. It's also what makes a Texas JP a *good* JP, even though there might be times in which the job depresses the hell out of you and stresses you out. At the end of the day, it's how you *begin* each day that counts. One of my favorite questions put to JPs in the many hours of conversations I enjoyed was, "What puts a smile on your face when you get up in the morning?" I didn't speak to a single judge who didn't give me *something*. The Honorable Mark Russo, JP in Rockwall County had this to say:

If you can't wake up every morning and not look forward to going to work, I'd say this is a job for which you need not apply. One thing I do that I love is give tours of the court to second graders and third graders. I let them put the robe on. It's to say, you can be this.

What puts a smile on *my* face? Realizing that I just gave the last word in my book to the justice of the peace who used to be a professional wrestler.

Now, how cool is *that*?

Notes

CHAPTER 1

1. John Detrixhe, "Entrepreneurs Are Thriving along the West Texas 'Death Highway,'" *Quartz*, May 13, 2019, accessed December 30, 2020, https://qz.com/1552685/entrepreneurs-thrive-on-us-highway-285-amid-permian-fracking-boom/.

CHAPTER 2

1. Obituary for Judge Joe B. Evins, Lux Funeral Home, accessed December 30, 2020, https://www.luxfhcares.com/obituaries/Joseph-Benjamin-Evins?obId=10546566.

2. Ronald W. Erdrich, "Howard County Justice of the Peace was Hall-of-Fame Rodeo Clown," *Eagle*, November 5, 2013, accessed December 30, 2020, https://www.theeagle.com/news/texas/howard-county-justice-of-the-peace-was-hall-of-fame/article_fbda8b56-4626-11e3-9d71-001a4bcf887a.html.

3. Mike Cox, "Armless Judge," *Texas Escapes*, July 7, 2007, accessed December 30, 2020, http://www.texasescapes.com/MikeCoxTexasTales/Armless-Judge.htm.

CHAPTER 6

1. Thomas Mitchell Shamburger, *Inquests: Living with the Dead* (Winona, TX: Proven Justice Inc.), 112, 122.

2. "Ex-Pastor's Murder Conviction Ends Four-Year Saga," ABC13/ KTRK-TV, January 23, 2010, accessed December 30, 2020, https://abc13.com/ archive/7235344/; Erin Quinn, "Justices of Peace Have Leeway in Dealing with Death Issues," *Waco Tribune-Herald*, February 7, 2010, accessed December 30, 2020, https://www.wacotrib.com/news/justices-of-peace-have-leeway-in-deal-ing-with-death-issues/article_13f7b9ad-e943-5441-bc38-70ed978dae65.html.

3. "Ranch Owner Clarifies How He Found Scalia Amid Conspiracy The-ories," CBS News, February 17, 2016, accessed December 30, 2020, https:// www.cbsnews.com/news/supreme-court-justice-antonin-scalia-death-con-spiracy-theories-texas-ranch-owner-clarifies/.

4. Tommy Witherspoon, "Out of the Flames: West JP Pareya Dealt with Branch Davidian, Fertilizer Plant Tragedies," *Waco Tribune-Herald*, April 18, 2018, accessed December 30, 2020, https://www.wacotrib.com/news/branch_ davidians/west-jp-pareya-dealt-with-branch-davidian-fertilizer-plant-trage-dies/article_fa253c75-70c8-5642-b0a8-a2ad31b8533c.html.

5. "Bodies of Firefighters, Residents Pulled from West Blast Bubble," *Waco Tribune-Herald*, April 18, 2013, accessed December 30, 2020, https://www. wacotrib.com/news/local/bodies-of-firefighters-residents-pulled-from-west-blast-rubble/article_5bf58fb8-e279-5431-97ea-ac128ad778e1.html.

6. "Timeline of Events: May 17, 2015 Twin Peaks Biker Shootout," *Waco Tri-bune-Herald*, May 18, 2016, updated August 11, 2016, accessed January 3, 2021, https://wacotrib.com/news/twin-peaks-biker-shooting/timeline-of-events-may-17-2015-twin-peaks-biker-shootout/article_01fe3e38-40f5-5574-9f4e-ce-7a509b1a1c.html.

7. Ashley Lopez, "Texas Doesn't Keep Track of Deaths Very Well, and It's Affecting Public Policy," KUT 90.5, NPR, September 2, 2017, accessed Decem-ber 30, 2020, https://www.kut.org/post/texas-doesnt-keep-track-deaths-very-well-and-it-s-affecting-public-policy.

8. Witherspoon, "Out of the Flames."

CHAPTER 7

1. Rachael Gleason, "Justice of the Peace Recalls Eighteen Years of Service," *Midland Reporter-Telegram*, March 15, 2014, accessed December 30, 2020, https://www.mrt.com/news/crime/article/Justice-of-the-peace-recalls-18-years-of-service-7406456.php.

CHAPTER 8

1. "Table 4: Motor Vehicle Traffic Fatalities, by State and Highest Driver BAC in the Crash, 2018," *Traffic Safety Facts: 2018 Data*, US Department of Transportation, National Highway Traffic Safety Administration, December

2019, accessed December 30, 2020, https://crashstats.nhtsa.dot.gov/Api/Public/ViewPublication/812864.

CHAPTER 9

1. Pierre Thomas, Jack Date, and Theresa Cook, "Judge Pushes Teens from Truancy to Triumph," ABC News, December 22, 2008, accessed December 30, 2020, https://abcnews.go.com/TheLaw/story?id=6512667&page=1; Ruth Campbell, "'ABC World News Tonight' Broadcasts Midland Feature," *Midland Reporter-Telegram*, December 22, 2008, accessed December 30, 2020, https://www.mrt.com/news/article/ABC-World-News-Tonight-broadcasts-Midland-7512948.php.

2. All references to misbehavior by Texas justices of the peace addressed by the State Commission on Judicial Conduct cited in this book are documented on their website: http://www.scjc.state.tx.us.

CHAPTER 11

1. "Justice of the Peace to Stop Doing Weddings After Supreme Court Ruling," *Everything Lubbock*, June 29, 2015, accessed January 3, 2021, https://www.everythinglubbock.com/news/justice-of-the-peace-to-stop-doing-weddings-after-supreme-court-ruling/.

2. "Interracial Marriage Stand Sparks Debate," United Press International Archives, January 7, 1983, accessed December 30, 2020, https://www.upi.com/Archives/1983/01/07/Interracial-marriage-stand-sparks-debate/8765410763600/.

3. All references to misbehavior by Texas justices of the peace addressed by the State Commission on Judicial Conduct cited in this book are documented on their website: http://www.scjc.state.tx.us.

CHAPTER 12

1. Jessica Pounds, "Seized Longhorn Nursed Back to Health, Ready for Adoption," *Cleburne Times-Review*, August 1, 2018, accessed December 30, 2020, https://www.cleburnetimesreview.com/news/seized-longhorn-nursed-back-to-health-ready-for-adoption/article_fb0743ea-950e-11e8-8698-9b8d-c19cf089.html.

CHAPTER 13

1. Carmen Goldthwaite, *Texas Ranch Women: Three Centuries of Mettle and Moxie* (Charleston, SC: The History Press, 2014), accessed December 30, 2020, https://books.google.com/books?id=-qSACQAAQBAJ&pg=PT124&lpg=PT124&dq=hallie+stillwell+inda+benson&source=bl&ots=vxUXP16uk-

g&sig=ACfU3U2-9n1daoBFqZugyH6h5HiJJcBMmA&hl=en&sa=X&ved=2a-
hUKEwjQsLXEsP_oAhXHK80KHWLuDHgQ6AEwAXoECAsQAQ#v=one-
page&q=hallie%20stillwell%20inda%20benson&f=falseFifteen.

CHAPTER 15

1. Jamey Boyum and KLTV Digital Media Staff, "Gregg County Justice
of the Peace Offers Free Gun Locks to Anyone in Need," KLTV 7, KSLA
News 12, December 3, 2019, accessed December 30, 2020, https://www.ksla.
com/2019/12/03/gregg-county-justice-peace-offers-free-gun-locks-anyone-
need/.

CHAPTER 16

1. "Historic Political Shift in Lamar County, 9 Elected Dems Join GOP,"
Republican Party of Texas, January 24, 2011, accessed December 30, 2020,
https://www.texasgop.org/historic-political-shift-in-lamar-county-9-elected-
dems-join-gop/.

CHAPTER 17

1. Elizabeth Campbell, "Johnson County JPs Want Their Salaries Increased,"
Fort Worth Star-Telegram, August 31, 2014, accessed December 30, 2020,
https://www.star-telegram.com/news/local/crime/article3871485.html.

2. "Population of Counties in Texas (2020)," World Population Review,
no date, accessed December 30, 2020, https://worldpopulationreview.com/
us-counties/tx/.

3. Texas Association of Counties, *Texas Association of Counties 2020 Salary Survey* (San Antonio, Austin, TX: TAC, 2020), accessed December 30,
2020, https://www.county.org/TAC/media/TACMedia/Resources%20for%20
County%20Officials/2020/Salary-Survey.pdf.

4. "Population of Counties in Texas (2020)."

5. Texas Association of Counties, *2020 Salary Survey*.

6. "Population of Counties in Texas (2020)."

7. Texas Association of Counties, *2020 Salary Survey*.

CHAPTER 18

1. Jim Atkinson, "Who's Judge Cole So Mad At?" *D Magazine*, January
1978, accessed December 30, 2020, https://www.dmagazine.com/publica-
tions/d-magazine/1978/january/whos-judge-cole-so-mad-at/.

2. Paul Burka, "The Law West of the Trinity," *Texas Monthly*, March 1980,
accessed December 30, 2020, https://www.texasmonthly.com/articles/the-law-
west-of-the-trinity/.

3. Kinky Friedman, "All Politics Is Yokel," *Texas Monthly*, April 2001, accessed December 30, 2020, https://www.texasmonthly.com/articles/all-politics-is-yokel/.

4. All references to misbehavior by Texas justices of the peace addressed by the State Commission on Judicial Conduct cited in this book are documented on their website: http://www.scjc.state.tx.us.

5. Hot Lotto Fraud Scandal, *Wikipedia*, n.d., accessed December 30, 2020, https://en.wikipedia.org/wiki/Hot_Lotto_fraud_scandal.

6. Ginger Allen, "Inside the Mind of Eric Williams: 'One of the Most Notorious Texas Killers,'" CBS DFW, January 31, 2019, accessed December 30, 2020, https://dfw.cbslocal.com/2019/01/31/inside-mind-eric-williams-notorious-texas-killers/.

7. Leigh Egan, "'He Wanted to Get Even': How a Former Lawyer Snuffed the Lives of Prominent Prosecutors Out of Rage, Jealousy," *Crime Online*, April 1, 2018, accessed December 30, 2020, https://www.crimeonline.com/2018/04/01/he-wanted-to-get-even-how-a-former-lawyer-snuffed-the-lives-of-prominent-prosecutors-out-of-rage-jealousy/.

8. Daniel Egitto, "Former Texas Judge Stockpiled Guns, Napalm Before Killing Two Prosecutors in Brutal Revenge Plot," *Oxygen Crime News*, October 14, 2019, accessed December 30, 2020, https://www.oxygen.com/killer-motive/crime-news/eric-williams-kills-mike-cynthia-mclelland-mark-hasse-revenge-napalm.

9. "Lockney J.P.'s Guilty Plea Draws Probation, Fine 01-16-2008," *My Plainview*, January 15, 2008, accessed December 30, 2020, https://www.myplainview.com/news/article/Lockney-J-P-s-guilty-plea-draws-probation-fine-8443210.php.

10. Review Tribunal Order in re Thurman Bill Bartie, delivered and filed April 16, 2004, State Commission on Judicial Conduct, accessed December 30, 2020, http://www.scjc.texas.gov/media/8097/inquiry90.pdf.

11. "Meet the Mayor and Council," Port Arthur, Texas, accessed December 30, 2020, https://www.portarthurtx.gov/333/Meet-the-Mayor-and-Council.

CHAPTER 19

1. Thomas Mitchell Shamburger, *Inquests: Living with the Dead* (Winona, TX: Proven Justice Inc.), 306.

Index

Note that there are no entries related to specific Texas cities and towns. Texas justice courts are connected jurisdictionally to the counties in which they are located and not to coincidental municipalities. For this reason, the geographic focus of the book is predominantly county centric, and reference to the cities and towns of the state is largely incidental to the material presented.